Still Captive?

History, Law and the Teaching of High School Journalism

By The Society of Professional Journalists'
Journalism Education Committee

The Editors

Rebecca Tallent, University of Idaho
Kym Fox, Texas State University
Butler Cain, West Texas A&M University
Mac McKerral, Western Kentucky University

NEW FORUMS

NEW FORUMS PRESS INC.

Published in the United States of America
by New Forums Press, Inc.1018 S. Lewis St.
Stillwater, OK 74074
www.newforums.com

Library of Congress Cataloging-in-Publication Data Pending

This book may be ordered in bulk quantities at discount from New
Forums Press, Inc., P.O. Box 876, Stillwater, OK 74076 [Federal
I.D. No. 73 1123239]. Printed in the United States of America.

ISBN 10: 1-58107-276-7
ISBN 13: 978-1-58107-276-1

Cover design by Tracy Ann Anderson

Table of Contents

Foreword

A few years ago in my role as national president of the Society of Professional Journalists, I asked our journalism education committee to take a fresh look at the state of high school journalism as taught in high schools across the nation.

The report you are reading is the result of that tenacious multi-year effort, and we are so much the better for it.

I believed then, as I do now, that high school journalism educators are on the front lines of a battle that will have a profound impact not only on the future of journalism but the vitality of our democracy.

Like many working journalists, I got my start in the business while working on my high school paper under the patient, but firm, guidance of a Christian brother who served as our newspaper adviser.

The valuable lessons learned back then – of accuracy, fairness, challenging assumptions, questioning authority and being accountable – went a long way to forming the journalist I am today.

And yet as this report documents, high school journalism education today is under a state of siege.

Hardly a month goes by that we don't hear about districts cutting their journalism programs and giving short shrift to nurturing the next generation of journalists.

Too often, administrators are mistakenly basing budget decisions on the cutbacks of the last few years among legacy media such as big metro newspapers.

And yet, reports of the demise of journalism, to paraphrase Mark Twain, have been premature and are greatly exaggerated.

Demand for the timely and accurate reporting of news has never been greater. And the young journalists graduating today are finding jobs albeit not always in the traditional places.

More troubling is this report's finding that the Common Core standards are being misused as the latest excuse to drop journalism from the high school curriculum.

There are very few disciplines that do a better job of teaching critical thinking skills, self-expression, analysis and intellectual independence than journalism. These are invaluable life skills, even for students who don't pursue a journalism career.

My hope is that this report will be read by school board members and administrators across the country and that it sparks a dialog about the need for a vibrant and relevant journalism education in every high school in America.

Our democracy depends on it.

John C. Ensslin
Former National SPJ President, 2011-12

Dedication

This work is dedicated to all high school journalism teachers and advisers. Thank you.

Acknowledgments

All the authors wish to thank:

Mark Newton, JEA president, and all JEA members who participated in this work. We could not have done this without you.

Howard Dubin, for his support and financial assistance with a grant from the Howard and Ursula Dubin Foundation.

John Ensslin and Sonny Albarado, two former Society of Professional Journalists national presidents who were the main support system for us during this project. Your encouragement is deeply appreciated.

Jill Jones for her tremendous work of interviewing high school teachers after the survey and for the creation of the graphs, along with her husband Nelson Sprinkle. Thank you!

The author of the Post-Hazelwood chapter gratefully acknowledges the guidance and research assistance of Frank LoMonte, executive director of the Student Press Law Center, in preparing this chapter.

The project coordinator also thanks Chris Vachon, SPJ associate executive director, for her assistance and guidance on the financial and contract issues.

Profile 1

ANN VISSER

Pella Community High School (public)
Pella, Iowa (800 students, 9-12)
Yearbook and Newspaper

A quiet lunchroom after newspapers are distributed, or after shiny new yearbooks have been handed out, is a sign of success for Pella Publications Adviser Ann Visser.

"We've had lots of other successes," Visser said. "We've won several awards, individual and as a group, but I think pleasing readers – pleasing our audience – is our best measure."

Visser, who has been teaching and advising student publications for 33 years (31 for Pella Community High School in Pella, Iowa), said that building sound journalistic programs has been the key to the respect those programs now enjoy.

"Of course we've had some challenges; this is a fairly conservative community," she said. "Sometimes people have questions about how and what we've covered."

PCHS yearbook and newspaper production, from planning and interviewing to page design, is the responsibility of publication students, Visser said.

"They cover things that are happening at the high school, the successes of groups at state and district contests, including more serious things, like building projects and community issues, if they connect to the school.

"They wrote about the building of a regional airport, for example, and a big controversy with one of the programs at school – the show choir – that required lots of time for practicing," Visser said.

Iowa's Student Free Expression Law (Iowa Code Sec. 280.22) extends protection for high school students against administrative censorship, she said, and affords administrators less of a risk of liability – as long as they stay out of content decisions.

"Students have the responsibility to cover things the way they should," Visser said.

Visser, a former JEA president, said the issues that typically get parents' or the community's attention are those "potentially explosive" topics, such as sex, pregnancy and drug use.

"People get nervous and don't like to think that their kids could be involved in or even go to a school where these issues might exist," she said.

But according to Visser, the PCHS administration has never tried to control student journalists, or the information they choose to present. "The students decide content, and if the administration has gotten calls, they've done a great job referring the calls to publication staffs," Visser said.

To make strong, ethical decisions, student editors need sound instruction in journalistic principles and ethics, Visser said. And administrators, who "hire responsibly," can trust well-trained advisers to help students make good decisions.

"Sometimes I go to them (administrators) to give them a heads up about something controversial coming up. It builds trust, and they're very receptive," Visser said, "but students won't shy away from things that are significant."

Visser, 57, graduated in 1979 from Northwest Missouri State University with a bachelor's of science degree in English and journalism.

"I wanted to be a sports reporter at *The Kansas City Star*," she said, "that was my dream." Instead she pursued another interest, teaching high school, in Gallatin, Mo.

When she started at Pella Community High School in 1983, "there was just one publications class, with yearbook and newspaper together," she said, "and no introduction class." Now the program boasts two sections of yearbook, two sections of newspaper (both print and online), and two introduction classes. Publication students earn English credits for the first two years of participation, then elective credit for the third and fourth years.

The student newspaper, *The Pelladium,* prints once a month, and has a regularly updated online edition. The 12-page monthly also is distributed to every home in the school district.

And when many schools are suspending print editions largely for financial reasons, Visser said the tradition is alive and well at PCHS.

"Students like to look at it, to feel it. They know they count on it to do a decent job of representing what's happening at the school," she said. "At lunchtime, 150 kids are reading the paper."

Visser said that along with increased student interest, support from administration has helped publications programs grow at her school. "They've been fabulous. They've provided money when needed, and have respected and encouraged me professionally," she said.

Separating yearbook and newspaper classes and being a full-time journalism teacher also was beneficial, she said. "It's definitely impacted my time," she said. Visser said she knows of several publications advisers who also must teach English classes.

Visser said the one thing that might help improve PCHS's publication programs the most would be to "not have to worry about the financial aspect. We are self-supporting – the students sell ads – but lots of time is spent coordinating sales and billing accounts," she said. "It would be nice to be able to just focus on the journalism, but I know that's not realistic."

Preface: How to use this Book

This book is the work of 14 separate individuals who came together out of a mutual passion: that of teaching journalism. Although all the authors are college or university professors, almost all of us began our journalism journey in a high school classroom. Most of us in a newspaper class, many of us in a yearbook class.

Unfortunately, not all of us are seeing the same enthusiasm for the subject that we remember. What we are seeing in our college classrooms are students who think they can jump right into being a sports analyst for a network or a fashion editor for a major publication, all as first jobs out of college. Many who come to higher education without a high school journalism experience come without the necessary critical thinking, creative thinking, collaborative and communication skills.

That is the reasoning behind this book: not just to discover the state of high school journalism, but a way to help teachers improve their own skills. This work is for teachers who either are or will be teaching high school journalism and people who are interested in preserving the programs.

The first part of this work is a look at the state of high school journalism in America in 2014. This includes a nationwide survey with the results in Section One. For teachers who want to argue for support in terms of newer technology, working with local professionals, additional certification or other issues, this section provides that information.

Section Two was developed because it became apparent early-on that many high school journalism teachers had no idea about the federal court laws which govern what they teach. The three chapters take teachers from the earliest history and laws through the Hazelwood decision and slightly beyond – cases that have significant impact on governance of scholastic news media.

Section Three turns back to the classroom itself and discusses the basics of high school journalism, how outstanding programs have survived, teaching the 4Cs, how teachers can best use available workshops and incorporate more professional assistance in their classroom.

The final section gives all the conclusions about what can be done to improve high school journalism, plus an annotated bibliography for anyone who wants to conduct further research in this subject, and brief biographical sketches of the authors and editors of this work. Also added is the original survey sent to 600 high school teachers.

It is the sincere hope of the SPJ Education Committee that this work is of assistance to scholastic programs throughout the country.

Section I

The State of High School Journalism 2014

Profile 2

CANDICE GRAVITT

Faith Lutheran Middle School and High School
(1,400 students, grades 6-12; private)
Las Vegas, Nev.
Broadcast and newspaper

Publications adviser Candice Gravitt could use a little more time, and perhaps, a bit more flexibility.

At Faith Lutheran Middle School and High School in Las Vegas, Nev., her broadcast and newspaper students meet for class 90 minutes every other day, which, according to Gravitt, is not nearly enough.

"I meet my high school block sometimes two days, sometimes three. We start at 8 in the morning and are done by 9:30 a.m. Technically, I can leave campus, but I have students working on stuff all day. So I hang around; I need to make sure the kids are getting what they need," she said.

Gravitt, 44, is a part-time teacher in Clark County School District. A former broadcast journalist, Gravitt advises two classes of middle school broadcast students and one combined class of high school broadcast and newspaper students. She's new this year to advising high school students, and advising newspaper and broadcast students in the same class has been a struggle, she said.

"When they come into class, an hour and a half is not enough time to get stories done and take photographs, not to mention editing and producing segments," she said. "And newspaper and broadcast are two different things."

Faith Lutheran is a private Christian school with 1,400 students in grades 6 through 12. Gravitt, who was hired five years ago to teach broadcast journalism as an elective class to seventh- and eighth-graders, was asked to take on the high school class when the newspaper adviser left to pursue a law degree.

"My background is in TV," Gravitt said, "and my passion is in teaching kids how to communicate, how to get up in front of people and ask questions. I don't want kids to feel like they don't have anything interesting to say.

"When my principal said, 'Let's put all these kids in one class and teach newspaper and broadcast together,' I had to figure it out. I decided to go online, to put all the news on an interactive website. We've done that successfully, although the writing and content isn't where I'd like it to be," she said.

Gravitt, who advocates the open forum, had been a producer for 10 years for the Las Vegas affiliates of ABC and CBS news. She also produced a talk show, "Point of View Vegas," for a local newspaper. And as a college student, she studied journalism at the University of Nevada at Las Vegas.

So teaching at a private, Christian institution that restricts content and limits free speech has been an adjustment for Gravitt. She said she was drawn to the school for the excellent education it offers her children, and for the Christian ideals her family values. She said she also feels she has a good rapport with administration.

"When I spoke to the administration last year, I was told that our broadcast, website and anything in print must represent the values of a Christian organization, to stick to the guidelines of the Bible," she said. "It was like, 'What would Jesus do?' We could not talk poorly about, or criticize, anyone or anything."

In addition, Gravitt said that Faith Lutheran student journalists cannot produce stories or voice opinions in print about teen pregnancy, drugs, alcohol, homosexuality or sex. Gravitt is in charge of monitoring content, she said, and it is her job to use her best judgment when deciding what to cover. "I signed a contract that I will follow a Christ-like morality," she said.

"I understand that, and I don't argue at all. I will talk to the administration when I have a question about a story, though."

A story that Gravitt said she was surprised could not run involved students allegedly sneaking off campus.

"I was blown away that we weren't allowed to do it. With my background, I wanted to get an undercover camera! The administration was worried that parents would sue," she said.

Looking ahead, Gravitt said she's excited about the growth and popularity of the program; next year she'll be teaching another section of combined broadcast and newspaper. She also is hopeful for a broadcast studio, she said, and wants to collaborate more with the middle school publications adviser.

"I do feel supported for what I do, and I know they want me to continue. I want to keep journalism afloat," Gravitt said.

Chapter 1

Introduction

▲ *Rebecca Tallent & Lee Anne Peck*

"I am grateful to journalism for waking me up to the realities of the world."

Eduardo Galeano, Uruguayan journalist

In May 2014 the Society of Professional Journalists (SPJ) called on high school administrators in Neshaminy, Pa., to stop censorship of the high school newspaper. As explained in the SPJ press release (SPJ, 2014):

> After editors at the Neshaminy High School student newspaper refused to print "Redskins" as the school's mascot name, the board of directors released a publications policy addressing what the students are and are not permitted to publish. SPJ believes the current version of the publications policy doesn't comply with the First Amendment or with Pennsylvania's student press rights law.

With similar censorship issues at other U.S. high schools, plus the loss of professional support for scholastic programs in cities that include Detroit and Seattle, can Galeano still be correct: Does journalism still wake people up to the realities of the world? When starting this journey, the authors asked several questions, including the following: Does high school journalism still exist, and does it encourage critical thinking plus other skills necessary for good citizenship?

What *is* the state of high school journalism in America? While delivery platforms for the professional field continue to shift and morph, journalism as a profession is alive and changing. However, there were serious questions about whether journalism was still surviving in secondary education.

Since the 1990s, technology has rapidly altered the media landscape: shifting traditional print and broadcast to digital platforms, and making deadlines constant, visuals more important and accuracy even more imperative. This leads to some important questions:

- What backgrounds do high school journalism teachers and/ or advisers have?
- Which students work with student media?
- Who has the final OK for airing or publishing student media work?
- Do student media have written guidelines to follow re: what is appropriate to cover?
- How are student media funded?
- What outside organizations help (or support) student media?
- What do our respondents believe is the main hindrance to doing their jobs—if any?
- What do respondents believe could improve high school journalism?

This is what the Society of Professional Journalists' Education Committee set out to discover starting in 2011.

Then-national SPJ President John Ensslin asked the committee members if they had heard of high school programs being eliminated because of the misconception by administrators that "journalism is dying." Starting with the two previous projects – 1974's "Captive Voices: The Report of the Commission of Inquiry into High School Journalism in America" and 1994's "Death by Cheeseburger: High School Journalism in the 1990s and Beyond" – the committee members researched the history of high school journalism – especially how federal laws have impacted teaching the subject. Several questions arose involving the relationship between high school programs and local professionals, the impact of high school workshops (sponsored either by professional news organizations or colleges and universities) and how some of the stellar programs have survived.

Along the way, committee member Dr. Lee Anne Peck developed a survey based on the 1974 "Captive Voices" report that committee chair Dr. Rebecca Tallent distributed electronically to high school journalism teachers involved with student media. These instructors results gave a picture of the state of high school journalism

– what the teachers believe they need or don't need. They also offer suggestions on how to improve journalism classes by showing administrators how four core concepts of journalism education (communication, critical thinking, creativity and collaboration) align perfectly with the common core standards for schools.

Students do not need to pledge their lives to journalism, but in taking the courses they can experience the core values in real time using real skills; these skills can translate into any profession. Along the way, those who take high school journalism classes report they are better professionally thanks to the skills they learned. In addition, the interviews with selected teachers and former journalism students show people believe these same skills have taught them to be better news consumers, and as a result, much better citizens because they remain aware of the issues they need to know to ensure democracy.

What was discovered as a result of this research is a mixed bag of good and bad news. While rays of hope exist, some of the results are not encouraging to professional journalists and university journalism programs – especially those who have let slide working with scholastic journalism. This work also proposes solutions for those issues.

What can be done? The following chapters explain the specific issues in detail but also provide solutions provided by high school teachers, college professors and media professionals.

Chapter 2

Beginnings: Method, Demographics and Basic Findings

 By Lee Anne Peck

To find out if then national SPJ President John Ensslin's concern about the elimination of high school programs was founded in reality, the SPJ Education Committee got to work. The committee's goal: to learn if high school journalism teachers and/or advisers were worried about their administrators cutting programs because "journalism is dying." The committee members had another concern, though: What was the status of high school journalism and censorship?

By modifying and updating the survey used in the 1974 study "Captive Voices," a questionnaire was created for pilot testing with high school journalism teachers and advisers during the summer of 2013. That fall, 10 high school teachers recommended changes and additions, ranging from giving more options for "the requirements for teaching courses" to listing "parents" as an option for the question about hindrances to their work.

After modification of the survey, which was a mixture of multiple choice and open-ended questions, a mailing list of high school journalism educators was obtained. Kelly Furnas, an assistant professor of journalism at Kansas State University and the executive director of the Journalism Education Association, helped by sharing JEA's mailing list. The JEA, founded in 1924, continues to be the largest scholastic journalism organization for teachers and advisers and was an obvious choice for finding participants.

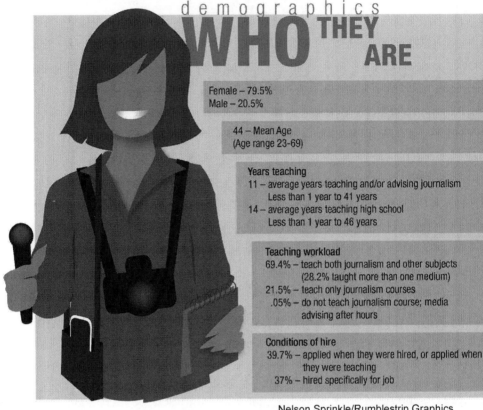

demographics

WHO THEY ARE

Female – 79.5%
Male – 20.5%

44 – Mean Age
(Age range 23-69)

Years teaching
11 – average years teaching and/or advising journalism
    Less than 1 year to 41 years
14 – average years teaching high school
    Less than 1 year to 46 years

Teaching workload
69.4% – teach both journalism and other subjects
    (28.2% taught more than one medium)
21.5% – teach only journalism courses
.05% – do not teach journalism course; media
    advising after hours

Conditions of hire
39.7% – applied when they were hired, or applied when
    they were teaching
37% – hired specifically for job

Nelson Sprinkle/Rumblestrip Graphics

JEA had 2,058 high school journalism members at that time. The sample size needed for a 95 percent confidence level with a margin of error of 5 percentage points would be 324 participants. Furnas created a systematic random sample of every third JEA member (686 names), which the education committee hoped would be enough to reach the recommended sample size of 324.

JEA could provide only mailing addresses for those 686 members; therefore, the education committee set upon the task of finding the 686 members' email addresses.[1] Eighty-six names (or their emails) were not usable for a variety of reasons – from teachers no longer being employed at the JEA-supplied school address to the inability to find an email address no matter how many methods the committee members tried.

With the help of an undergraduate student, the survey questions (Appendix A) were entered into the online survey software Survey-Monkey. The survey was emailed February 9, 2014, with a letter (Appendix B) explaining the purpose and importance of completing the survey.[2] Two more letters encouraging JEA members to respond were sent. The survey was taken off line on March 8, 2014.

Although the number of survey respondents did not reach the recommended sample size of 324 during that month, it did reach 258 respondents, which is a response rate of 43 percent. Participants came from 47 states.[3] The number of respondents gave the researchers a bit higher than a 90 percent confidence level with a margin of error of 5.71 percentage points.[4] Basic descriptive results, or frequencies, were determined by SurveyMonkey while SPSS 20.0 was used for additional tests.

Demographic information and basic results follow.

The respondents

As mentioned above, 258 high school journalism teachers or advisers attempted the survey titled "The status of high school news media in the 21st century." Respondents included 79.5 percent females and 20.5 percent males. The respondents' mean age was 44 with respondents ranging in age from 23 to 69.[5]

More than one-third (37 percent) became a media adviser and/or journalism teacher because they were hired to do the job. More respondents (39.7 percent) reported, however, that they applied when they were hired or applied while they were already teaching. Teachers and/or advisers assigned to their jobs came in at 12.5 percent. About 11 percent stated a variety of other reasons for doing their work as media adviser or journalism teacher.

Where they work

Using *National Geographic* magazine's five regions of the United States, (http://education.nationalgeographic.com/education/maps/united-states-regions/), the following areas of the country are where respondents worked:

Midwest region: 30.4 percent
West: 25.2 percent

Southwest: 19.3 percent
Southeast: 17 percent
Northeast: 7.5 percent
U.S. Military: 0.3 percent

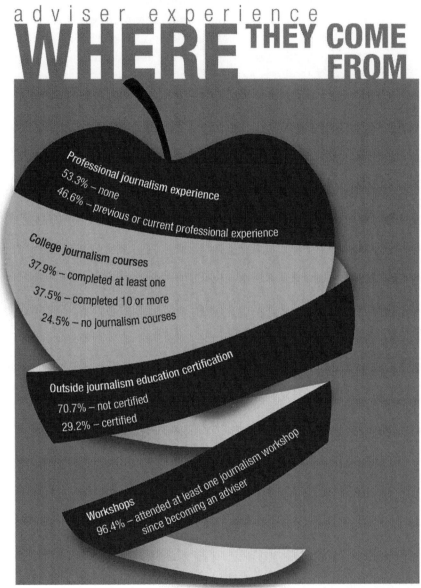

adviser experience

WHERE THEY COME FROM

Professional journalism experience
53.3% – none
46.6% – previous or current professional experience

College journalism courses
37.9% – completed at least one
37.5% – completed 10 or more
24.5% – no journalism courses

Outside journalism education certification
70.7% – not certified
29.2% – certified

Workshops
96.4% – attended at least one journalism workshop
since becoming an adviser

Nelson Sprinkle/Rumblestrip Graphics

Most respondents (50.1 percent) reported they lived in a smaller city or suburb with a population fewer than 150,000. Thirty-one percent said they lived in cities with a population of 150,000 or more. Nineteen percent said their schools were in a rural or consolidated school district. Five respondents said they taught in a high school with fewer than 100 students; 11.4 percent reported teaching in schools with 101 to 500 students and 14.6 percent said they taught at schools with 501 to 1,000 students. Twenty percent said they taught at schools with 1,001 to 1,500 students; 26 percent, the largest number, reported teaching at schools with 1,501 to 2,000. Twenty-two percent said they teach at schools with 2,001 to 3,000, and 3.9 percent taught at schools with up to 4,000 students.

Most of the respondents (88.5 percent) taught at public schools while the remaining respondents taught at private schools. Forty-four respondents, or 17.3 percent, said their school was predominantly minority, and 60.6 percent said their high schools were predominantly non-minority. A little more than one-fifth (20.4 percent) reported they taught at a school with roughly an even balance of minority and non-minority students. Four participants said they did not know what the breakdown was at their schools.

The teaching

The 258 respondents' average number of years teaching high school was 14 years with respondents reporting they had taught from less than one year to 46 years. Not all had taught journalism during their entire teaching careers, however. The average number of years teaching and/or advising journalism students was 11 years with respondents reporting they had taught and/or advised journalism from less than one year to 41 years.

Most respondents, 69.4 percent, taught both journalism and other subject areas, mostly English courses, while 21.5 percent taught only journalism courses. A small percentage, 4.7 percent, taught no journalism courses but did their media advising after regular school hours.

Of the 258 respondents, 28.2 percent reported they taught or advised more than one medium, and those 73 answered questions about each medium they taught or advised. Therefore, when combined, the following media had these numbers of teachers or advisers answering questions about their areas of journalism used in the study[6]:

Newspapers (online and/or print)	175
Yearbook	114
Television news	33
Magazine	18
Radio news	1
TOTAL	**341**

The majority of the 73 respondents who said they taught or advised more than one medium taught both newspaper and yearbook although some teachers said they advised more than these two areas, adding magazine or television to the mix.

Respondents' journalism experience

Almost one-fourth (24.5 percent) of the respondents had no journalism courses in college; however, 37.5 percent said they had completed 10 or more and 37.9 percent had at least one course. Almost 30 percent (29.2) had received journalism education certification through an outside organization, such as JEA; 70.7 percent had no outside certification. The majority of the respondents (96.4 percent) said they had attended at least one journalism workshop since becoming a high school journalism instructor and/or media adviser.

The requirements for teaching journalism in each respondent's respective state generated a variety of answers; however, more than one-fourth (25.7 percent) reported no requirements exist while more than one-fifth (21.4 percent) reported they did not know if their states had requirements. Fifty participants (19.8 percent) said college journalism coursework was a requirement; requirements written in the "Other" category ranged from Language Arts Certification to Career and Technical Education certification to English certification.

Almost half (46.6 percent) reported previous or current professional experience with 53.3 percent reporting no experience. Of those who reported professional experience, which included internships, most worked as newspaper reporters, writers and editors and a small number worked at television and radio stations. A handful worked in advertising, marketing or PR while an even smaller number worked in graphic design.

For those who have the duty of advising student media, 81.8 percent are paid a stipend of some sort for their work. Some (13.7 percent) do not receive any extra pay for the extra hours of work with a student media organization. The others who answered this question said they worked part-time or were volunteers so no additional stipend was involved.

A little more than one-fourth (25.9 percent) of the respondents said they believed their journalism courses or their school's student media were in danger of being eliminated. About seven percent said they did not know what the status of their programs might be while 68 percent said they were not worried at all. Respondents gave many reasons for their belief about why their programs might be eliminated, but one of the main reasons was an emphasis on the required (Common Core) curriculum; another reason reported by respondents, however, was a lack of student interest.

According to many of the study's respondents (63.5 percent), the most important purpose of having student media is to teach the skills of "communication, critical thinking, creativity and collaboration".[7] Twenty-three percent said providing a forum for student expression was the most important. The remainder of the answers were too diverse to have a large percentage.

What is being taught?

Respondents were able to check "all that apply" from a list of technological skills, which follows; the use of design software was most prominent with photography skills high on the list, too:

> Use of design software: 92 percent
> How to shoot photos: 89.3 percent
> Use of photo-editing software: 89.3 percent
> Use of social media: 70.3 percent
> How to shoot video: 37.9 percent
> Use of video editing equipment: 37.5 percent
> How to create audio: 21.7 percent

Write-in responses included writing skills, accounting and use of WordPress.

WHAT'S BEING TAUGHT

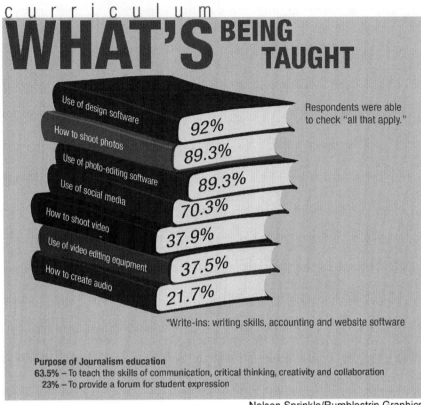

Use of design software **92%**

How to shoot photos **89.3%**

Use of photo-editing software **89.3%**

Use of social media **70.3%**

How to shoot video **37.9%**

Use of video editing equipment **37.5%**

How to create audio **21.7%**

Respondents were able to check "all that apply."

*Write-ins: writing skills, accounting and website software

Purpose of Journalism education
63.5% – To teach the skills of communication, critical thinking, creativity and collaboration
23% – To provide a forum for student expression

Nelson Sprinkle/Rumblestrip Graphics

Requirements to participate with student media

If students want to participate in student media, the requirements vary from school to school. From the list of responses available to respondents, the following was reported:

Must be enrolled in relevant journalism course: 33 percent
Must have taken a journalism course: 23.4 percent
Anyone welcome: 27.9 percent

Most write-in responses to this question included that staff participation included some type of application process.

Slightly more than two-thirds of respondents (67.5 percent) said their student media have no written guidelines for what topics are appropriate to cover for a high school audience, yet in another question the majority of the advisers and/or teachers (88.7 percent) said they place limitations on what can be aired or published. The kinds of limitations reported range from possibly libelous material to invasion of privacy and obscenity or sexual content.

About a third of the advisers and/or teachers (34.6 percent) said their student media's work is always reviewed by their administration before being published or being aired. However, 52.2 percent reported their student media never have a pre-publication or pre-airing review from the administrators. The rest of the advisers said "sometimes" they deal with prior review from their administrators.

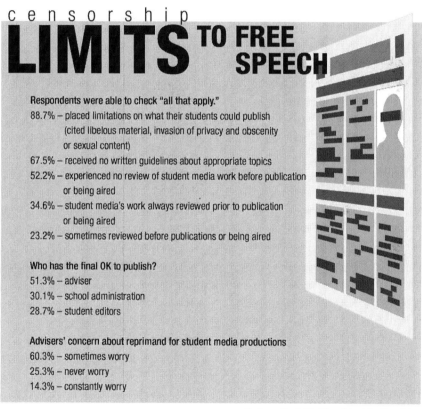

censorship
LIMITS TO FREE SPEECH

Respondents were able to check "all that apply."

88.7% – placed limitations on what their students could publish
(cited libelous material, invasion of privacy and obscenity
or sexual content)

67.5% – received no written guidelines about appropriate topics

52.2% – experienced no review of student media work before publication
or being aired

34.6% – student media's work always reviewed prior to publication
or being aired

23.2% – sometimes reviewed before publications or being aired

Who has the final OK to publish?

51.3% – adviser

30.1% – school administration

28.7% – student editors

Advisers' concern about reprimand for student media productions

60.3% – sometimes worry

25.3% – never worry

14.3% – constantly worry

Nelson Sprinkle/Rumblestrip Graphics

When it comes to who has the very final OK of student-created work before it airs or is published – and here teachers could answer for each medium they advise, which caused duplications in some responses – 51.3 percent of the respondents said they do as adviser or teacher; 30.1 percent said the school administration has the very final OK. For 28.7 percent of the respondents, the student editor or producer has the final say.

Fourteen percent of the respondents said they were constantly worried their journalism teaching and/or student media advising will be reprimanded because of student work that creates a controversy while 60.3 percent said they were "sometimes" worried. About a fourth of the respondents (25.3 percent) said they were never afraid of being reprimanded.

Nelson Sprinkle/Rumblestrip Graphics

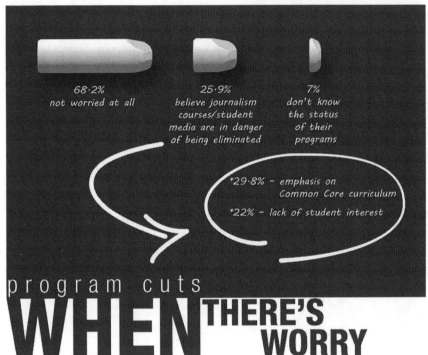

68·2%
not worried at all

25·9%
believe journalism
courses/student
media are in danger
of being eliminated

7%
don't know
the status
of their
programs

*29·8% – emphasis on
Common Core curriculum

*22% – lack of student interest

program cuts

WHEN THERE'S WORRY

Negatives and positives

One of the last questions on the survey (Appendix A) asked the following: "If you believe something hinders your job as a journalism instructor and/or adviser, what do you think is the problem? Check all that apply." Responses follow[8]:

No support from other faculty	17.2 percent
No support from administration	13.8 percent
No support from school district	13.8 percent

No support from state Board of Education   10 percent
No support from parents   9.2 percent
Interference from parents   4.6 percent
No interest from students   26.8 percent
No money for updating necessary equipment 38.7 percent
Not applicable (no significant problem)   35.7 percent

roadblocks
HOW ADVISERS ARE HINDERED

Respondents were able to check "all that apply."

38.7%	no money for updating equipment
26.8%	no interest from students
17.2%	no support from other faculty
13.8%	no support from administration
13.8%	no support from school district
10%	no support from State Board of Education
9.2%	no support from parents
4.6%	interference from parents
35.7%	no significant issues

Nelson Sprinkle/Rumblestrip Graphics

As shown above, more than one-third said having no money for updating equipment hindered them from doing their jobs. However, more than one-third also said they had nothing hindering them from doing their jobs. "No interest from students" was chosen by more than a fourth of the respondents.

Participants also shared what they believe would improve high school journalism today. And so, what does this all mean 40 years after "Captive Voices" and 20 years after "Death by Cheeseburger?" The current status of high school journalism is explored and explained in the next two chapters.

Endnotes

1. The JEA does not sell its members' email addresses, only regular mailing addresses.

2. Five $100 Visa gift cards were offered as an incentive to complete the survey.

3. Alaska, West Virginia and Vermont were not represented.

4. Sample size was determined by raosoft.com.

5. The JEA does not keep demographic information on their members; the only information that is tracked is the medium in which members teach.

6. Note that even though the teachers or advisers answered questions about two or more media, they completed only one set of demographic questions.

7. Because the mailing list of the JEA became part of this study's sample, it is not unusual that more than half of the respondents said that the JEA's 4 C's—communication, critical thinking, creativity and collaboration—were noted as the most important.

8. The survey offered no "other" option.

Chapter 3

Research Questions, Answers and Concerns

 By Lee Anne Peck

This research attempts to determine the current status of high school media via a questionnaire sent to high school journalism teachers and/or advisers via a random sample of Journalism Education Association (JEA) members. By looking at the 1974 "Captive Voices" and the 1994 "Death by "Cheeseburger" reports, one can see what situations have stayed the same and what has changed over the past decades.[1] The research questions the SPJ Education Committee wanted to answer included the following:

- **RQ1:** What backgrounds do high school journalism teachers and/or advisers have?
- **RQ2:** Which students work with student media?
- **RQ3:** Who has the final OK for airing or publishing student media work?
- **RQ4:** Do student media have written guidelines to follow re: what is appropriate to cover?
- **RQ5:** How are student media funded?
- **RQ6:** What outside organizations help (or support) student media?
- **RQ7:** What do our respondents believe is the main hindrance to doing their jobs – if any?
- **RQ8:** What do respondents believe could improve high school journalism?

Finally, both the "Captive Voices" and "Death by "Cheeseburger"" reports listed recommendations to improve high school journalism. Which recommendations still make sense today?

The "Captive Voices" project

Why "Captive Voices"? In 1973, the Robert F. Kennedy Memorial[2] created a commission to report on the status of high school journalism.[3] According to Franklin Patterson, the commission's chairman, the memorial's original interest in high school journalism evolved from two surveys: One survey showed that high school faculty advisers to newspapers "in one way or another" favored censorship, and the other study indicated that less than 1 percent of U.S. professional journalists were minorities ("Captive Voices", p. xiv).

The commission members responsible for "Captive Voices" supported the *Tinker v. Des Moines Independent School District*[4] (1969) ruling and firmly believed the First Amendment did apply to high school students. In other words, when students enter their high schools, they shouldn't lose their rights to free expression; school administrators are not publishers.

The commission originally had four areas of inquiry: (1) censorship, (2) minority participation, (3) journalism and journalism education status and, (4) professional (or established) media's perceptions. Both qualitative and quantitative methods were used to compile its report, which Jack Nelson[5] edited and prepared. Members held town hall meetings; surveyed student editors, administrators, and journalism teachers and advisers; and did a content analysis of almost 300 school papers.

However, when the report *Captive Voices: High School Journalism in America* was published in 1974, it met with criticism. According to John Bowen, the author of the 1976 article titled "Captive Voices: Another Look," the original report created "a wide and continuing controversy over the status of scholastic journalism among principals, advisers, members of the professional media and members of the country's scholastic press organizations" (p. 3).[6]

Naysayers said the report was guilty of generalizations and over-simplifications. The main point of "Captive Voices" was this: Censorship of high school journalists and their publications remained a problem even though the courts continued to favor students and their advisers as cases came to light.

Because of the allegations against the report, Bowen decided to do his own survey to seek answers that would either duplicate or reject the conclusions of the Kennedy commission – namely, the findings of widespread censorship and of the low priority high school journalism classes experienced. Bowen (1976) concluded the following from the information he gathered:

> It seems obvious that the report of the Robert F. Kennedy Commission's "Captive Voices" is guilty of sweeping generalizations and over-simplification. However, some specific charges were seemingly upheld while in some cases there is not enough conclusive evidence. There is valid evidence to indicate that censorship is unreasonable in enough cases to make it a problem worth further investigation. (p. 17)

Bowen's research concluded that the original "Captive Voices" report, overall, "painted a representative picture of what was happening in the high schools" ("Cheeseburger", 1994, p. 77). In other words, suspicions from the past were confirmed in some areas, and "the report was seen as a legitimate call for strengthening the high school press" (p. 80).

The report concluded with 47 suggestions. Although some criticized "Captive Voices," many others helped create changes suggested in the report. The commission responsible for "Captive Voices" hoped its study would be the beginning of reform for scholastic journalism – and so it was. For instance, because of "Captive Voices," the Student Press Law Center was created in 1974. The SPLC was a joint project of the Robert F. Kennedy Memorial and the Reporters Committee for Freedom of the Press. JEA, established in 1924, became even more active, and with the help of two organizations – NAA and ASNE – distributed "Project Outreach" to professional news associations. The publication explained how professionals could support high school newspapers. JEA also created national certification tests for high school faculty advisers. A member of the Kennedy commission, Sister Ann Christine Heintz, and Kennedy Memorial fellow Craig Trygstad began publishing an independent teen newspaper *New Expression* in Chicago with a staff of mostly minority students. Soon these independent youth newspapers were published in many large U.S. cities.

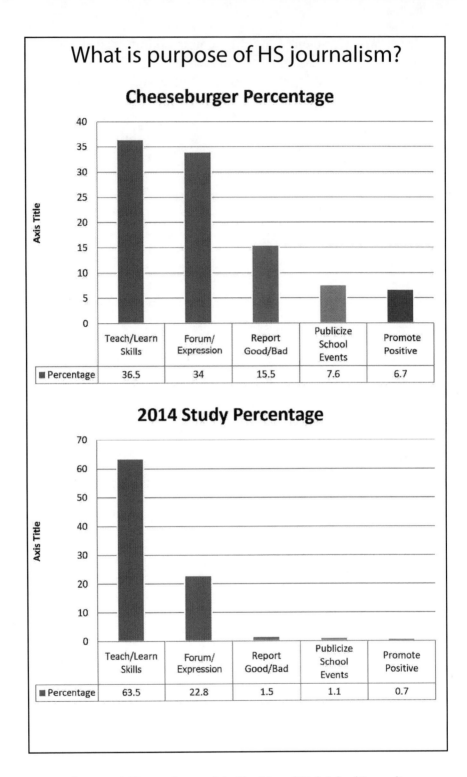

What is purpose of HS journalism?

Cheeseburger Percentage

	Teach/Learn Skills	Forum/ Expression	Report Good/Bad	Publicize School Events	Promote Positive
Percentage	36.5	34	15.5	7.6	6.7

2014 Study Percentage

	Teach/Learn Skills	Forum/ Expression	Report Good/Bad	Publicize School Events	Promote Positive
Percentage	63.5	22.8	1.5	1.1	0.7

Twenty years later: The Freedom Forum's Death by "Cheeseburger"

Charles Overby was the president and CEO of the Freedom Forum when the 1994 *Death by Cheeseburger: High School Journalism in the 1990s and Beyond*[7] was published. At the beginning of the report, Overby explained the following:

> High school journalism is being threatened by budget shortages, community indifference, poor teacher training and occasional outright hostility from school administrators. ... all high school students deserve vehicles of expression and communication. This idea is at the core of The Freedom Forum's mission of free press, free speech and free spirit. (p. vi)

The commission responsible for "Captive Voices" hoped its study would be the beginning of reform for scholastic journalism – and so it was. However, by 1994, the 1988 Supreme Court decision in Hazelwood School District v. Kuhlmeier reversed the way school officials saw the student press. (See Chapter 7 for more information.) With that concern in mind, "Death by "Cheeseburger"[8] provided recent research about high school journalism, provided a content analysis of 233 school newspapers and reported on several interviews with people involved in or who had been involved with high school journalism.

It should be noted that Jack Dvorak, the former director of the High School Journalism Institute at Indiana University, did a research report published in 1992 titled "Secondary School Journalism in the United States"; many of his findings appear in "Cheeseburger" and will be mentioned later in this chapter. Also, Tom Dickson – then of Southwest Missouri State University – published survey information from 364 high school teachers and/or advisers in 1990, and his findings are shown via infographics in "Cheeseburger". More than three dozen individuals helped research and compile the report.

The "Cheeseburger" report suggested 12 steps for improving high school programs (p. 147), including the following:

School broadcast media should be integrated with newspapers

to serve diverse student interests and talents and to let electronic media, including broadcast, cable and electronic bulletin boards become a part of high school journalism. News organization and schools should recognize the place, and need for support, of all modes of information delivery. (p. 148)

The reviews of "Death by Cheeseburger" were positive and appreciative.[9] Bruce Konkle, an associate professor at the University of South Carolina, stated the following at the end of his 1995 commentary in the Student Press Review:

"Cheeseburger" accomplishes what it set out to. It gives readers insights into critical scholastic journalism issues through features and informational graphics. In its own way, it updates "Captive Voices" and gives readers vignettes that help tell some of the stories of high school journalism in the 1990s and beyond. (p. 31)

The following sections discuss the first seven research questions; the final question, RQ8, gets its own chapter following this one.

RQ1: The teachers: What backgrounds do journalism teachers and/or advisers have?

When the 1974 "Captive Voices" report summarized the status of journalism faculty/advisers' media backgrounds, it highlighted that its surveys showed a majority of teachers had little or no journalism background (more than 50 percent) and had little interest in taking their jobs in the first place; only 32 percent had requested their journalism jobs (Nelson, 1974, p. 89).

The "Captive Voices" commission also reported university schools and departments of journalism were occupied with the training of professional journalists, not journalism educators. This has "contributed to the dearth of qualified high school teachers," the report stated (p. 89). English teachers were the most likely to end up as the adviser of the newspaper. Specifically, the 1974 report stated:

The low priority usually accorded journalism by school administrators discourages teachers from participating and disheartens many of those who do participate. While athletic teams, bands, and pep squads rarely suffer from lack of funding, high school media are in a constant financial squeeze. … journalism teachers also frequently are required to bear unfair burdens of heavy scheduling, inadequate compensation, and – in cases where they buck the tide of censorship – job insecurity. (Nelson, 1974, p. 91)

"Captive Voices" made it clear that journalism teachers, classes and publications were a low priority with administrators, and how journalism was taught in the United States was far from consistent. "Death by Cheeseburger" declared 20 years later it was hard to fight that old image. "Far too many educators and administrators rank journalism with metal shop, rather than Shakespeare. At worst, it's viewed as a dumping ground for hard-to-handle students" (Freedom Forum, 1994, p. 17).

"Cheeseburger" also lamented poorly prepared teachers:

From state to state, the standards by which teachers are certified as qualified to teach the subject vary wildly or don't exist at all. Standards for what constitutes good curriculum are uneven, too. Censorship clashes in some schools put many a teacher's neck on the chopping block and warp his or her students' understanding of the First Amendment. (Freedom Forum, 1994, p. 11)

"Cheeseburger" noted that experts thought the shortage of college-trained journalism teachers correlated with the small number of colleges offering majors in journalism education. "Over the last 10 years, some campuses have stopped offering bachelor's degrees in journalism education because of budget cutbacks, a lack of demand and other reasons," the report stated (Freedom Forum, 1994, p. 13).

So, 20 years ago, the teaching and advising of high school journalism had many of the same problems from 40 years ago. And, if one looks at high school journalism history at the beginning of the 20th century, many of these worries were the same then. (See Chapter 5.)

Today, is *anything* better? Many teachers *do* care about teaching journalism and teaching the subject correctly – and many more have the qualifications to teach and advise student media. Almost half (46.6 percent) said they had some kind of professional media experience. More than one-fifth of the current study's respondents (21.5 percent) teach only journalism courses while the majority of respondents teach both journalism courses and other subject areas (69.4 percent). Most teachers who teach in both areas stated English classes were what they taught – a situation that has been the norm since journalism showed up in high schools decades ago.

About one-fourth (24.5 percent) said they had taken no college journalism courses; however, more than a third (37.5 percent) reported taking 10 or more college journalism courses. Unqualified people still teach journalism courses or advise student media today, but many teachers and/or advisers have much more training and skills.

How did teachers and/or advisers come to be in their current position? Although half of respondents (49.6 percent) said they were hired or assigned to the job of journalism teacher and/or adviser, 39.8 percent said they actually applied for the work. If one compares this to the information from 40 years ago (when 32 percent requested the job), this has not changed much.

RQ2: Which students work with student media or take journalism courses?

Encouraging results come from the question about the ability range of journalism students and/or student media staff. Although the majority of the respondents (65.4 percent) said they had a diverse mixture of student ability in their classes or on their student media staffs, 31.7 percent reported they had mostly high-achieving students. Only a small number of teachers and/or advisers reported their student media comprise low achievers.

Similar results came from the question about the motivation of respondents' student journalists. More than half said their students ranged from highly motivated to no motivation (54.4 percent); however, 37.9 percent said they had mostly motivated students.

In 1974 when "Captive Voices" survey respondents reported on the same two questions, the answers were somewhat similar to the current report: 67.3 percent said they had a diverse mixture of students and 20.3 percent reported working with mostly high-achieving students.[10] For the question of student motivation, "Captive Voices" respondents (57.6 percent) said they worked with a diverse mixture of students while 38 percent said they worked with highly motivated students.

One of the five sections in "Captive Voices"' is dedicated to mi-

nority participation – or the lack thereof. The commission concluded the following via interviews with high school students, teachers
and professionals: "In the first place, there are relatively few faculty
members – black and white – with [a] zeal for recruiting minorities
for journalism" (p. 55). The commission's findings included the ob-
servation that minority access to journalism participation included
financial issues at mostly minority schools, failure of schools to help
minority youth develop reading and writing skills, and lack of high
school journalism organizations and journalism professionals encouraging participation by minorities (p. 77). The commission also
noted that most high school counselors knew nothing about opportunities in journalism.

"Captive Voices" provided no concrete statistics about participation by minority students in student media or journalism classes.
Professionally, though, the American Society of Newspaper Editors
conducted its own survey in 1973 and found minority staffing at U.S.
newspapers to be three-fourths of one percent, or .0075 (p. 56). In
fact, the report found recruitment of minorities by newspapers had
decreased and "the sense of urgency for hiring minority journalists
that began with the urban riots of the 1960s had tapered off" (p. 57).

Christopher Callahan published a study, "Race and Participation in High School Journalism," in 1998. He notes that 1978 was
the year when the American Society of Newspaper Editors set a goal
of having newsrooms reflect the racial makeup of the country by
2000. By 1994, more than 20 years after the 1973 ASNE study, the
percentage of minorities was 10.5 percent. Callahan also points out
that although many newspaper minority-recruiting programs were
created, few programs targeted high school students (p. 46). He did
discover in his 1998 study that predominantly minority (black) high
schools (67.5 percent) had fewer newspapers compared to 91.7 percent of "white plurality" schools (Callahan, p. 49).

In "Death by Cheeseburger" minority student involvement was
explained as follows:

> The words from "Captive Voices" still apply. It is still too often
> true that school newspapers generally are dominated by college-
> bound middle-or upper-class students, with those of low income
> or of a vocational bent participating in minimal numbers. This
> results in an elitism that excludes cultural and ethnic minorities as
> well as racial minorities. (Freedom Forum, 1994, p. 31)

The average percentage of white journalism students or staffers at high schools was 80.6 percent, a 1992 JEA survey reported, with 525 of its members responding (p. 34). Other participation percentages included 6.5 percent Hispanic, 5.6 percent African American, 5.3 percent Asian American and 1 percent Native American.[11]

The current study found participation in high school journalism was "mostly minority" students in 17 percent of the schools while "mostly non-minority" came in at 67.3 percent. An equal balance of minority and non-minority students involved in journalism was at 17.2 percent of the schools.

Today's yearbook staffs had the highest percentage of minority student participation with 23.9 percent while television had the lowest with 12.1 percent. However, if one takes the "equal balance" of minorities and non-minorities percentages and adds them to the minority participation and the nonminority participation, the percentages change to approximately 25 percent minority and 75 percent nonminority. It should be noted no significant correlation was found between the makeup of school and students' participation in journalism courses or student media. According to the U.S. Census Bureau, however, the following is predicted:

> Minorities, now 37 percent of the U.S. population, are projected to comprise 57 percent of the population in 2060. (Minorities consist of all but the single-race, non-Hispanic white population.) The total minority population would more than double, from 116.2 million to 241.3 million over the period. (www.census.gov)

Although the percentages seem a bit better than 20 years ago, more recruiting still needs to be done.

If students do want to participate in student media, the requirements vary from school to school. From the list of responses available to survey respondents of the current study, the following was reported:

- Must be enrolled in relevant journalism course: 33 percent
- Anyone welcome: 27.9 percent
- Must have taken a journalism course: 23.4 percent

Most write-in responses (15.6 percent) to this question said staff participation included some kind of application process. The "Captive Voices" study showed there were "less stringent requirements for publication staffs in minority schools" (p. 193); however, the current study does not show any significant correlation. Forty years ago, 59.6 percent said no experience was necessary and anyone was welcome; today's study shows basic journalism knowledge and/or good grades are important to be a member of student media staffs.[12]

RQ3: Who has the final OK for airing or publishing student media work?

"Captive Voices" reported 40 years ago that 75 percent of advisers had the final OK for publishing student work, 11.7 percent said student editors did while 13.3 said school administrators did. In contrast, 44.5 percent of today's high school journalism advisers report they have the final OK, 24.8 percent say their student editors have the final OK while more than one-fourth, 25.7 percent, say the administration has the final OK – which is quite different than 40 years ago following the 1969 Tinker decision.

"Death by Cheeseburger" was published after the 1988 *Hazelwood* decision, and student publication censorship is prominently discussed via two separate chapters. "Cheeseburger" reported via Dickson's 1992 study that 36 percent of advisers said their principals either "on occasion" or "quite often or always" read their student publications before they were published. The current study found 33.4 percent of newspaper and yearbook advisers said administrators either "always" or "sometimes" did a pre-publication review. It appears not much has changed since *Hazelwood* or since the "Cheeseburger" report.

The current study found that 37 respondents (14.3 percent) said they were constantly worried their journalism teaching and/or student media advising would be reprimanded because of student work that creates a controversy while 60.3 percent said they were "sometimes" worried. Sixty-five respondents (25.3 percent) said they were never afraid of being reprimanded. What is alarming today, however, is that almost three-fourths of the respondents reported they are constantly or sometimes afraid of reprimand. What needs to be done so these teachers are not afraid to do their jobs?

Twenty years earlier, "Cheeseburger" reported from Tom Dickson's 1992 study that 28 percent of advisers did not worry at all about facing controversies with the administration because of student work; however, 9 percent said they worried "quite a bit" and another 63 percent said they worried "not too much" (p. 121). The percentages from today and 20 years ago are very similar. The good news is that when "Cheeseburger" was published only five states had passed positive legislation regarding student press rights; today, the SPLC reports that 10 have now passed legislation (http://www. splc.org/knowyourrights/statelegislation.asp).[13]

RQ4: Do student media have written guidelines to follow re: what is appropriate to cover?

The majority of high school journalism teachers and/or advisers in the current study (66 percent) said they have no guidelines to follow for deciding which topics are appropriate to cover for a high school audience; 33.1 percent said they do have guidelines, and less than 1 percent said they didn't know if there were any available.

Of the respondents who did have guidelines, the majority (65.7 percent) were self-created with newspaper and magazine teachers and/or advisers explaining they did everything, from modifying Student Press Law Center (SPLC) guidelines to "cobbling together ideas from various student journalism web sites." The majority of yearbook and television broadcast advisers reported they created them with their staffs and re-evaluated them each year while some were staff-created then approved by administrators. Of those who said they had guidelines to follow, only 6.4 percent said administrators or the Board of Education provided them.

Teachers and/or advisers do, however, put limitations on what can be aired or printed. Forty years ago, "Captive Voices" reported 41 percent of faculty/advisers placed limitations on what students could publish, and 20 years ago "Cheeseburger" reported 43 percent of advisers said some stories were not covered sometimes or fairly often because of subject matter. Exactly what they limited was not explained in either study; however, anecdotal cases were provided such as a pulled Planned Parenthood article ("Captive Voices", 1974, p. 4) and a story about alcohol poisoning stopped by the principal ("Cheeseburger", 1994, p. 117).

The current study found, though, that 90.7 percent place limitations on what can be published or aired. Those who said they put limitations on student media listed the following for legal, ethical, personal or aesthetic reasons:[14]

- Potentially libelous/libelous: 92.5 percent
- Obscenity/sexual content: 87 percent
- Invasion of privacy: 79.2 percent
- Language or visuals that cause a material and substantial (physical) disruption to the learning process: 72.7 percent
- You (or others) have a legitimate pedagogical concern about the language or visuals: 46.1 percent
- Too controversial, inappropriate for our school community: 39.9 percent
- Too controversial, inappropriate for our broader community: 20.5 percent
- Content critical of the school (its employees, student clubs, athletics, etc.): 7.1 percent [15]
- Violation of FCC rules/regulations: 54.8 percent

One can see that the legal limitations are necessary; however, some limitations seem to be a teacher's choice.[16]

Censorship Issues

As mentioned earlier, one of the outcomes of the "Captive Voices" study was the creation of the Student Press Law Center. Now, 40 years later, the non-profit SPLC is as active as ever. "Cheeseburger" reported thoroughly on the center nearly two decades after its creation. In 1992, more than a quarter of the 1,713 calls to the center concerned censorship (26.8 percent) with libel/privacy questions coming in second (13.6 percent). It should be noted that more than half of the total number of calls came from private or public colleges (62.7 percent), yet almost one-fourth (22.3 percent) came from private or public high schools.

Currently, according to SPLC's website (splc.org), about 2,500 student journalists, teachers and others contact the SPLC every year for help or information. Frank LoMonte, SPLC's executive director since 2008, notes in an email that SPLC does not keep statistics on calls or emails because it would be too overwhelming. However, he says, from what he and his staff can track, about 60 percent of the calls received today are from high school students.

"They do range greatly, but the most common [inquiry] is press freedom," he says. "Copyright is generally the second most–asked inquiry, and I think, online publication—whether or not information can be placed online—is third" (personal communication, May 13, 2014). In November 2013 during the National High School Journalism Convention in Boston, Kent State University's Center for Scholastic Journalism on behalf of SPLC administered a survey to 531 students and 69 advisers about their experiences with censorship.[17]

According to a Feb. 18, 2014, SPLC press release, 32 percent of the student respondents and 39 percent of advisers said school administrators had told them not to publish or air student-created work. Also, 32 percent of the students said a school official always reviews their work before it is published or aired, and 42 percent of advisers said someone other than students had the final say for the content of the student media they advise. Because of the above situations, both students and advisers said they had applied self-censorship. Nine percent of the advisers also reported their positions had been threatened by school officials because of content decisions made by their students.

In Tyler Buller's 2011 *Journal of Law and Education* article, "Subtle Censorship," retaliation against high school journalism advisers is addressed. Instead of student-created work being censored directly by administrators, the adviser's job is instead threatened. According to Buller (2011), "This retaliation exploits a loophole in student journalists' protections, results in indirect censorship and shills student speech."

Buller's comprehensive article argues the best way to prevent reprisal against journalism advisers is via state legislatures that should adopt statutes that prohibit this kind of retaliation, grant students a cause of action and require local school districts to adopt policies to protect student publications (Buller, 2011). Buller, an attorney and a former student journalist, presents wording to use and suggestions on how to save advisers and their students from unfair censorship.

RQ5: How are student media funded?

Forty years ago, "Captive Voices" reported student publications were mostly funded by the sale of publications and/or from advertising (66 percent), but 38.7 percent also received funds from the school.[19] The report noted almost a quarter (24.3 percent) of the newspapers relied on fund-raising, but it also noted that in minority schools, the newspaper was less likely to have school funding and had to depend on raising funds through a variety of means (p. 196). Although most schools 40 years ago used offset printing for publishing their newspapers more than any other method, minority schools tended to mostly mimeograph their papers (p. 195).

"Cheeseburger" (Freedom Foundation, 1994) devoted one of its 10 chapters to "Black ink, red ink: Dollars and cents of high school newspapers," noting "by the standards of most media outlets, high school newspapers are a cheap form of expression" (p. 68). No media executives need to be paid, and the basic costs, such as teachers' salaries and classroom space, are provided by the schools. "Cheeseburger" stated the majority of newspaper advisers typically receive a stipend of about $1,000 for the extra hours they put into advising the newspaper staff (p. 68).

In 1994, equipment costs came from a variety of sources. A computer might be donated or bought with school funds; software and a camera might be bought with advertising revenue. In addition to the cost of equipment, however, there were printing and film costs (Freedom Forum, 1994, p. 70). What "Cheeseburger" found, however, was that if there was a lack of funds, there was a lack of diversity (Freedom Foundation, 1994, p. 71). In other words, just as financial gaps existed between suburban and urban schools, the same existed between high school journalism programs.

Today, more than one-third of the respondents (38.7 percent) reported they fund their student media through a "mixture of methods," including funding from the administration, advertising sales and fund-raising. "Advertising sales" was the next most frequently answered response (21.4 percent) to how student media were funded with "school administration" coming in third (18.8 percent).[19] However, 16.6 percent of respondents chose "other" to explain how student media were funded at their schools. Perkins grants were noted as one way of raising money for student media, but several teachers said they paid for print issues themselves (because "the school administration does not contribute") and, apparently, according to respondents in this category, more newspapers and magazines are going online. That's good news; however, one instructor said she had to pay for upgraded software. Some newspapers are photocopied (which is similar to being mimeographed 40 years ago). One respondent, though, did report that the local newspaper printed the high school newspaper for free.

Forty years ago, the majority of faculty advisers of high school newspapers (34.3 percent) reported most of the work they did with student publications was done during class time, so there was no extra compensation. Some (32.7 percent) received a bit of relief from their teaching load, and 22.3 percent carried a full load but received extra salary for their work with the newspaper (Nelson, 1974, p. 192).[20] Five percent said they carried a full load yet volunteered their time as adviser. As mentioned above, according to "Cheeseburger," the majority of high school newspaper advisers 20 years ago typically received a stipend of about $1,000 for the extra hours they put into advising the newspaper staff.

Today, 81.8 percent of this study's respondents said they received a stipend for the student media they advise along with their base salary; however, 13.7 percent reported they receive no extra pay for being a student media adviser. Other responses (4.9 percent) varied between outside volunteers to part-time work. If one looks at the teachers and/or media advisers who teach only journalism courses or teach a couple of journalism courses and the rest in another subject area, 92.8 percent of these respondents are paid a stipend of some kind; however, the amount of the stipend was not asked in the current study.

RQ6: What outside organizations help (or support) student media?

The SPJ Education Committee also wanted to learn how media professionals and colleges or universities helped respondents. More than half (56.1 percent) said media professionals made no contributions to their high school student media while 53 percent said nearby colleges or university journalism programs also made no contributions. Almost one-fourth of the respondents (23.6 percent) reported they receive no help from either. One-fourth of the respondents, therefore, are fending for themselves. Almost a third (30.3 percent) of "Captive Voices" respondents said they received no contributions from either, so perhaps the situation today is slightly better.

The biggest help in 1974 from university journalism departments came via workshops for high school journalism students, "Captive Voices" (Nelson, 1974) respondents reported (59.3 percent). Today, 32.4 percent of this study's respondents said university journalism programs provided workshops. This is a substantial drop in contributions. "Cheeseburger" did not touch on how universities might help high school journalism teachers and/or advisers; however, the report did include a chapter, "Good news, bad news: Newspapers' investment in local high school journalism," on how local media (newspapers) were helping – or not helping – high school journalists and their advisers.

"Cheeseburger" (1994), which reported video would be an important component to add to high school journalism in the future, suggested five ways community newspapers could get involved with high school newspapers:

1. To bolster schools and to rescue journalism programs threatened by budget cuts, indifference, censorship and poorly trained advisers.
2. To recruit young talent – especially ethnic minorities – into the profession.
3. To connect with young people, so journalists can do a better job of covering them.
4. To cultivate newspaper readership among young people, so they develop an appetite for news.
5. To instill an appreciation of First Amendment freedoms in students, who become better citizens and in the process enrich democracy. (p. 50)

"Cheeseburger" also reported on an American Society of News Editors (ASNE) survey of 234 newspapers about how they helped high school journalism programs. The most answered choice (41 percent) was "high school journalism seminars" (Freedom Forum, 1994, p. 53). Thirty percent of the newspapers reported they printed high school newspapers although it was not clear if they did this for free.

(See Chapter 13 for additional information on how professionals help high school news media.)

Today only 20 percent of high school journalism teachers and/or advisers said working professionals provide workshops; 53.7 percent said, however, that professionals speak to their classes when asked. Almost half of the respondents 40 years ago reported that guest speakers from local papers came to speak when asked; 39.3 percent said that the local newspaper printed their students' articles in their publications. Offering scholarships and internships to high school students seems to be a very low priority for local news media.

Speaking of scholarships, only 11.3 percent of the current study's respondents said universities provide them to their high school students while 4.9 percent said professional media organizations offer them; 18.9 percent reported professional media offer internships to their students.

RQ7: What do our respondents believe is the main hindrance to doing their jobs — if any?

No money for updating necessary equipment	38.7 percent
No interest from students	26.8 percent
Not applicable (no significant problem)	35.7 percent

As shown above and mentioned previously, more than one-third said having no money for updating equipment hindered them from doing their jobs. "No interest from students" was chosen by more than one-fourth of the respondents.

More than one-third, however, said they have nothing hindering them from doing their jobs, but the teachers and advisers who believe they have hindrances could use some outside help.

One reason the SPJ Education Committee wanted to explore the current status of high school journalism was because of the rumor that some high school journalism programs or student media were in danger of being eliminated. Although many of the respondents said they did not believe there was a danger (68.2 percent), 24.4 percent said "yes" they believed there was that danger and 7 percent said they really didn't know.

Although some of this study's respondents reported stressful situations, Reinhardy, Maksl and Filak published "A Study of Burnout and Job Satisfaction Among High School Journalism Advisers" in *Journalism & Mass Communication Eduction* in 2009, using the Maslach Burnout Inventory. With 563 advisers responding, the researchers found that these participants "are not experiencing burnout at any level" (Reinardy, Maksl, & Filak, p. 345). The respondents "indicate normal levels of emotional exhaustion," which is balanced by "high levels of personal satisfaction" (p. 352). The researchers concluded journalism advisers are happier than other secondary school teachers, noting, however, there is "room for further research" (p. 353). Agreed. With some advisers working extra hours with no extra pay and with almost one-fourth of respondents believing their journalism programs or student media might be cut, this is a situation worth re-investigating.

Respondents gave many reasons for their belief about why their programs might be eliminated, but one of the main reasons was an emphasis on the required (common core) curriculum, which does not include journalism. Another reason reported by respondents, however, was a lack of student interest. Why this lack of student interest exists also needs to be explored through additional research, interviewing the high school students themselves.

The responses to RQ8: "What do respondents believe could improve high school journalism?" will be answered in the next chapter.

Endnotes

1. In both of the previous reports, yearbooks were not considered as part of the studies although yearbooks have a long, rich history in American junior highs and high schools. The current study included yearbook advisers because they are part of the JEA membership.

2. According to www.nndb.com: "Since its inception in 1968, The Robert F. Kennedy Memorial has aimed to fulfill the legacy of Robert Kennedy through promoting the full spectrum of human rights within the United States and throughout the world."

3. The study cost $65,000 and was carried out by a 22-member commission over 15 months.

4. See Chapter 11 for more information.

5. Nelson was a Southern-born reporter and Pulitzer Prize winner famous for covering civil rights.

6. Bowen, J. (1976, January) Captive voices: Another look. *Communication: Journalism Education Today*, 3-23.

7. The reports title comes from a 1971 satirical article in a North Carolina high school newspaper that described eating at the school's cafeteria; the article was titled "Death by a cheeseburger." Because of this article, the paper was shut down and its adviser fired.

8. The report was conceived and led at that time by Alice Bonner, Freedom Forum's director of journalism education, and by Judith Hines, Freedom Forum's program officer for journalism education.

9. For more information, see the annotated bibliography. See citations for Konkle, B., Walsh, M., Andrew, R., and Hernandez, D. H.

10. "Cheeseburger" did not have a similar question for comparison.

11. "Other" or No Answer" made up 1 percent.

12. "Cheeseburger" did not specifically answer this question.

13. The 10 states are Massachusetts, Pennsylvania, Arkansas, Illinois, Iowa, Kansas, Colorado, California, Oregon and Washington state.

14. Respondents were able to check as many answers as applied.

15. These answers were compiled from those asked in the 1974 "Captive Voices" and the 1994 "Death by Cheeseburger" reports.

16. The current study did not ask for specific examples.

17. The results are not intended to present a random sampling of students and advisers; instead they are an anecdotal indication of experiences. The results were released in conjunction with Scholastic Journalism Week, which began Feb. 17, 2014.

18. Respondents (faculty advisers) were able to check as many answers as applied.

19. Note that 33.6 percent of the responses came from yearbook advisers who said they sell their books for funding.

20. No specific dollar amount was provided.

Chapter 4

Recommendations: Then and Now

 By Lee Anne Peck & David Burns

"Too few schools have journalism programs, and when they don't, they lose out on a great educational opportunity."[1]

Ninety-two (or 35.7 percent) of the current study's respondents chose to answer the following open-ended question: "Do you have suggestions on how scholastic journalism can be improved?" Some of these respondents provided more than one suggestion. Their responses were categorized, and this chapter outlines the top three areas. In addition, it compares current survey responses with data gathered 20 and 40 years ago. Specifically, comparisons are made with Jack Nelson's 1974 report titled, "Captive Voices" and The Freedom Forum's (1994) "Death by Cheeseburger" study, which provided snapshots of the state of scholastic journalism in Watergate Conspiracy-era America and the mid-1990s respectively. Also, this chapter refers to findings by Childers (2012) in his collection of essays titled, *The Evolving Citizen: American Youth and the Changing Norms of Democratic Engagement.*

Current respondents clearly state that where student media once attracted the best and brightest students, those students now choose to instead take college credit-earning AP courses. Survey comments also indicated teacher/advisers lack moral, physical and financial support from peers and especially administrators as well as training and networking opportunities – leading to low morale and feelings of isolation. Thus, this chapter is divided into three sections indicating the need for (1) curriculum reform, (2) comprehensive training and (3) financial support.[2]

Curriculum Reform

Of those responding to the open-ended question, 35.9 percent said curriculum reform would improve high school journalism. Chocked full of 47 suggestions, the "Captive Voices" report stated in its "Toward Action" chapter that "the ability to communicate effectively is a vital function of education in a democracy" (p. 143). The message: This ability can be taught in journalism courses.

Childers (2012) shared similar insight. In the chapter titled "American High School: Teenagers and Scholastic Journalism," he states: "If one wants to get a better understanding of the changing nature of democratic engagement, as seen through the eyes of American youth, the public school system seems to be the place to look" (p. 29). He writes that the subset of high school journalists is important for two reasons:

> Perhaps even more so than other students, a high school journalist has to be aware of his peers as a group with shared cultural norms and ideas. ... The second reason high school students are important is that there is evidence to suggest these students may grow up to be informational leaders and more involved citizens.[3] (p. 43-44)

But how does a young person perceive what democracy is today – that is, if he or she thinks about democracy at all? In a post-Sept. 11 world, even adult perceptions of American democracy have changed. A decade of wars in Iraq and Afghanistan may have imperceptibly influenced how America's youth think about democracy, their role in that democracy and even the need for a Fourth Estate. Childers (2012) believes teenagers should be taken more seriously: "Dismissing American youth and clinging to old notions of democratic engagement will not do," he says (p. 52). Instead, he says, young people understand their roles as democratic citizens in a different way because of the changing world in which they live. Reading and listening to student journalists will give one insight into what is important to them – and it's not just cell phones and video games.

Forty years ago, "Captive Voices" recognized journalism education could play a vital role in our democracy. The "Captive Voices" commission envisioned a high school journalism curriculum that extolled the right of free expression and encouraged inquiry and investigation – the foundations of a critical thinker, in other words. It recommended the following:

> Journalism education (should) be broadened in concept beyond traditional publications programs to the central curriculum so that all students will have the opportunity to elect courses that deal with the significance of media in contemporary society and that offer opportunities for free media expression. (p. 144)

The Freedom Forum's "Death by Cheeseburger" (1994) offers a dozen recommendations less-detailed than those in "Captive Voices." Ones similar to the above suggestion follow:

> Principals, administrators, school boards and parents must recognize the value of student expression for an effective education. High schools need policy guidelines or state laws that allow student journalists to exercise First Amendment press rights responsibly. … Students deserve clear teaching regarding the role of free expression within a democratic society and the responsibility of those who have access to the means of expression. (p. 147)

Educator suggestions for up-to-date high school curriculum in the current report may be more practical and less lofty; they simply want consistency. They see excellent students choosing to get a jump on college through AP courses rather than getting involved in their school's media enterprises. The survey respondents call for Common Core national standards for journalism courses and the creation of AP journalism classes. They want journalism classes to count for English class credits.[4] As one respondent wrote:

> The toughest issue facing scholastic journalism is enrollment because the course is not given the credit it deserves for teaching critical thinking skills and the practical, real-world, diverse experience it provides students. Finding a place for such a course within the coursework required for graduation would [be] immensely beneficial.

Another respondent added it was not just a matter of perspective (choosing college-level courses over extracurricular activities) but perception. School media are often not valued or supported by the front office: "Administrations, for the most part, don't respect the hard work of both teachers and students, or they treat the publications more like a PR tool for their campuses. They have no idea what it takes to produce a publication." Other respondents said some high schools don't even offer a journalism class; student media organizations are just an after-school activity.

Forty years ago, the "Captive Voices" report asked that journalism courses be added to "the central curriculum." Twenty years ago, "Death by Cheeseburger" recommended more administrative and academic support. Today, it appears high school journalism is still waiting for both.

Comprehensive Training

"It is important that journalism advisers find out what the new trends are and what new journalists are being required to know and do."

"I wish there was some protection for students/advisers. I am sometimes harassed about mistakes or published stories or prevented from even allowing kids to write stories."

As it was noted both 40 years ago and 20 years ago, more than one-fourth (27.2 percent) of those who answered the current question said comprehensive training needs to be done –administrators need to be tutored on the importance of having student media, student media instructors need better training, and student journalists need to be challenged by well-trained teachers/advisers. This area frustrates teachers and/or advisers a great deal. Many comments seemed to indicate they believe they are feverishly pedaling but going nowhere. One teacher's comment seemed especially poignant: "I think journalism needs a 'narrative,' or a definition. I find that students don't know what journalism is."

In the 1994 "Cheeseburger's" list of 12 suggestions for improving high school journalism programs, suggestion (or step) No. 3 stated: "Journalism teachers should be well-trained and qualified at the highest level with a thorough grounding in reporting and editing, ethics, First Amendment law and the newspaper business" (p. 147). The 1974 "Captive Voices" said, "The quality and general availability of the journalism experience in the schools should be dramatically improved" (p. 143). Not much has changed since then.

If the need for high school students to understand the role of journalism in a free society has remained unrealized for 40 years, the future does not look much better. For college students who aspire to teach high school journalism, they will have a hard time finding a university that offers courses toward that aspiration. When those who know about such university programs were asked where a list of universities could be found, they knew of no list.

However, Candace Perkins Bowen, the director of the Kent State University Center for Scholastic Journalism, said her center does have a link on its website listing requirements or certifications to teach high school journalism in all 50 states. "Each state seems to have a different requirement, and, thus, different courses might be offered," Bowen wrote in an email (personal communication, July 30, 2014). "Exactly what defines 'a program' might vary from one course to an entire major, depending on what that state requires."

She added, "So I can tell you, Kent State, Ball State, Kansas State, Michigan State, University of Iowa all have pretty active journalism teachers prep programs. I think South Carolina and North Carolina do or did. There are some at Eastern Illinois University. That's all I know about for sure."

Adam Maksl, an assistant professor at Indiana University Southeast and expert on youth media and media literacy, said in an email (personal communication, July 29, 2014) he suggests teachers who want training should consider the voluntary certification that the Journalism Education Association (JEA) offers: "With public school teachers having to demonstrate that they are 'highly effective' per federal and state regulations, many have been using the 'certified journalism educator' and 'master journalism educator' certifications from JEA."

Maksl also mentioned the American Society of Newspaper Editors/Reynolds High School Journalism Institute in his email: "It is a summer workshop program that has trained (free of charge) more than 2,000 teachers over the past dozen or so years (first supported by [the] Knight [Foundation], and for the past five or so years, [by] Reynolds)."

Tom Dickson's (2001) study "Trends in University Support of Scholastic Education" investigated whether university journalism and mass communication programs had lost interest in scholastic journalism in past years. At the end of the 20th century, Dickson found significantly fewer institutions were involved in activities related to preparing future journalism teachers. The current study suggests this trend has continued. To add to the problem, many college-level journalism programs themselves are in a state of flux.

"The job can be isolating and overwhelming, and advisers do not often have time to look beyond their workloads for help."

Many journalism teachers and/or advisers feel isolated in their endeavors, and, therefore, 15.2 percent of those who answered the open-ended question wished for more networking opportunities. With whom do they want to network? Forty years ago, the "Captive Voices" commission suggested teachers, advisers and/or students do the following:

- Connect with organizations in the community traditionally concerned with the protection of First Amendment rights, which includes the established media (p. 141);
- Connect with the local established media to increase understanding of professional journalism as an institution (p. 142); and
- Encourage minority students to participate in and connect with summer high school journalism programs (p. 142).

The "Captive Voices" study also suggested the established media reach out to journalism high school teachers, advisers and students. "This should be done through such activities as short-term internships, regular consultations with youth, journalism projects, and financial support and professional expertise to enrich and broaden student participation in summer workshops," the report stated (p. 145).

The "Captive Voices" commission suggested non-media community organizations such as the American Civil Liberties Union, local bar associations, colleges and universities, cable TV franchises, youth development foundations and local and state teachers associations could provide networking opportunities as well (p. 149). "Cheeseburger's" final suggestion 20 years ago was specifically about networking: "Students and teachers should have opportunities to use the services and attend meetings of state and national press organizations" (p. 148).

The teachers and advisers who answered the current survey desired an increased connectedness with the at-large community. One respondent wished for the following:

More connections between public schools and local college journalism programs, more business connections, more local journalism field trips, webinars in which students can participate during the school day; it should not be up to the journalism/newspaper adviser to go out and find the connections—college programs and businesses should be seeking out the public schools.

They want more support.

Another pertinent comment from a hopeful respondent was that JEA continue to enlist and maintain mentors to advise first- and second-year advisers as a remedy for the isolation many advisers feel. One participant mentioned joining JEA's national and state chapter as a crucial first step toward improving her high school journalism program. Another suggested the same: "Get more beginning teachers to visit JEA/NSPA [National Scholastic Press Association] conventions." If there is no one to sympathize or network with in the high school itself, JEA and other scholastic journalism organizations offer both practical and moral support to beginning teachers and seasoned educators.

"When administrators recognize the myriad ways in which journalism speaks to the Common Core, and parents see the tangible results of such studies (overall improvement in writing, academic performance, not to mention wonderful examples of student work), perhaps it will become a key content area and highly valued components of secondary education."

Financial Support

The quote that opens this section is reminiscent of one in "Captive Voices:" "The low priority usually accorded journalism by school administrators discourages teachers from participating and disheartens those who do participate" (p. 91). Such administrative attitudes do not help when it comes to funding journalism programs.

Twenty years ago in "Cheeseburger," the message was the same: Low priority equals low funding. Suggestion (or step) No. 9 stated: "Schools must have adequate funding to afford the materials, resources and adviser compensation necessary to produce a good newspaper every month" (Freedom Forum, 1994, p. 148). The step continues: "Faculty, administration, parents and outside media organizations should work with newspapers to make certain they have enough basic funding to publish on a regular basis."

Of the respondents who answered the open-ended question, 17.4 percent said they wished for financial support: to cover operational costs (such as printing or website costs), in the form of academic scholarships, to attend regional or national high school journalism conferences, and to update technology. They also wished for more financial support for teachers who want to be more involved with professional educator associations such as JEA and NSPA.

Many respondents struggle to keep their programs alive as economically strapped school systems parse out scaled-down budgets. One adviser said, "The focus is on athletics." Another strategized: "I am thinking of dropping our print paper next year and going strictly online because it is so expensive." The respondent added, "I also only have one computer (my teacher station) to use to publish print editions and update the website, which we do daily." A magazine adviser explained her staff must share one 8-year-old computer with the newspaper staff: "I am hoping we can save enough for a laptop."

Many high school journalism programs are struggling with little or no funding and a lack of up-to-date technology. Ironically, today's technology potentially could lower production costs for schools. However, technology updates require at least an initial outlay of cash and getting funding from an apathetic administration may prove more difficult. One respondent suggests bypassing school budgets entirely: "Perhaps some of the big technology companies and media corporations should create grants for these struggling programs." Interestingly, this idea mirrors a suggestion made two decades ago in the "Cheeseburger" report.

It may be easy to see increased funding and/or technology improvements as panaceas for high school journalism programs' many woes, but those would be shortsighted solutions to a far more complex problem. If high school journalism is to survive, journalism must have a place in school curricula, supported by school budgets and recognized among teachers' professional development options. As one teacher said, high school journalism "needs the 'respect' afforded to other academic disciplines by school administrations, colleges and, especially, state credentialing offices to ensure qualified teachers." Without those measures, high school media educators will continue to feverishly pedal, but go nowhere.

Endnotes

1. Quotes throughout this chapter are from open-ended question answers from this study's participants.

2. Other suggestions were made; however, many – although good – were not mentioned as often as others. They included the need for legislative advocacy and for more publicity about courses/student media and better recruitment of both talented students and teachers.

3. Childers did an analysis of seven high school newspapers over 45 years of publication.

4. Forty years ago, the "Captive Voices" commission suggested schools offer academic credit "for work done by students involved in out-of-school media."

Section II

History and Legal Issues for High School Journalists: How We Got Here

Profile 3

TERRY DURNELL

Lee's Summit North High School; public (1,800 students)
Lee's Summit, Mo.
TV, film adviser

When it comes to advising high school media, Terry Durnell said the story that really matters is about students who succeed despite expectations.

Durnell, 53, has seen plenty of success in her 21 years as an educator, including 1,200 awards won by media students, state and national recognition for her schools' publications, plus plenty of kudos for her own hard work.

But according to Durnell, it's those students who wander on the fringes, who might not seem as successful in the traditional sense, who typically find a way to succeed in publications.

"Most (advisers) look for the top kids," Durnell said. "I've never been that way; if you want to come in, I'll work with you how you are."

Durnell advises broadcasting and film at Lee's Summit North High School (LSNHS) in Lee's Summit, Mo. Throughout her 17 years at LSNHS, she's also advised the yearbook and newspaper. Her career began at a 400-student high school in Arizona where she advised students on the yearbook staff.

Her former students work professionally as journalists, as actors and stuntmen for the Arizona Film Commission, and as documentary videographers for national film companies. One works for National Public Radio, she said, and another teaches and advises publications at a nearby high school.

Yet the success stories that Durnell celebrates the most are much closer to home.

"I had a kid who took special education classes, with ADHD and dyslexia, who wanted to be in yearbook. I wasn't sure about it, and during first semester he was Mr. Social and ended up failing. He came back second semester and asked me if there was any way I'd let him stay.

"I told him, 'If you show me you're really interested, and maintain an 'A' or a 'B,' you can stay in the class,'" Durnell said. "He had found a family in here, and that kid got an 'A,' and continued to work hard. His senior year he took first place at nationals for photography. He was also first in state and was named student journalist of the year."

It's always, Durnell said, about what students can do.

A blind student approached Durnell with hopes of becoming part of the TV broadcast team. He had an interest in working professionally on radio, and thought the experience would help him get there.

"We figured out a way to make it work," Durnell said. "I had him find a partner to work with. He does storylines, voice-overs and conducts interviews, and his partner does the filming."

The news program, which is broadcast every three weeks, has a magazine format with two-minute packages about stories related to school. Students collaborate to produce storyboards, interview sources, and to film and edit video. In film class, students produce public service announcements, music videos and short films.

Durnell said the students' work has always been supported by administrators at her school – she's working with her fourth principal in 17 years – and there has never been any censorship or prior review in the yearbook or broadcast programs.

"The current newspaper adviser has had some censorship, but that was because the story was given to the principal before it was published. That opened up a bunch of issues," she said. "I'd rather ask for forgiveness than to ask for permission."

Durnell, who majored in journalism at Evangel University at

Springfield, Mo., said she teaches her students about student press law and firmly supports free speech in the publications at LSNHS.

"As an adviser who has done yearbook camps and journalism workshops, I see so many journalism teachers who don't know the law, and so many not as willing to take a stand for free speech, as I'd like them to."

And although Durnell said she's always had a "positive environment" in which to work – healthy budgets, a stipend for advisers and plenty of computers – the workload has been heavy, and she admits to burnout. She said she stopped advising yearbook three years ago.

"It definitely had worn me slick," she said. "I worked 12 months a year, and many weekends, nights and holidays. The burden to get it done still lands on the adviser. If the students drop the ball, it lands in the adviser's lap."

She also had a new family to consider "and all the new requirements of teachers. And there's No Child Left Behind requirements, and Common Core coming," Durnell said.

"The load for all teachers is becoming overwhelming," she said.

Her new schedule includes an introduction to broadcast class, advanced broadcast, advanced video technology, and a new class that she said has renewed her energy and teaching spirit, an International Baccalaureate (IB) film class.

She said she considers it another success. "This is what I get to do!"

Chapter 5

High School Journalism Pre-1960

 By Lee Anne Peck

"Most superintendents regard journalism as a mere extension of an English course, and – Heaven preserve us! – that anyone who knows English must necessarily know journalism. It is a constant source of surprise to newspapermen how many persons think of the ability to write English and journalism as synonymous."

Myles T. McSweeney, night city editor,
Boston Daily Record (1947)

Since the early 1900s, much has been published about the pros and cons of teaching high school journalism. Typically, in its early years, English teachers with little or no journalism experience taught journalism and/or advised yearbook and newspaper staffs. The teacher/advisers often lacked equipment, funds and/or support from administrators. Many in those first decades, however, worked many extra hours with both exhaustion and passion, believing in the many benefits of teaching journalism at the high-school level, including the opportunity to teach about democracy, the First Amendment and citizenship. The majority believed, too, they should not be censors.

Bruce E. Konkle, a professor of journalism at the University of South Carolina, tackled the early history of high school journalism in his comprehensive research paper "A Preliminary Overview of the Early History of High School Journalism in the U.S.: 1775-1925," which he presented in August 2013 at the annual Association for Education in Journalism and Mass Communication (AEJMC) convention.[1] Konkle concluded more research needed to be done, however, and called his 90-plus-page work "preliminary"; he stated that he hoped his effort would encourage others to continue the pursuit of scholastic journalism history (Konkle, 2003).[2]

Following the time period Konkle studied, a substantial number of books, essays and research articles about high school journalism continued to be published. By 1960, the research showed the challenges of teaching high school journalism remained the same. However, by 1960, research showed that more girls than boys worked on publication staffs, and not many high school staffers continued to study journalism in college. A brief history of high school journalism from its beginnings to 1960 follows, compiled via a selection of relevant articles.

Beginnings

In his article, Konkle said *The Student Gazette*, handwritten in 1777 by William Penn Charter School students in Philadelphia, had been identified as the first-known high school newspaper, but he points out that some researchers say it's best to believe papers published regularly in the mid-1800s were the first. The first yearbook, *The Evergreen*, was published in 1845 at Waterville Academy in New York, and the second-known annual was published in 1846 at Hopkins Grammar School in New Haven, Conn., according to J. Cutsinger and M. Herron in their 1996 book *History Worth Repeating* (Cutsinger & Herron, 1996).

Laurence R. Campbell, sometimes referred to as "the father of high school journalism," writes in his 1940 dissertation that some type of high school journalism courses were offered in 1900 at North High School in Des Moines, Iowa, and in 1910 at Kearny High School in Kearny, Neb. (Campbell, 1940). In the December 1910 School Review journal, Horace Mann School's teacher Allan Abbott published "High-School Journalism." On the article's first page, Abbott wanted to "make clear why . . . this journalistic activity is a vital force for good, to show how it reacts on the editors and on the school, and how it can be helped by the friendly co-operation of some interested teacher" (Abbott, 1910, p. 657). He outlined how school publications should operate and warned "a teacher adviser" should never be two things: "one is a censor, the other is an editor-in-chief" (p. 666). Why? Because of the following:

> Nothing could be more surely fatal; the student body are quick to detect the voice of Jacob, no matter if the hairy hand of Esau signs the editorial. They are even ready to imagine dictation from a teacher where it does not exist. And the moment they think that discussion in the columns of their paper is not free, the paper loses their respect, and is no longer a power in the school. The teacher adviser should tell his editors *how*, and not *what*, to write. (p. 666, author's italics)

In other words, journalism teacher/advisers should not interfere – only offer guidance.

Frances M. Perry writes about the supervision of school publications in the December 1919 issue of *The English Journal*; the author points out the danger of English teacher as censor and discusses the problems of not offering journalism courses *yet* having a school paper. Perry explains: "The English teacher's first aid to the student paper should be given in the classroom, not as criticism of the paper, but in modification of his course to include and enforce instruction of which the paper reveals the need" (Perry, 1919, p. 618). What happens, Perry says, is that the adviser who has the responsibility of the rogue newspaper staff will be responsible for:

> … the correctness of the paper and with no time or authority to have the work submitted by students and corrected and revised by them, would in many cases, however reluctantly, slip into the habit of retouching and rewriting the copy he approved, until the paper ceased honestly to represent student ability but would instead be faculty work regularly paraded in public as student achievement. (Perry, 1919, p. 618)

That's when "a press club" should be considered if no class offers journalism instruction. "English instructors figure more or less prominently in these meetings as they make themselves wanted," according to Perry (p. 620).

Four decades later, in John A. Boyd's 1960 *Journalism & Mass Communication Quarterly* article about high school journalism instruction, Boyd reports on a survey of Indiana high school journalism teachers. He concludes the following:

1. If the newspaper advisership is to become a desirable position and if the school is to be well represented to the public, administrators will have to hire qualified advisers and see that they are not overloaded.
2. There is a need for a definite educational program in the state for qualifying journalism teachers.
3. There is a need for a common course of study adopted by the state for teachers to use as a standard.
4. Student publications play an important role in the school and community as well as in the development of the student, so administrators cannot afford to overlook the importance of a qualified adviser and an adequate and more standardized journalism program. (Boyd, p. 587)

Boyd's study and his recommendations are a good representation of the needs of high school journalism teachers and programs throughout most of the United States in the 1960s.

Keeping journalism alive: Pre-1960s

Maurice W. Moe wrote "Amateur journalism and the English Teacher," published February 1915 in *The English Journal*. To help budding writers become interested in journalism, he both promotes and explains how to use membership in the United Amateur Press Association of America to high school journalism teachers. He provided this description: "The United Amateur Press Association of America 'was established in 1895 for the purpose of bringing amateur writers together to share their creative writings, exchange ideas, and encourage printers and desktop publishers to produce newsletters from their home print shops'" (Moe, 1915).

Moe wrote that he believed teachers and students alike "will be stimulated to write prolifically, and others will be given an interest in composition they would not otherwise have known" (p. 115). Anything written by teachers or their students could be submitted to the organization for possible publication.

In a 1922 *School Review* article by W.C. Reavis, "Student Publications in High School," the author writes that a student newspaper is an important medium of communication; however, high-school papers can also have major problems. Reavis says it is imperative that a capable adult oversee "the project" (Reavis, p. 514). "The success of the paper depends on this individual ... who cannot take things for granted at any time" (p. 515). He added the paper also needs competent, enthusiastic students for staff positions; momentary enthusiasm by student staff and the adviser is not acceptable (p. 515). The author strongly concludes "a policy of open-mindedness" and freedom of expression needs to be considered for both the staff and the student body.[3]

In the 1924 *Educational Review* article titled "The Value of High School Publications," H.N. Sherwood says the high school newspaper can be compared to athletics. Because the administration prescribes the regular high school curriculum, the students rebel – "no student helped plan it, in other words" (Sherwood, p. 20). Why are newspapers so valuable? Sherwood states, "They furnish an opportunity for youth to learn the art of meeting responsibility. The only agency that compares favorably with this one in rendering a similar service is athletics," the author says. However, the author also points out that the high school newspaper is more refined and wholesome than athletics, and calls for "careful study and supervision."

In 1924, *The English Journal* published two articles describing innovative publication efforts by two high schools, one in Freemont, Ill., and one in Elmsdale, Kan. In her February article, Clara Ryan (p. 129) explains how Freemont High School saves money on publishing its school newspaper. The local newspaper, the *Journal-Standard*, publishes students' news stories twice a week, therefore, saving the high school money. She describes the many benefits of such an arrangement, including the following:

> Business men are no longer being constantly approached, by both the semi-monthly (newspaper) and Annual (yearbook) staffs, for ads. Therefore, they are more ready to support the one publication. The project has led to a feeling of unanimity between Freeport's daily newspaper and the high school, a thing to be desired in any town. The students greatly appreciate the co-operation of the *Journal-Standard*; the daily's staff is most anxious each year that the high-school continues its news columns, for the school's activities are "covered" more thoroughly than would be possible,

otherwise. . . . The readers of high-school news are increased from 800 (the student enrollment) to perhaps 15,000 of Freeport's citizens. (Ryan, p. 130)

Money-saving tactic, yes. However, the article makes clear many more advantages can happen when the students' stories are published in the local newspaper.

The other article, "A Unique Project in High-School Journalism" by Vera E. Fawcett published in the April 1924 issue of *The English Journal,* explains how students at the Elmdale (Kan.) Rural High School published a country newspaper for three years. Titled the *Elmdale News,* the newspaper serves a previously unfulfilled purpose as the community publication, providing information about community affairs and school activities. Senior students are responsible for the writing and editing, and also for the newspaper's finances. A student business manager takes care of ad sales. Fawcett describes the situation as follows:

> The common criticism, that high school English does not function in the lives of the students, can be answered easily by a project of this kind. . . . My journalism class devoted part of their time to study of civic improvement, which bore fruit in several interesting editorials. . . . Incidentally, they are learning to correct their own mistakes and to write clear, forceful English. Mistakes in print under the public eye mean so much more than they do when they are red-inked on a theme page. (Fawcett, p. 278)

The importance of – and the problems with – high school journalism

The 1930 textbook, *Student Publications* by G. C. Wells and Wayde H. McCalister, discusses the publication of newspapers but also addresses the problems of the yearbook, or annual. The authors discuss surveys done by high schools which show that "the yearbook is gaining in popularity in some sections of the country while in others it appears to be losing" (p. 98). Although in the late 1920s some high school administrators indicated "the annual is not worth the cost in time and money" (p. 99), the yearbook continued to thrive in almost all U.S. high schools. In fact, a 1930s master's thesis study by G. Gordon Granberg found "opinions seem to indicate that the high school annual is here to stay. It must, however, become more an integral part of the high school in order to attain its proper place in the activities of the school" (p. vii).

Granberg also says yearbooks should be "a more complete yearly record of student life and the activities of the school" (p. x). The 1947 guidebook *Yearbook Architecture* states: "The yearbooks of the future will continue to serve their readers as a history of the year's educational activities at their schools, completely told in picture and story, well printed and illustrated and durably bound in permanent form" (p. 5).

In 1932, Myra McCoy wrote in *School and Society* about the importance of offering at least one course in high school journalism. She reports a school newspaper performs valuable services such as the following:

- It interprets the school and its activities to students, parents and the community;
- it unifies the student body and faculty and raises the morale of the school;
- it helps to fix standards of conduct, scholarship and athletics;
- it vitalizes composition and is most effective agent for teaching clearness, conciseness and vividness of style. (p. 245)

However, she stresses, the newspaper needs appropriate guidance because "without careful training of staff members and adequate supervision of the work of the editorial and business departments . . . it is obvious that few of the benefits mentioned would accrue" (p. 245). She notes few people know the amount of work that goes into supervising a school publication, but the experience and training students receive via working on the student newspaper is incomparable—especially when it comes to writing skills.

Jesse Grumette notes in a 1938 *Education Digest* article that a high school journalism curriculum can be excellent training for citizenship, although naysayers believe no space exists in the curriculum for a course "so purely vocational in nature" (p. 42). A journalism course, however, can teach both media literacy and critical thinking. To further clarify this position, Grumette expresses the following:

> If every citizen were taught to examine newspapers in the critical way in which students in this course are, it would be much more difficult for an unscrupulous chain of newspapers to create a war scare or return to office by a landslide a mayor who has been definitely proved to be thoroughly corrupt. (p. 43)

For democracy to survive, schools need to teach its importance, and high school journalism courses could possibly be the place for this to happen, Grumette says.

By 1940, hundreds of articles and books had been published about high school journalism; Konkle's 2013 paper – mentioned above – offers extensive bibliographies of such in its appendices. Edward H. Redford writes in the January 1940 issue of *School and Society,* it is time for a concrete philosophy of high school journalism to be created: What are the ends being sought? He blames this void on how quickly the journalism curriculum had grown since 1920. "It was a fad," Redford writes (p. 83). But now it is time to "get our feet on solid ground" (p. 85).

He provides "a scattering" of observations to help organize some basic principles for high school journalism. Redford also states that education for citizenship is of utmost importance in a student's education, and that includes knowing the importance of guarding freedom of speech and freedom of the press. In other words, learn about democracy by living it. He lists 23 ideas for high school teachers – from discouraging the use of awards and artificial recognitions to opening up journalism courses to everyone, not just those "who will do well in competition" (p. 85).

In the same 1940 issue of *School and Society,* Laurence R. Campbell discusses the educational backgrounds of journalism teachers, stating the importance of journalism teachers having specialized training for their jobs. Through a national survey in which 613 teachers from 48 states participated, he created a "picture" of high school journalism teachers (p. 87). He found evidence that journalism teachers are more likely to teach courses in English than in any other subject—but have no specific training in journalism.

Campbell also reported that administrators tended to make no provision for time in which to supervise publications during regular class periods. He also said that "principals in supposedly modern secondary schools thrust the task of sponsoring publications upon anyone who happens to be an innocent bystander – a new teacher who has to take whatever he gets or an older teacher who cannot handle study hall" (p. 87). He reports 16 of the 613 teachers who answered his survey had a degree in journalism while 20 respondents had no degree at all. Many respondents noted their inadequacies, he said.

"Perhaps this is a bleak picture," he writes (p. 89). More than half of the teachers reported they liked their journalism teaching more than their non-journalistic teaching. More than one-third were members of scholastic or professional journalism organizations. Campbell concludes with the following:

> It seems apparent that despite the fact that teachers of journalistic activities are teachers of superior general ability and general education, they are not so effective as they should be because in many instances they lack the specialized preparation for their work, which they should have. To assert that they are to blame for this situation would be unfair, for many of them have done remarkable jobs despite lack of funds, equipment and cooperation. (p. 89).

The teachers are, in general, not indifferent to their work; however, Campbell points out that "it is the school administrators, the heads of schools and departments of education and the superintendents of state departments of public instruction who are indifferent."

In 1957, Clifford F. Weigle, a Stanford university journalism professor, published in *Journalism and Mass Communications Quarterly* the results of two surveys[4] about the influence of high school journalism on career choice. Weigle explains newspapers have been facing a shortage of qualified male applicants for open editorial positions; according to the author, though, "newspapers themselves have been behind other industry in developing adequate personnel procedures and in adopting aggressive policies for the recruitment of new blood" (p. 39).

Weigle creates a hypothesis that low enrollment in college journalism programs correlates with low interest on newspaper staffs (mostly from males) in the high school setting. Twenty-three percent of the advisers said that newspaper men talking to school classes "seldom presented journalism as a desirable career" (p. 42.)

Advisers tended to underestimate, Weigle said, the rate of pay experienced editors and reporters could earn, and they also believed it was difficult to find a job. When former high school student editors were queried, only 3 percent of the "boys" who said they liked to write and had been successful at high school journalism wanted to pursue journalism as a career. All in all, Weigle found that journalism had turned into a girls' pursuit (p. 44).

To solve some of the many problems mentioned above, Northwestern University's Medill journalism professors created the first high school journalism workshop in 1930. According to Lester Benz in his Journalism and Mass Communications Quarterly article published in 1959, a survey conducted at the State University of Iowa in fall 1958 reported the number of high school journalism summer workshops conducted by college journalism programs had grown to 19 and showed five more were planned for summer 1959 while other colleges had plans for 1960 and beyond. Benz came to the conclusion via his study that "programs of this type offer an outstanding opportunity for schools and departments of journalism to render a much-needed and desired service to high schools" (p. 56). For more information on the history of journalism workshops and their current status, see Chapter 12.

Until the 1960s, student publications operated with their rights intact – and if there were problems, they were not discussed in national news. In the 1960s, however, students' freedom of speech became an issue, and years later their rights as student journalists were questioned.

Endnotes

1. Konkle's paper won the AEJMC Scholastic Journalism's Laurence R. Campbell Research Award.

2. Konkle stresses that eventually researchers will need to address the 235-plus years of scholastic journalism. Information comes from more than 500 theses and dissertations, about 2,000 journal articles, 130-plus journalism textbooks and other supplemental resources for students and advisers. Konkle says in addition to the above resources from scholastic press association resources, state department of education curriculum archives and membership record of scholastic press associations need to be searched.

3. Reavis also says annuals, or yearbooks, can be more than just photos of students.

4. The first study questioned high school journalism advisers in central California; the second study questioned college freshmen who had been high school editors.

Chapter 6

High School Journalism: 1960 to Hazelwood

 By Suzanne Lysak

He has been a professor in Georgia Southern University's education department for nearly 30 years, but Michael Moore has vivid memories of his first year as adviser to a high school student newspaper in Beaver Falls, Penn. It was 1983; he was teaching English. He had taken a journalism course while attending high school in the same area. As a junior and senior, he did some sports writing for the local newspaper, the *Beaver County Times.* But Moore admits he had no idea what he was in for when he was selected for the job of advising the student staff of the *Cougar Connection.*

"It changed how I do teaching," Moore reflects now. "I mean it was a life-changing experience for me."

Before his experience guiding his student reporters and editors, Moore said teaching "was pretty much a traditional kind of thing … I never really thought about my literature classes and my other classes as being classes where I could change my role to being that … more of a coaching role, more of the students actually setting the agendas, doing the work, making the major decisions on what we were doing and how we were going to do it and everything.

"My approach was, this is their newspaper," Moore said (personal communication, December 2013).

This meant the students took the lead in confrontations with school administrators about certain articles. Moore offered his opinion, but ultimately let the students decide how far they were going to take their case. It also meant they would learn the meaning of the adage "pick your battles" and the art of negotiation.

When challenged by an angry football coach and three school principals about a story examining why the team was 0 and 4 early in the season, the student staff at first unanimously voted to publish the story. After all, it did not name names and instead focused on an analysis of certain plays that had not worked in the team's favor. But then Moore talked to them about what was at stake: They would lose the future cooperation of the administration and coaches.

"So we made a deal. We made a deal [with the administrators], we would self-censor, we would move some things around until they were satisfied in exchange for more money and carte blanche on writing an article about teen pregnancy, which they balked at but they eventually went for it. That kind of thing happened all the time" (personal communication, December 2013).

Years later, Moore is still negotiating, but now as a journalist himself. In addition to his college teaching, he writes a column on education issues for the Savannah (Ga.) *Morning News*. He notes he and his editor have the occasional, expected, disagreement.

"It's a conservative newspaper so a lot of times we go back and forth about some of my pieces. Georgia is one of those states where the principle school funding comes from the state, so I'm pretty critical of what they choose to fund and what they don't fund and why they fund it. So he's always doing the balancing act with me like I used to do. So it's kind of fun to negotiate and compromise and make deals" (personal communication, December 2013).

Moore's limited journalism experience before he became a high school newspaper adviser is not unusual in the tradition of American high school journalism. In fact, in a 1960 *Journalism & Mass Communication Quarterly* article, "High school journalism in Indiana," John Boyd reported 58 percent of newspaper advisers he interviewed had not had any college journalism courses when they started as advisers. Sixty three percent of the first year advisers he interviewed at high schools in the state "were not originally employed to be newspaper advisers." The rate of turnover in advisers was high. "More than 50 percent were in their first five years as advisers," Boyd (1960) noted.

In the recommendations that emerged from his findings, Boyd

maintained "It should be recognized that journalism courses and activities need to be directed by teachers with specialized training." Furthermore, he urged, "To assure better trained publications advisers, the state should set up more stringent requirements for certification to teach journalism courses and/or advise student publications, and much more care should be made in the selection of journalism instructors."

Also in the years leading up to the landmark U.S Supreme Court *Hazelwood* decision, there is plenty of proof – both anecdotal and academic – that high school journalists struggled with censorship. In his 1976 book for the Journalism Education Association, *Captive Voices: Another Look*, high school newspaper adviser John Bowen referred to the original 1974 report prepared by the Commission of Inquiry into High School Journalism, which found "Censorship and the systematic lack of freedom to engage in open, responsible journalism characterize high school journalism;" and that "Censorship is generally accepted by students, teachers and administrators as a routine part of the school process. This has developed into the most pervasive kind of censorship, that imposed by students … themselves" (Bowen, 1976). The original "Captive Voices" report also maintained that pervasive censorship "has created a high school press that in most places is no more than a house organ for the school administration."

Bowen's *Captive Voices: Another Look* sought to determine if the Commission report accurately reported the realities of high school journalism. Bowen surveyed 175 high schools that had student newspapers. At each school, advisers, principals and editors were asked to complete the survey. As he was working as adviser to *The Lakewood High School Times* in Lakewood, Ohio, at the time, Bowen acknowledged "more surveys were sent to Ohio schools than out of state."

One of the 22 student editors who responded to Bowen's 1976 survey and commented anonymously had this feedback about censorship: "We are not allowed to criticize administrative decisions; to mention the use of any sort of drugs, criticize cafeteria food, or criticize coaches or athletic teams. Our proofs are read and censored by the principal before they are shipped to the printers. Our adviser believes in self-administered censorship, but his hands are tied due to administrative pressures."

But another high school editor responding to the survey commented (Bowen, 1976): "We are able to print controversial issues without censorship from the administration. The one problem we face is financially; we do not receive as much money as we would like from sources other than advertising." In fact, 13 of the 22 student editors responded that they did not feel restricted in publishing controversial materials.

For their part, 21 of the 43 newspaper advisers who answered Bowen's survey said yes, they had been censored or had themselves censored student work (five within court-protected censorship guidelines) while 18 answered no. One adviser offered "I have guided, not censored" while another said "a former principal who wanted nothing negative about the school" had censored some articles.

The differing views and experiences on censorship might also be reflected in the fact the three groups that Bowen surveyed also had differing views in their responses to the question: "What should the role of the high school press be?"

One student said "To inform students of everything concerning their school, their future, their community," while another said "It should be having the experience of writing, reporting and layout techniques. Being able to edit copy and learn the experience of what a newspaper provides for people. A paper should be entertaining and interesting, to draw attention to it" (Bowen, 1976).

A principal responded to the same question about the role of the high school press: "A step toward future and present good journalistic procedures, responsible yet sensible. Sometimes, in spite of the Kennedy Commission report, there is a failure to remember that high school students are just that – high school students. Their level of maturity is not always responsible enough to have what is called a free press."

An adviser to a high school newspaper answered that the role of the high school press is "Similar to the public press with the exception that youthful writers need guidance and advice and instruction on press responsibilities and rights."

Applying his survey results to the original "Captive Voices" report, Bowen wrote, "Students, advisers and principals strongly reject the idea that the high school paper is merely a house organ for the administration." Bowen (1976) also concluded there was "general agreement only on the Commission charge that 'censorship often takes the most pervasive form: self-censorship by students themselves because of fear and lack of a tradition of a high school press," and noted "There also seems to be support that 'censorship and the systematic lack of freedom to engage in open, responsible journalism characterize high school journalism' is not true to the degree indicated by the Commission." But Bowen (1976) also noted "There is valid evidence to indicate that censorship is unreasonable in enough cases to make it a problem worth further investigation."

It's worth noting that as Bowen and others sought to discern the status of high school newspapers in the early 1970s, there was at least one call to abandon a printed publication and regular journalism class. That call came from Eugene E. Balazs, principal of Monument Mountain Regional High School in Great Barrington, Mass. He expressed frustration in his December 1970 *The English Journal* article "High School Journalism is Dead! Dead! Dead!" at the lack of student interest in his school's journalism class, which produced the school newspaper. He noted that "school activities make it difficult to retain a student staff through two consecutive issues, let alone a school year." Balazs' solution was to turn to video and establish a "living news programming class" that was taught by the school's acting and directing instructor. With the school already wired for closed circuit television and equipped with cameras and other electronic equipment, an in-school news service was started. It then morphed into a class called "Television" at the expense of journalism and speech classes, which were cancelled.

"Enrollment problems disappeared, for acting and directing students, public speaking students, electronics students, creative writing students, and art and music students swarmed to register," Balazs (1970) wrote. As for the loss of the journalism class, Balazs maintained in 1970, "I am certain that today's student will get all the journalistic practice he needs in providing deadline copy for the telecasts ..."

While many high school newspapers certainly experienced turmoil over both their mission and viability in the 1970s, the so-called "underground newspapers" and satirical publications that emerged in greater numbers in the 1980s struggled more with censorship that often threatened their existence. An April 20, 1986, article from the *Los Angeles Times* by staff writer Jennifer Warren noted that school district administrators paid $22,000 and were required to apologize to two Fallbrook High School students who were suspended for publishing an unauthorized newspaper titled *The Hatchet Job*, which the school district had labeled "obscene and libelous." In return for the settlement and apology, the students dropped their lawsuit against the district (Warren, 1986).

Similarly, an Associated Press story published in *The Victoria (Texas) Advocate* on Dec. 19, 1986, recounts the story of a Bryan High School student who in 1984-85 distributed an alternative publication called *Twisted Times*. While the school administration was aware of the publication, the student did not seek approval and was suspended for two days after the *Twisted Times* sponsored a contest to draw a likeness of the principal. The student protested, and according to a Spring 1986 report from the Student Press Law Center, the Bryan Independent School District agreed to clear his record of the suspension since it violated a state law banning suspension of a student for minor violations of school rules. See Anonymous (1986), and Associated Press (1986), for related information.

In many of these cases involving "underground" publications, it was policies requiring administrators' approval of student work before it could be published and distributed that was at the center of the dispute. It was certainly the issue cited at the start of a protracted battle at Fridley High School in Minnesota in the spring of 1985. As reported by *Minneapolis Star Tribune* staff writer Paul Gustafson in March of 1986, student publishers of Fridley's underground *Tour de Farce* newsletter were told they would be suspended if they distributed additional issues without first getting approval of the content. In a *Star Tribune* article in July of the same year, Gustafson (1986) refers to the suspension of three student *Tour de Farce* publishers after an issue that made fun of vandalism at a teacher's home. Ultimately, a 1987 federal court ruling sided with school administrators and upheld the students' suspensions, which the school administrators said was due to vulgar language used in *Tour de Farce* that also advocated violence against teachers.

American high school newspapers also have a rich history of serving as a reflection of the times in which their student reporters and editors live. In a December 1984 *Philadelphia Inquirer* article by staff writer Sue Chastain, Wayne Brasler is identified as "the nation's unofficial historian of the high school newspaper." Chastain (1984) also noted Brasler was the long-serving adviser to a high school newspaper in Chicago and had judged student journalism competitions for many years. Brasler said high school newspapers are "magic mirrors. They reflect the times better than any history book could." Also quoted in the Inquirer article is C.J. "Skip" Leabo, at the time a professor of journalism at Texas A&M. He recalled judging entries for the National Scholastic Press Association from 1961 to 1967 (Chastain, 1984).

"It was a wild, turbulent time," Leabo said. "The whole world was changing. A lot of people, including high school students, were coming to grips with reality. That's when high school newspapers started changing from adolescent gossip sheets into real newspapers."

But jumping ahead to the 1980s, Leabo told the *Inquirer*'s Chastain that the sense of activism had faded. "The spirit and the times are blander now. The firebrands are dampened," he said. Two student journalism advisers quoted in the article confirmed this; Ann Doughtery, cited as adviser to the student newspaper at a high school in Folsom, Pa., said "It's tough to get them to go out in the community," while Sister Maura Williams, adviser to a Catholic school paper in Drexel Hill, Pa., noted "They like to run polls, like who's their favorite teacher, that sort of thing" (Chastain, 1984).

Also reflecting on the state of high school journalism in the 1980s, Brasler, the well-known Chicago high school newspaper adviser, said the time period saw a "... great deal of censorship and coercion seeping back in, particularly in the Southern states." But it seems some of the censorship was voluntary; in the article, Chastain (1984) spoke with high school newspaper advisers who willingly show their school administrators, prior to publication, any articles they think might be controversial.

And yet the period immediately before the 1988 Hazelwood decision was not without examples of serious student journalism. Take the case of the monthly student newspaper *New Expression*, which was profiled in an Associated Press article by reporter Sharon Cohen; the story ran in the *Orlando Sentinel* in July 1985. Cohen reports the staff of *New Expression* was drawn "from more than two dozen Chicago-area public and parochial high schools and five colleges."

Just how seriously the students took their reporting is reflected in the opening line of Cohen's 1985 story: "Every day after the final school bell rings, Sister Ann Heintz's kids go to work – investigating gangs, the cocaine trade and once, even, a pornography ring."

The paper, Cohen reported, operated on a budget of $110,000 a year; about a third came from advertising, and the rest from donations and foundations. The adviser, Sister Heintz, delivered the paper to 80 schools herself – by truck. The AP article detailed the negative reaction the paper and its hard hitting stories sometimes received. Sister Heintz recalled how running a Planned Parenthood ad prompted letters to Catholic schools, urging that students not work at the paper. "One school burned the paper on the patio," Heintz said. And yet she remained undeterred, telling the reporter, "Journalism is something ... that has to be set on fire. High school is a period when values are developing" (Cohen, 1985).

Captive Voices: Another Look author John Bowen (1976) echoed that sentiment with his recommendation that "Administrators and teachers should realize that a student publication is a place for learning the principles of journalism. It is a learning laboratory where they might make mistakes, but they will also learn from them. And if they are learning, through professional instruction and use of full First Amendment rights (the responsibilities come with proper education in the rights), they will stop making mistakes and act responsibly and maturely."

Chapter 7

Post-Hazelwood: The courts debate "forum" and "legitimate" educational concerns

 By Nerissa Young

Proponents of student media rights point to the *Tinker v. Des Moines Independent Community School District* (1969) case as the precedent that establishes civil rights in a school setting. But what the U.S. Supreme Court giveth in *Tinker*, it taketh away in *Hazelwood School District v. Kuhlmeier* (1988) a generation later.

U.S. Circuit Courts of Appeal and the Supreme Court have spent the ensuing 25 years since *Hazelwood* trying to decide the questions left unanswered in it and *Tinker*. The answers have whittled away broad student rights articulated in Tinker.

Most students attending school are minors, and teachers and administrators perform an "in loco parentis" function, the courts have ruled. Hence, they give wide latitude for school officials to "protect" students from student expression deemed unsuitable for a variety of reasons. The Supreme Court has ruled consistently that it is not a court's duty to educate students. Achieving that is a school district's prerogative.

Case law and the survey (Chapter 2) show 40 percent of administrators exercise that prerogative.

The right to a free press is a natural extension of the right to free speech. This chapter confines itself to federal cases involving student publications. Unless otherwise noted, case information comes directly from court opinions.

A review of Tinker

Courts wrestled with defining the essence of freedoms granted in *Tinker* to delineate high school newsroom practice exceptions stated in *Hazelwood*.

They identified student behavior presented in Tinker as "pure" speech – separate from speech under the auspices or sanctioned approval of a school district.

In its 7-2 decision in *Tinker*, the Supreme Court majority uttered these words to which every schoolhouse free-speech advocate clings: "It can hardly be argued that either students or teachers shed their constitutional rights to freedom of speech or expression at the schoolhouse gate. This has been the unmistakable holding of this Court for almost 50 years."

Ironically, with regard to "in loco parentis," local parents helped plant the seed for the *Tinker* case.

In December 1965, some adults and students in the Des Moines Independent Community School District met in a home and decided to show their opposition to the Vietnam War by wearing black armbands during the Christmas season and by fasting December 16 and New Year's Eve (*Tinker v. Des Moines*, 1969). The parents of John Tinker, 15; Mary Beth Tinker, 13; and Christopher Eckhardt, 16, attended that meeting and supported the plan.

Principals in the school district became aware of the plan to wear the armbands. They met December 14, 1965, and adopted a policy that would require students who wore armbands to school to remove them. A student's refusal would result in suspension until he or she agreed to return to school without an armband. The respective parents knew of the policy before their children wore the armbands to school.

Mary Beth Tinker and Eckhardt wore theirs December 16. John Tinker wore his Dececember 17.

The Supreme Court's majority focused on the district's preemptive strike, noting that the policy anticipated a disruption of the educational process without knowing that would occur.

"The school officials banned and sought to punish petitioners for a silent, passive expression of opinion, unaccompanied by any disorder or disturbance on the part of petitioners," wrote Justice Abe Fortas in the majority opinion. "There is here no evidence whatever of petitioners' interference, actual or nascent, with the schools' work or of collision with the rights of other students to be secure and to be let alone."

In reversing and remanding the 8th U.S. District Court of Appeals' decision that school officials acted correctly, Fortas wrote the fear of disruption is not sufficient to prohibit speech.

"Any word spoken, in class, in the lunchroom, or on the campus, that deviates from the views of another person may start an argument or cause a disturbance. But our Constitution says we must take this risk, and our history says that it is this sort of hazardous freedom — this kind of openness — that is the basis of our national strength and of the independence and vigor of Americans who grow up and live in this relatively permissive, often disputatious, society."

The majority also noted the narrowness of the policy. It banned only armbands. Other students in the district had worn to school election buttons and even the Iron Cross, a traditional symbol of Nazism. In other words, the policy targeted armbands because of their symbolic and particular viewpoint.

"Freedom of expression would not truly exist if the right could be exercised only in an area that a benevolent government has provided as a safe haven for crackpots," Fortas wrote. "The Constitution says that Congress (and the State) may not abridge the right to free speech. This provision means what it says."

Justice Potter Stewart wrote in his separate concurring opinion, "Although I agree with much of what is said in the Court's opinion, and with its judgment in this case, I cannot share the Court's uncritical assumption that, school discipline aside, the First Amendment rights of children are co-extensive with those of adults."

He said children are captive audiences without the full capacity to make individual choices regarding First Amendment guarantees. Stewart's note that children's rights are not "co-extensive with those of adults" became the basis of later decisions that school administrators have authority to protect students from themselves.

In his dissenting opinion, Justice Hugo Black noted the majority viewed the armbands as "symbolic" or "pure" speech and their finding suggests the high court took upon itself "the decision as to which school disciplinary regulations are 'reasonable,'" instead of leaving that to school officials.

Black added students wore the armbands with the deliberate purpose of distracting other students.

"Uncontrolled and uncontrollable liberty is an enemy to domestic peace," Black wrote.

"This case, therefore, wholly without constitutional reasons in my judgment, subjects all the public schools in the country to the whims and caprices of their loudest-mouthed, but maybe not their brightest, students. I, for one, am not fully persuaded that school pupils are wise enough, even with this Court's expert help from Washington, to run the 23,390 public school systems in our 50 States."

Justice John Harlan wrote in his dissenting opinion "that school officials should be accorded the widest authority in maintaining discipline and good order in their institutions."

Later courts would weave threads of the opinions of Stewart, Black and Harlan to create the position that minors do not possess the same rights as adults and that school officials should have broad discretion in determining what is best for students.

The burden established by Hazelwood

The *Hazelwood* decision arrived at the Supreme Court via a school district's appeal (by school administrators) from the 8th U.S. Circuit Court of Appeals. The Supreme Court ruled 5-3 that administrators maintained the right to censor a school newspaper.

Staff members of the *Spectrum*, the newspaper at Hazelwood East High School in St. Louis County, Mo., originally sued the school board after the principal deleted two pages of articles from the May 13, 1983, issue. Stories on those pages dealt with student pregnancy and the impact of divorce on students (*Hazelwood v. Kuhlmeier,* 1988).

In evaluating the decision of Principal Robert E. Reynolds to censor, the Supreme Court considered how the newspaper operated:

- Students created content in the school's Journalism II class.

- The adviser was a salaried teacher for the district, and a portion of her salary was designated for advising the paper.
- The school board paid the printing costs – partially offset by advertising sales – and bought supplies and textbooks for the Journalism II class.
- The Spectrum circulated 4,500 issues every three weeks to students, school personnel and community members.
- As practice, the adviser submitted page proofs to the principal before publication.

The principal's concerns involved girls quoted in the pregnancy story. Reynolds said he believed they could be identified by the details in the story even though the story used false names for them. He wanted to protect student privacy. Reynolds also took issue with references to sexual activity and use of birth control, which he deemed inappropriate for younger students.

And the paper identified a student quoted in the divorce story, in which the student made critical comments that Reynolds believed merited a response from the student's parents and/or their approval. A subsequent version of the story omitted the student's name, but Reynolds did not know that, he said.

Reynolds thought it better to delete two pages instead of censoring the entire issue, he said. The court brief stated the principal didn't realize the staff – to address his objections – could make changes to the stories before printing to address his concerns. His decision deprived students from reading other stories on those pages about teenage marriage, runaways, juvenile delinquents and a general article on teenage pregnancy. The principal did not object to those stories, he said.

The 8th U.S. Circuit ruled for the students and deemed the paper a public forum for student viewpoints.

The Supreme Court referenced four cases in determining what constitutes a public forum: *Hague v. Committee for Industrial Organization* (1939), *Widmar v. Vincent* (1981), *Perry Education Association v. Perry Local Educators' Association* (1983), and *Cornelius v. NAACP Defense & Educational Fund Inc.* (1985).

Public and Nonpublic Forums

The Freedom Forum in Washington, D.C. – a nonpartisan foundation that champions the First Amendment – provides these definitions on its Web site:

- A traditional public forum includes streets, parks or other similar places where community members meet and exchange ideas. The state may not restrict speech based on content except for a compelling state interest, and any regulations must be narrowly tailored to serve that interest.
- A limited or designated public forum is public property opened to the public for expressive activity. Examples include university meeting facilities, municipal theaters and school board meeting rooms. Clear governmental intent to create a limited forum is required. A lack of intent is not considered a designation. As long as the forum is open, the same regulation restrictions apply as with a traditional public forum.
- A nonpublic forum includes light posts, prisons, military bases, polling places, a school district's internal mail system and airport terminals. The state may impose time, place and manner regulations, but restrictions must be viewpoint neutral, which means speech cannot be regulated simply because state officials disagree with the viewpoint.

In *Hazelwood*, the Supreme Court examined school board policy and the school's curriculum guide in determining which type of forum existed at Hazelwood East.

Justices quoted the board's policy that "school sponsored publications are developed within the adopted curriculum and its educational implications in regular classroom activities." Further, the Journalism II course description stated students would learn journalistic skills under deadline pressure and "the legal, moral, and ethical restrictions imposed upon journalists within the school community."

Although the board's policy delineated the school district's responsibility for the newspaper, the Supreme Court ruling embraced the idea that newsroom practice trumps policy. The practice at Hazelwood East was for the faculty adviser to select editors, schedule publication dates, decide the number of pages in each issue, assign story ideas, help students develop stories, review quotes, edit stories, select and edit letters to the editor and work with the printing company.

In reviewing policy and practice, Justice Byron White in the majority opinion wrote that even though the policy statement published in the *Spectrum* stated the newspaper accepts all rights of the First Amendment, "it does not reflect an intent to expand those rights by converting a curriculum newspaper into a public forum."

He added: "Accordingly, school officials were entitled to regulate the contents of *Spectrum* in any reasonable manner. It is this standard, rather than our decision in *Tinker*, that governs this case."

White distinguished the *Tinker* case from the *Hazelwood* case this way: *Tinker* asked whether school officials can censor a student's personal expression at school, while *Hazelwood* asks whether a school may censor speech at district-supervised events that the public may perceive as speech sanctioned by the school district.

White concluded: "Educators are entitled to exercise greater control over this second form of student expression to assure that participants learn whatever lessons the activity is designed to teach, that readers or listeners are not exposed to material that may be inappropriate for their level of maturity, and that the views of the individual speaker are not erroneously attributed to the school."

White even extended that control to grammar and editing mistakes.

"Instead, we hold that educators do not offend the First Amendment by exercising editorial control over the style and content of student speech in school-sponsored expressive activities so long as their actions are reasonably related to legitimate pedagogical concerns," White wrote.

The debate on what constitutes a "legitimate pedagogical concern" continues today.

The majority also opened the door for what could have a chilling effect on college and university student media as well as high school: "We need not now decide whether the same degree of deference is appropriate with respect to school-sponsored expressive activities at the college and university level," stated a footnote in the court's majority opinion.

Justice William Brennan wrote the dissenting opinion.

"When the young men and women at Hazelwood East registered for Journalism II, they expected a civics lesson," Brennan wrote.

He said students expected to learn about their First Amendment rights and responsibilities while working on the *Spectrum*.

"In my view, the principal broke more than just a promise," Brennan said. "He violated the First Amendment's prohibition against censorship of any student expression that neither disrupts classwork nor invades the rights of others, and against any censorship that is not narrowly tailored to serve its purpose.

"The Court today casts no doubt on *Tinker*'s vitality. Instead, it creates a taxonomy of school censorship, concluding that *Tinker* applies to one category and not another … Nor has this Court ever intimated a distinction between personal and school-sponsored speech in any other context."

Brennan concluded: "The case before us aptly illustrates how readily school officials (and courts) can camouflage viewpoint discrimination as the 'mere' protection of students from sensitive topics … The young men and women of Hazelwood East expected a civics lesson, but not the one the Court teaches them today."

The post-Hazelwood climate

By the time the Supreme Court issued its Hazelwood opinion Janurary 13, 1988, the 9th U.S. Circuit Court of Appeals faced a similar case. When the circuit court issued its opinion in November 1988, it looked to the *Hazelwood* decision for guidance.

Burch v. Barker (1988) involved an unofficial student newspaper distributed May 20, 1983, at a senior picnic. The paper, *Bad Astra*, was distributed at Lindbergh High School, in Renton, Wash. Five students produced the paper off campus at their expense and without the knowledge of school officials.

A parent, the president of the Lindbergh High School Parent Teacher Association and a mother of one of the students, placed copies in school faculty and staff mailboxes.

Bad Astra, a four-page newspaper, included articles critical of administration policies governing student activities and attendance, a mock teacher evaluation poll and poems by Stephen Crane, Edgar Lee Masters and Langston Hughes. The students printed 350 copies.

The principal disciplined the five students by placing letters of reprimand in their files but did not find anything objectionable in *Bad Astra*. He issued the reprimand because students failed to follow a 1977 Renton School District policy requiring official approval for student-written material before distribution on school property or at school functions. This policy did not apply to official school publications.

Between *Bad Astra*'s distribution and the lawsuit, the Renton School District revised its prior approval policy regarding unofficial student publications. A much more detailed policy emerged, which added language that allowed principals to ban distribution if the content criticized school officials or advocated violating school rules.

The court opinion written by Judge Mary Schroeder stated: "There was no evidence that *Bad Astra* had interfered with the operation of the high school or impinged upon other students' rights ... Defendants showed that a few teachers who had been mocked in the newspaper became emotionally upset, but the distribution caused no violence or physical damage, nor did it interfere with classes ... We thus are confronted with a unique and ironic situation in which a school has punished students for distribution of material which both sides acknowledge could not be suppressed under the First Amendment."

The 9th Circuit ruled that *Hazelwood* affirmed student rights to speech, as decided in *Tinker*, while determining school officials did not have to promote student speech.

"This case, unlike *Hazelwood v. Kuhlmeier,* concerns a policy aimed at curtailing communications among students, communications (sic) which no one could associate with school sponsorship or endorsement. We therefore hold this policy does violate the First Amendment."

The court found the Renton policy too narrowly tailored, which did not allow for the rights articulated in *Tinker*, and that it amounted to prior restraint.

Once the Supreme Court set forth its decision in *Hazelwood,* it left the job of delineating the finer points to U.S. district and appellate courts (Schulman, 2011).

In *Dean v. Utica Community Schools* (2004), the U.S. District Court for Michigan's Eastern District, Southern Division, determined a school district could not censor a student newspaper article because of its viewpoint and that *Hazelwood* didn't apply because the article did not raise a legitimate educational concern.

Katherine (Katy) Dean was a student at Utica High School and a staff reporter and sports co-editor for the *Arrow,* the school newspaper. During a February 2002 meeting, staff member Dan Butts suggested reporting a story about a pending lawsuit against the school district. Joanne and Rey Frances lived near the district's school bus garage. They filed suit, claiming bus diesel fumes caused a nuisance that violated their privacy and threatened their health.

Dean and Butts viewed a videotape of a school board meeting during which Joanne Frances spoke. They interviewed the couple at their home.

Adviser Gloria Olman told the students to get a statement from school officials. Dean interviewed Principal Richard Machesky, who said he did not know about the lawsuit. Other district officials refused to answer Dean's questions, citing a policy of not commenting on pending litigation. When Olman again sought Machesky's advice, he directed her to community relations, which had earlier denied Dean's request for a comment.

The story went to the printer March 7, 2002, for publication in the March 15, 2002, edition of the *Arrow.*

Machesky acquired a copy of Dean's story before publication and raised the issue of what he deemed unreliable sources — a reference to the use of pseudonyms, an unnamed school district employee and health research quoted from a *USA Today* story. He passed the story to the assistant superintendent who passed it to the superintendent, who ordered the story's removal based on the position that pending litigation was inappropriate content for the school newspaper.

The superintendent did not know students could revise the story. Even though a community newspaper, *The Macomb Daily,* published Dean's article a few days later, the superintendent refused to reconsider.

At the time of litigation, students published the *Arrow* monthly and paid costs by selling advertising. The students received academic credit for a journalism course.

The students controlled the content and production of the paper from setting the advertising rates to assigning stories. Olman advised students, offered critical analysis and checked grammar. The *Arrow* was distributed to students, community members, other schools, parents and alumni. Previous topics covered included teenage sex, suicide, drug and alcohol abuse and sexual orientation. Olman – who taught journalism, newspaper, desktop publishing, yearbook and English classes – had never been told to remove a story.

Judge Arthur Tarnow wrote in the opinion: "If the role of the press in a democratic society is to have any value, all journalists – including student journalists – must be allowed to publish viewpoints contrary to those of state authorities without intervention or censorship by the authorities themselves. Without protection, the freedoms of speech and press are meaningless and the press becomes a mere channel for official thought.

"Based on the evidence in the record, the Court finds the *Arrow* is a limited public forum because it has been opened for use by the public for speech and discussion concerning matters that are relevant to the Utica High School community and its readership. Even if the Arrow is a non-public forum, the defendant's suppression of Dean's article was unreasonable."

In determining newsroom practice, the judge noted that for 25 years, no Utica administrators attempted to influence the editorial process for any student newspapers. After the decision to remove Dean's article, no official since attempted to influence the editorial process.

Tarnow determined the decision to remove came with no educational concerns and was strictly viewpoint related.

Seven years later, *R.O. v. Ithaca City School District* (2011) made its way to the 2nd U.S. Circuit Court of Appeals. But the U.S. Supreme Court on October 2011 denied a petition to hear the case.

The case involved efforts to publish in the Ithaca High School newspaper, *The Tattler*, a stick-figure cartoon depicting sex acts. "R.O.," a minor, was on the newspaper staff throughout high school and served as editor-in-chief his senior year.

In the opinion issued by the U.S. District Court for the Northern District of New York, Judge Norman Mordue (*R.O. v. Ithaca City School District*, 2009) gave the complaining students the proverbial half a loaf. While the court supported censorship in this particular instance, it found the paper served as a limited public forum.

Mordue wrote the school board did not open *The Tattler*'s content for anyone's use, which would have created a public forum. Further, the student code of conduct provided for the district to exercise control over libelous, obscene and disruptive content. That standard was in place before the 2005 guidelines were adopted upon which school administrators relied.

Determining the type of forum, the level of student control over content and practice versus policy became key issues in the case. The nameplate identified the paper as *The IHS Tattler,* and the paper's website address, the name of the school and its mailing address accompanied the nameplate.

The paper's disclaimer about who determined content changed three times between May 2001 and February 2005. The first version called it the "student-run newspaper of Ithaca High School" and "an open forum." The second version included the same language. The third version deleted the "open forum" language.

The Ithaca school district paid a stipend to the adviser and for *The Tattler*'s production and office costs, and the newspaper staff sold advertising. The press run was 3,000, and about one-third of those landed off campus in grocery stores, coffee shops, bakeries and other businesses.

Two faculty advisers served during the time R.O. worked on *The Tattler*'s staff, but the court record noted disagreement among advisers regarding their roles.

The first testified she saw her role as advisory only. She intervened if stories included potentially libelous or obscene information or urged a violent disruption of school activities.

The second adviser testified she participated fully and equally in the production process, which included reviewing page proofs of every issue and editing them for revision. After students made changes, the adviser reviewed final proofs and sent them to the printer.

The district's student code of conduct included the following language, "The school has the right to halt distribution of materials that would materially and substantially interrupt the educational process or intrude upon the rights of others."

The May 2004 issue of *The Tattler* included a personal ad soliciting the 2005 class president for an "intimate relationship." The adviser said the staff slipped it in after review without her approval. She canceled the June issue.

In October 2004, *The Tattler* staff distributed a survey to IHS students to gauge their level of confidence in the principal's job performance.

The paper published the results, unfavorable to the principal, in the November 2004 issue. Staff members then conducted a survey of faculty regarding the principal's competence and published results in the December 2004 issue (*R.O. v. Ithaca City School District*, 2009).

The pleadings suggest the students got on the wrong side of good will before they found themselves on the wrong side of good law.

During production for the January 2005 issue, the adviser received page proofs on which a cartoon accompanied a former student's article titled, "Alumni Advice: Sex is Fun." The cartoon depicted the inside of the Health 101 classroom. The class blackboard showed eight stick-figure drawings depicting sexual positions and the phrase "Test on Monday" beneath the cartoon.

The adviser pulled the cartoon but allowed publication of the rest of the issue.

Mordue noted student editors did not appeal the removal of the personal ad or the cartoon.

The January issue included other material that caused controversy. One story explained how students could successfully cheat in a class and named the teacher in whose class students thought they could cheat. An article about a local restaurant included the descriptions of "smackin' a ho," "colla greens" and "pimpin' cane." That prompted a restaurant employee to write a letter to the school district complaining about racial slurs and hurt feelings.

The adviser threatened to resign after repeated conflicts with the staff. She wrote a set of guidelines and suggested the district implement them, which it did in late January.

The one-page, six bullet-point guidelines stated the adviser would approve all stories before assignment and edit and approve all content before publication.

Editors again sought to publish the stick figure cartoon in the February issue, this time with a serious story about how the school taught sex in health class. The adviser approved the article but rejected the cartoon. This time, R.O. appealed.

The adviser resigned within days, and the principal denied R.O.'s appeal. The principal found the cartoon obscene and unsuitable for immature students, he said. R.O. appealed unsuccessfully to the superintendent. Without a faculty adviser, the school canceled the March, April and May 2005 issues.

The controversy corresponded to a letter sent to school district parents urging them to be vigilant because school administrators and personnel overheard anecdotes about an increase in drug and alcohol use and risky sexual behavior among the district's middle and high school students.

R.O. and company sought an alternative method of expression by independently publishing *The March Issue*. The front page contained part of the cartoon with the stick figures obscured by a black circle and the word "CENSORED" beneath it. The unedited cartoon and an article about the censorship appeared inside.

R.O. asked the principal's permission to distribute *The March Issue* to homerooms. His request included page proofs for the principal and superintendent because district policy required approval before distribution. The superintendent declined, saying the paper "would cause material and substantial interference with the educational operation of Ithaca High School."

R.O. appealed the same day and the superintendent again denied permission. This time, she noted the cartoon was obscene, offensive and potentially confusing for young readers. The cartoon would interfere with the school district's health curriculum and make light of the serious subject of sexual relations.

The circumstances created the perfect storm for a clash between the responsibility of educators and student civil rights.

Mordue concluded the district provided a limited public forum and students could retain reasonable control over the content. And he found the newly adopted guidelines were not drawn to only serve the district's pedagogical concerns. He saw value in the cartoon because it tried to deter students from risky sexual behavior.

But the court ruled the district successfully argued that readers could consider the cartoon "district-sanctioned" speech because the district funded all aspects of *The Tattler*. Hence, the reference to "half a loaf" and the appeal to the 2nd U.S. Circuit Court of Appeals.

Judge Jose Cabranes (*R.O. v. Ithaca City School District*, 2011) wasted little ink in the 2nd Circuit's opinion by affirming the lower court's decision. He said the Supreme Court in *Bethel School District v. Fraser* (1986) determined school officials have the right to censor "lewd, indecent or offensive" speech. Ithaca officials were entitled to prohibit distribution of *The March Issue*. Further, *Hazel-*

wood provided leeway because the school-sponsored speech in *The Tattler* related to educational concerns.

The standards by which a school district may constitutionally censor student speech as articulated in *R.O. v. Ithaca City School District* (2011) are:

- School officials may prohibit speech that is less than the legal definition of obscene, which includes vulgar, lewd, indecent or plainly offensive speech (*Bethel v. Fraser School District,* 1986).
- School officials may prohibit school-sponsored speech when the censorship is related to pedagogical concerns (*Hazelwood v. Kuhlmeier School District*, 1988).
- School officials may censor speech that is not obscene or school sponsored if it causes a material disruption in the school (*Tinker v. Des Moines Independent Community School District*, 1969).
- School officials may censor speech that they believe encourages illegal drug use (*Morse v. Frederick*, 2007).

Hazelwood extended to college and university campuses

Two student media cases allowed federal courts to consider the boundaries of *Hazelwood* on college campuses.

In *Kincaid v. Gibson* (2001), the 6th U.S. Circuit Court of Appeals ruled that Kentucky State University officials violated student rights by confiscating copies of *The Thorobred*, the campus yearbook, because administrators did not like the content.

Judge R. Guy Cole Jr. wrote in the majority opinion that university practice gave broad freedoms to student editors and created a limited public forum.

That pro-rights attitude shifted in the final decision in *Hosty v. Carter* (2005), a case that extended *Hazelwood* to college and university campuses, and prompted some state legislatures to pass laws declaring campus newspapers "public forums" (Overbeck, 2006).

In *Hosty*, the 7th U.S. Circuit Court of Appeals allowed an administrator's defense of ignorance of the law when she literally stopped the presses from printing the campus newspaper because she didn't like the content.

Tinker reflects on case nearly 50 years later

During 2013 and 2014, Mary Beth Tinker participated in a nationwide tour to educate students about the case and their rights in *Tinker v. Des Moines Independent Community School District* (1969). She said in 2014 that the fight was worth it. "It's a way of life that's so worth living – to use your rights, to speak up, to stand up" (personal interview with M. Tinker on July 18, 2014).

Tinker said she never felt alone even though she was the only student at Harding Junior High to wear an armband. Parents, local church members, people throughout the country and the world showed their support in person and in letters, she said.

Tinker shunned the term "hero" and described herself as an ordinary person doing a small thing. "That's what moves the world forward," she said.

Tips for today's student media advisers

- Don't help school administrators censor student media. If a policy is in effect, follow the minimum requirements.
- Make the case to students that the responsibility of power should outweigh the power of power, not for purposes of self-censoring but to perform work that will garner community support in the event of attempted or outright censorship.
- Develop relationships with student-rights advocates, individual school board members, and district boards of education.
- Develop relationships with community media and college journalism programs. It will improve the professionalism of student media and provide allies when administrators attempt to control student media.

- Create a paper trail of appeals at the school level and upward. Judges appreciate plaintiffs who have exercised all options before filing a lawsuit.
- Judges look at practice more than policy. Make sure daily practices of student media show students exercise control over content.
- Amend policies to include "public forum" rather than "open forum" because the latter term causes a legal hurdle.

Section III

What Can be Done

Profile 4

WILLIAM LOVE

Sandpoint High School (public, 1,000 students)
Sandpoint, Idaho
Newspaper (print and online)

When William Love accepted a journalism teaching position at Sandpoint High School (SHS) in Idaho, he suspected it might be a challenge.

Love hadn't focused on journalism in college. He hadn't even studied teaching. He graduated from Boise State University with a bachelor's degree in English literature.

"I was the best-read cab driver in Boise," he said.

He had taken a news writing class, however, and was drawn to journalism as a profession. He landed his first job at the *Newport Miner*, a small weekly in northeastern Washington state, and later became a sports reporter and editor at the *Idaho Press-Tribune* in Nampa, Idaho.

"I spent three years there, and went through furloughs – it was 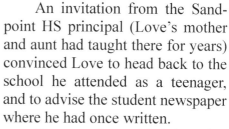 a tough time for the business. The newspaper seemed shaky," Love said.

An invitation from the Sandpoint HS principal (Love's mother and aunt had taught there for years) convinced Love to head back to the school he attended as a teenager, and to advise the student newspaper where he had once written.

"I sort of stumbled into it," Love said. "I got classroom experience through PTE (Idaho Professional-Technical Education) and worked on a temporary license."

Five years later, Love, now 37, teaches six sections of journalism, including introductory classes, newspaper production classes, and photography and graphic design classes. The student newspaper, *Cedar Post*, is available online as well as in print; the goal is 10 editions a year, Love said.

"I feel really lucky to have this position," he said. "At our school, the journalism program has been a huge part of the school for decades. The kids want to be part of the history and tradition."

Yet with all the program's past and recent successes – the *Cedar Post* staff finished third nationally in its division at JEA's 2014 convention in San Diego, six students won individual awards there, and *Cedar Post*'s editor-in-chief was named Idaho journalist of the year – Love said that taking over the program wasn't exactly easy.

"At first it was difficult – those first hard days in the classroom, developing the program, and developing the curriculum," he said.

He had become the fifth adviser in as many years, and Love said that the program had suffered for it.

"I started with two kids," he said, "which grew into nine. The editor-in-chief had done a lot of work to fill the class, and I've been working ever since to build numbers."

Love said he thinks the frequent turnover in his position, and the temporary dwindling of interest in the program, had to do with previous advisers "not being a good fit." Love said he feels comfortable with the administration at SHS, however.

"Our principal has been supportive since I've been here," he said. "She does get upset sometimes, but she does understand. She believes in students' rights to free speech and to choose content." That is something that Love takes seriously.

"I have been in her office, however, but it's been more of a fairness issue," he said.

Love said he reminds students to think about what they're doing, and to consider "who's going to get the call the next day," he said.

There are currently 25 student journalists on the *Cedar Post* staff. SHS is a rural, consolidated school of 1,000 students, an hour from the Canadian border. Right now, the program is well-supported, but Love said he worries what might happen if finances continue to tighten. The journalism program is under a funding umbrella with other technical programs such as welding and sewing, he said. No

English credit is offered, but students can earn one credit to satisfy a technical education requirement.

"The district budget is getting smaller and smaller, the population has dropped; that's a huge factor in how they determine which classes to keep," he said.

Financially, Love said the paper gets a "little bit" from the school and receives federal funding to purchase equipment. He said the paper has 18 iMacs and four DSLR cameras.

"We support the printing by selling advertising," he said.

In addition to financial security, Love said it would be "really helpful" to have a high school journalism program, a northern Idaho organization, to better serve his students.

"The state journalism program at the high school level is not very strong," he said, "and geographically, it's too hard to get to conventions. It's a 12-hour bus ride."

Love said this sort of access to training and competition would help get kids excited, and could introduce them to available careers.

"Giving these kids an opportunity like this is just awesome," Love said. "When we went to San Diego (JEA), a few of these kids had never ridden on an airplane before, and some had worked six months to buy a ticket."

Chapter 8

Stellar High School Programs That Have Adjusted with Time

By Jeff South

It was 1995. In February of that year, *Newsweek* published an article titled "The Internet? Bah!" and predicted it was a passing fad. This was, after all, B.G. – Before Google. The first Web browser, Mosaic, had launched only two years earlier. Today, with about 3 billion Internet users and 1 billion websites worldwide, it's easy to forget how barren the online landscape was two decades ago. There were just 16 million Internet users around the world – and only 20,000 websites – in 1995.

Back then, Jim Streisel, the adviser for the *HiLite*, the student newspaper at Carmel High School in Carmel, Ind., had every right to be skeptical when his staff of student journalists proposed creating a website. And Streisel responded the way the best high school journalism advisers would: Go for it!

"The students said, 'We want to start a website.' It was a novelty at the time, of course," Streisel recalled (personal communication, April 15, 2014). "But now we're used to having a digital format."

Indeed, the *HiLite* has morphed from a biweekly broadsheet in the 1990s into a print, online and multimedia juggernaut. It includes a monthly full-color tabloid newsmagazine; a 24/7 website chock-full of news, features, opinions, photos, blogs, polls and interactive features; and a robust presence on Twitter, Facebook, YouTube and other social media platforms. Moreover, Streisel's students developed the Greyhound Media Network (named for Carmel High's mascot), which aggregates content not only from the *HiLite* but also from the school's other media operations: the *Pinnacle* yearbook, CHTV television and WHJE radio.

"We are not about awards. We are about our readers," Streisel said. "If we serve our readers well, the awards will come." And they have: Since 1995, the *HiLite* and its website have won 11 Gold Crowns from the Columbia Scholastic Press Association, 11 Quill & Scroll George H. Gallup Awards and seven Pacemaker awards from the National Scholastic Press Association. The *HiLite* newspaper was inducted into the NSPA Hall of Fame in 1997.

Common traits
of successful programs

Carmel High illustrates several key reasons why scholastic journalism programs flourish at certain schools. It has, for example, a knowledgeable and dedicated adviser who puts the ball squarely in the students' court. "I challenge them to explore," Streisel said. "In order for something to work, students must be behind it, or it won't last."

Moreover, the school's administration has been behind the journalism program, allowing Streisel's students, with his guidance, to do their job. A common trait of successful scholastic journalism programs is "an administration that understands the value of the school having a student voice," said Mark Newton (personal communications, June 13 and June 18, 2014), president of the Journalism Education Association and a journalism teacher and media adviser at Mountain Vista High School in Highlands Ranch, Colo.

In standout programs, the school administration realizes that journalism is an integral co-curricular activity, as important as sports, student government or student clubs. Administrators show that support in their policies toward the student press – designating student media as open forums and allowing students, with their adviser's input, to make all content decisions, Newton said. Good administrators also provide a level of financial support – so students can attend conferences and workshops and buy equipment and software for student media. "Supportive administrators send the message that 'This is important; we want to empower our students to do good journalism.'"

Another contributor to success is motivated students – and that comes back to having an adviser who can inspire them. Working for the school newspaper or yearbook, after all, is typically an elective course that students must juggle with competing demands.

"The only way to succeed is for students to develop the ability to work together," Newton said. "You want them to see the impact of journalism, and to understand that they're leaving a legacy."

Newton said scholastic journalism advisers often ponder the recipe for success – what the top programs have in common. There is no cookie-cutter formula. But stellar programs that have evolved and thrived share certain traits, he said.

"Anecdotally, we know it's important to have an adviser who's really engaged – who sees the value in what they're doing." That value is not necessarily or strictly journalistic (teaching students how to be reporters and editors). Newton said the overarching value is education in general: Through scholastic journalism programs, young people learn ideas and skills that will prepare them for life – for doing well academically, socially, as citizens and in whatever careers they choose.

It is also important for advisers to be "connected with people like them," Newton said. This might mean having a partner at the same school (with one teacher overseeing the school newspaper and the other the yearbook, for example); being a member of the state press association; and being involved in the Journalism Education Association and other professional groups. These connections provide a support system as well as opportunities for leadership and professional development, Newton said.

A support system is important because advisers can feel isolated and on their own. They face a lot of pressure navigating tough issues and helping students make solid decisions about what to publish or not publish.

In quality programs, Newton said, advisers are knowledgeable, of course: about the law, ethical issues, journalism in general, technology and news industry trends. They also must be willing to take informed risks and not be afraid. "You have to make hard choices on things that will have a profound impact. It's hard when you know your yearbook is going to be read by everybody for years to come; that's a lot of pressure" for both advisers and yearbook staffers.

Advisers must provide guidance but also let students make decisions. "I learned early that it's not about me – it's about the kids," Newton said. "My role is to support them and engage them in making choices – and if necessary, defend them in their choices later on."

In many ways, an effective journalism adviser is like a coach for an athletic team. In fact, Newton earned bachelor's and master's degrees in physical education (he also holds a bachelor's in journalism education and a minor in English education, all from the University of Northern Colorado) with an eye toward coaching or serving as director of athletics. He didn't go that route after all, but he said scholastic journalism and sports have a lot in common.

"There are, in my opinion, many similarities – a committed and dedicated group of individuals comes together for a common cause," Newton said. "I see advising as being the same as coaching." In both athletics and journalism, participants must work as a team, set goals, strive for excellence, practice regularly and continuously improve.

Those qualities exist at Mountain Vista High School – and it's no surprise that the school's *Eagle Eye* newsmagazine has won a slew of national honors, including NSPA Pacemaker awards in 2010 and 2013. (In addition, Taylor Blatchford, the *Eagle Eye*'s co-editor in chief, was the JEA National High School Journalist of the Year for 2014.) The school's *Aerie* yearbook also received NSPA Marks of Distinction. Moreover, Mountain Vista has won all-state honors in both the newspaper/magazine and yearbook competitions of the Colorado High School Press Association in 2011, 2012 and 2013 – the only school to accomplish that feat.

While awards are nice, Newton said, the biggest reward in scholastic journalism is serving the community and watching students grow.

"Having a viable journalism program at a school – one that is empowered to cover all the news, 'good' and 'bad' – is the glue that holds together the community. It's real, and the community sees – maybe even expects – quality journalism in a democracy," he said. "Are people who were exposed to or participated in quality scholastic journalism programs in high school and college more active citizens? I would think so. Are adults interested in student voices and opinions? Are schools, and the adults who run them, better because of quality student media? I would think so. And, we know 'journalism kids do better.'"

Scholastic journalism programs usually do better when they are organized as for-credit classes, not extracurricular clubs. "The class is the key to it all," said Adrienne Forgette (personal communication, June 22, 2014), the student media adviser for Darlington School in Rome, Ga.

That was clear from a survey conducted in November 2013 by Michael Simons, the yearbook adviser at West High School in Painted Post, N.Y., and Forgette, then at Martha's Vineyard Regional High School in Oak Bluffs, Mass. They surveyed 37 advisers of award-winning yearbook programs, from Virginia to California. Almost every award-winning program functioned as an academic class – not a club. "If my school ever changes our program to a club, I would have to seriously consider whether or not I would continue to advise it," one respondent wrote (Simons & Forgette, 2013). "I'm not sure a yearbook staff can survive in competition with sports and drama and band, etc."

Another common refrain from the survey's respondents was that great programs have a "culture of excellence." One adviser wrote: "I think the expectation of excellence – the culture of leaving it better than it's found every year – must never be lowered. Yearbook kids need to know they are the most important people in their school because they are the Memory Keepers." Another respondent added, "At this point, my program runs on tradition. The next group does not want to let the editors who taught them and the hundreds before them down." (Simons & Forgette, 2013)

Forgette said (personal communications, June 22 and June 23, 2014) that she fostered such a culture during her six years as a publications adviser at Northern High School in Owings, Md., by treating journalism as "a varsity sport. We competed nationally, and I required that commitment from the students." Forgette also started each school year with an unusual event – a "wedding ceremony" for yearbook staff members: "They would get married to the book." Students dressed up and recited vows; they video-recorded the ceremony – one mother even provided a wedding cake. That may sound hokey, but Forgette said it pushed the students to produce highly celebrated yearbooks.

Against that backdrop, here is a sampling of other schools with high-quality student media – outstanding scholastic journalism programs that have adjusted with time.

Carmel High School, Carmel, Ind.

Streisel said (personal communications, April 15 and April 23, 2014) that a key to long-term success at the *HiLite* is fostering a culture of excellence. "We must build a culture of journalists – students who believe in the program, who believe in what they're doing, who believe that journalism is an important thing to share with readers," he said. "That takes time to develop."

It develops as students assume responsibility for student media: They must make the decisions, with their adviser's input. "Once you have established a culture of excellence, nobody wants to break that," Streisel said. "They will do everything in their power to maintain that level of quality."

There will be bumps in the road, of course. "Kids are going to make mistakes. It's inevitable," Streisel said. "One of the most important lessons is to learn from your mistakes – to learn how to minimize mistakes and avoid the same mistake in future."

He has developed a system to transmit his program's culture – to pass on the skills and institutional knowledge – from one year's crop of students to the next. Each spring, Streisel selects the *HiLite* editors for the following year. The outgoing editors then have at least a few months to mentor their incoming successors. This makes for a smooth transition, Streisel said. And when school resumes in the fall, the *HiLite* won't miss a beat: Readers will pick up the same high-quality journalism.

Carmel High School, which has 4,800 students, is "a big community to cover," Streisel said, and the student media operation is correspondingly large. He teaches five newspaper courses a semester and has 90 students, from sophomores to seniors, on the *HiLite* staff. Streisel said his goal is not to channel students into journalism careers; it's to teach students skills that can apply to various academic areas and life in general.

"I happen to be using the common language of journalism to teach students. What I'm teaching students are transferrable skills," he said. "Some students may go on to study journalism in college.

A lot of our students have been standouts as college journalists and beyond. But most of our students are not here because they plan to pursue a degree in journalism. However, working on the *HiLite*, they will learn so much more than journalism: management skills, people skills, problem-solving skills, how to think critically, how to find information, how to vet information."

Streisel credits the administration of his school and school district for supporting student journalism.

"We couldn't do what we do without their support," he said. "The administration here understands the role of student journalism. They understand that it's not a bad thing for the student media to talk about things that are controversial. It's a good thing – because then, they will be discussed in a responsible way.

"Schools without student media are setting themselves up for problems. The information is out there, and it will get shared somehow. Would you prefer to have it shared in an environment with an adviser and student journalists who are familiar with media ethics and responsibility – or would you rather let students spread rumors?"

Granite Bay High School, Granite Bay, Calif.

The Granite Bay Gazette is a multi-section broadsheet with tabloid inserts, covering the range of student interests from hard-hitting school news and engaging features to sports and music. The paper, which has been inducted into the NSPA Hall of Fame, feeds the school's student-driven website, GraniteBayToday.org. Granite Bay's student journalists have won NSPA Pacemaker awards and CSPA Gold and Silver Crowns and been recognized as among the best in California.

If *The Gazette* feels as professional as the nearby *Sacramento Bee*, it might be because its adviser, Karl Grubaugh (personal communications, June 17 and June 23, 2014), works there as an occasional copy editor and freelance reporter. Out of college, Grubaugh started as a social studies teacher and later attended the Missouri School of Journalism for his master's degree; he contemplated a career switch before gravitating back to teaching and journalism advising. In 2008, the Dow Jones News Fund named him its National High School Journalism Teacher of the Year.

Grubaugh said the best high school journalism programs have

advisers who understand the First Amendment and the role of the press in a democratic society. Finding such advisers is no easy task.

"There's no credential to teach journalism in California. Journalism teachers are overwhelmingly English teachers – occasionally a social science person," Grubaugh said. "They're rarely trained journalists. They typically are English teachers who want to teach Shakespeare," and they agree to take on the role of journalism adviser at the request of administrators who see the school newspaper strictly as a public relations tool. Once such teachers survive probation and get permanent job status, they pass the advising duties to another newbie.

Grubaugh shatters that mold. He has been a teacher for 30 years and a journalism adviser for almost 20 years, with the past 15 at Granite Bay. "I've brought some longevity to the gig. I've got professional experience; students appreciate that. And I understand how the law works in California," where student journalists enjoy greater press freedoms than in many other states.

With his administration's support, *The Granite Bay Gazette* and its website cover the gamut of school news, from achievements in sports (banner stories about winning the state championships in football in 2012 and girls' volleyball in 2013) to controversial issues (such as in-depth looks at drug use and sexuality).

"We're going to tell stories that are going to be positive. But we're also doing investigative stuff and digging in on sensitive types of stories that are not necessarily stories principals are all that keen to see a lot of readership about," Grubaugh said. For example, a Gazette reporter recently wrote a 1,500-word article about binge drinking, including an interview with the mother of a student who had died from alcohol poisoning in 2008. The story noted that college-style binge drinking had seeped into high school culture and examined "what that looked like in our community," Grubaugh said.

"My kids quickly learn that I'm not a censor. The last thing I'm going to be is a censor. What I'm going to do is be a check of the system – to make sure they're doing the stories they've taken on appropriately, that they're doing them professionally, the kinds of things that would hold up to scrutiny in the professional workplace."

Grubaugh said student journalists step up "once they realize they're going to be doing this for an audience not of one teacher or one classroom of 30 students, but for an audience of hundreds or thousands." Students respond responsibly when they see "they're not lassoed and held back by restrictions other than the same kind of restrictions that the professional press tries to abide by," such as libel law and the SPJ Code of Ethics.

"I tell them, 'You guys are journalists. You're student journalists. You're learning – you're going to make more mistakes than pros will make.'" Grubaugh said he assures students he will help catch those mistakes or at least correct them and prevent repeats.

"For bright, talented students, once they get a glimpse of that and get that first byline, there's no stopping them." Grubaugh said he realizes that most of his students will not pursue journalism careers, and that is OK. But they all will emerge with "a greater appreciation for the First Amendment and its role in a democratic society, and the ability to write clearly and coherently and well, and take stuff from multiple sources and turn it into a readable report – that kind of a skill is going to serve you no matter what you're going into: medicine, engineering, law, whatever."

Granite Bay's student media operation has maintained a standard of excellence even as it has expanded and innovated in recent years; it launched its school news portal and showcases broadcast stories, including multidimensional videos focused on "Every 15 Minutes," a public service campaign against drunken driving.

Grubaugh inspires students to excel by invoking the "carpe diem" scene from the movie *Dead Poets Society*, in which Robin Williams, in the role of an English professor, has his students lean into a trophy case of photographs of a boarding school's long-ago graduates and whispers their advice: "Seize the day, boys. Make your lives extraordinary." At his "boot camp" at the start of each school year, Grubaugh invites staff members of *The Granite Bay Gazette* to contemplate a similar message as they scan 15 years of the newspaper's front pages and awards on the classroom wall.

"I have this time line of scholastic journalism excellence up on the wall in our lab, and I tell them there's a huge legacy here.," said Grubaugh. "The legacy of excellence is one that if you are here, you are called to maintain that kind of commitment to the quality of work done by the people who came before you. It's goofy, but that's a meaningful moment for them. They see that this is something bigger than themselves, and they don't want to drop the ball. It's a culture thing."

Columbus North High School, Columbus, Ind.

Columbus North represents the direction many scholastic journalism programs are headed: Beginning several years ago, it converged its media operations. An umbrella organization, Columbus North Student Media, was formed to provide "full, balanced and ethical coverage of the people and events of CNHS in print, on the air and on the web" (Columbus North High School, 2014). Both of the school's print publications – *The Triangle* newsmagazine and *The Log* yearbook – funnel content to http://cnhsmedia.com. The website also includes the Bull Dog News Network, the school's multimedia/broadcast program of daily announcements and other information.

The program's advisers are Kim Green (personal communications, June 18 and June 22, 2014), who has been a teacher for 36 years and focuses on *The Triangle* and *The Log*, and Rachel McCarver, a "digital native" who joined the faculty seven years ago and focuses on the website and multimedia products. They work with a staff of more than 130 students. Over the past decade, Columbus North's student media program has garnered more than 50 national honors, including NSPA Pacemaker awards, CSPA Gold and Silver Crowns and Journalism Education Association's Best in Show recognitions. Another measure of the program's success came about five years ago when the high school started an alumni association: The first scholarship it created was for communications.

Green taught journalism and English and advised student publications during the first 10 years of her career and then shifted to English classes exclusively when her sons became competitive swimmers. After moving to Columbus North, she found she might be laid off – and, partly for job security, she offered to oversee the school newspaper. The journalists she has mentored are glad she did: Green is a fierce guardian of the First Amendment, as demonstrated by a battle over *The Triangle*'s independence in 2005.

That was the year the student newspaper published a four-page report headlined "That Other Sex." It was about oral sex, including its prevalence among students ("One in ten teenagers have had it," the story stated) and its medical and psychological risks (as documented by health and religious authorities). The trigger for the article was the perceived acceptance of oral sex among many young people: "43 percent of teens see it as not as big a deal as sexual intercourse."

Some residents, including members of the school board, objected to the story. David Clark, the principal of Columbus North High School, supported Green and her students. (Clark does not see or approve articles in the student newspaper before publication. In this case, however, the editors gave him a heads-up, anticipating community reaction.) Clark said at the time (Student Press Law Center, 2005) that he believed the package would inform students of the dangers of oral sex and help them make responsible decisions.

"It's a tough subject for parents to broach," he said. "As a parent, I was uncomfortable with it. But the students (journalists) were absolutely compelling in their argument that this affects the community."

The controversy shook up the school board. Some members wanted to institute a policy of prior restraint on student journalists: to require them to get the administration's approval on each issue of the school newspaper before it goes to press. The board ultimately voted 5-2 against prior restraint – a vote of confidence that Green said (personal communications, June 18 and June 22, 2014) preserved the paper's status as an open forum.

"We survived that and even have come out stronger, with our editors saying, 'Whatever you do, don't censor yourself.' We're doing the right thing; we did it the right way," Green said. "Those things kind of make my hair gray, but if they (the students) do it right, I back them 100 percent. And I told them, 'You know, it's not about me keeping my job. They can shut us down at any time. So if you're going to use the First Amendment, it isn't to try to test the waters. It isn't to try to use it on something ridiculous. It's serious business, so use it for serious business.' And they have."

Columbus North's student journalists have continued to tackle tough subjects, ranging from dating violence to cat dissections in anatomy class. Increasingly, they are using multimedia storytelling to complement the print publication.

"It's a comfortable step for these kids," Green said. "In addition, we have several alumni who are in the business and report regularly that turning out grads who can tell stories on multiple platforms gives them an edge in the market."

But student media's emphasis, Green said, is broader than that:

"We have a culture of, this isn't just a program that produces products; it's a program that engages kids. I think the most important thing for students to understand is why we do what we do, and also that they have a ton of transferrable skills that go with them out into the world, at college and in the workplace."

Journalism education embodies the reforms and forward-looking pedagogies that many experts have been urging schools to adopt, Green said. "They talk about 21st century skills that we want to give our students. That's what journalism is. We've been doing project-based learning forever. And I'm not afraid of it – I'm not afraid of empowering kids to make their educational decisions."

Whitney High School, Rocklin, Calif.

Like Columbus North, Whitney High School also has a converged student media program. It encompasses the school's yearbook, called *Details*; its newsmagazine, *The Roar;* and a dynamic news website, Whitney Update, which features slideshows, videos and other multimedia as well as social networking tools. All of the platforms, especially the yearbook, have won top awards from organizations such as the National Scholastic Press Association, the Columbia Scholastic Press Association and the Journalism Education Association. Moreover, Sarah Nichols (personal communications, June 17 and June 24, 2014), the student media adviser at Whitney High School, was JEA's Yearbook Adviser of the Year for 2010.

Nichols' student journalists have beats and produce content across platforms. A soccer reporter, for example, might write breaking-news coverage on game day for Whitney Update and social media, then craft a longer-shelf-life news feature for the newsmagazine and archive photos and memorable moments for the yearbook.

Many advisers are reluctant to converge their student media staffs, Nichols said. They are more comfortable keeping the newspaper and yearbook in separate silos and fear that convergence is "too much to handle, too many things to juggle." But Nichols believes a converged media operation offers distinct advantages: "I think that the more we focus on the skills and the less on the medium, the more our students benefit, and so they become so much more versatile and marketable."

She has her student journalists focus on "what storytelling is and how each of the platforms is going to offer something different." This requires a cultural shift in the student newsroom, Nichols said. To serve audiences today, reporters must be prepared to live-blog an event as it happens, then write a recap for the Web and produce a long-form follow-up for the newsmagazine. Student journalists also must engage the audience in a conversation – for example, by posting photos to Instagram.

To succeed in this multimedia environment, Nichols said, a scholastic journalism program must develop a "culture of experimentation." She encourages her students to find and try new tools – embeddable time lines, for instance; they learn these tools on their own, following tutorials they can find on Google and YouTube. If the tools prove useful, students then teach them to each other.

That strategy allows Nichols to concentrate on teaching higher-level principles and core writing and visual communication skills. "It would be impossible to teach every kind of multimedia tool; things pop up every hour. So I really focus more on the skills and the critical thinking and 'Do you know how to verify that? Do you know what the most important piece of this story is? Does this story need photos? Do you know how to interpret the data?' That's a huge challenge at the high school level. We focus more on that, and the tools are secondary."

In excellent student media operations, Nichols said, advisers must internalize "a willingness to keep learning. This job changes every day, and so if we're not willing to move with it and embrace some of these new ideas, then we can't share them with our students. The common link among successful programs is the idea that students are going to lead the way. They're going to know so much more" than their adviser. For example, Nichols said her students know computer coding – and she doesn't.

Advisers must be comfortable "with knowing that the kids are going to surpass us, and that we're just going to teach and advise and expose them to things, and question them and play devil's advocate, and help make sure that they are still practicing sound journalism," Nichols said. "Even though they might try some tool I've never heard of, I'm OK with that. I'm not afraid of that. And I'm not afraid of them experimenting. I trust them."

Nichols trusts her staff to do hard-hitting stories on sensitive topics, from suicide to #YesAllWomen. For two years in a row, students covered the arrest of a Whitney High School teacher on charges of having inappropriate relationships with students; the students' stories were so solid that professional media outlets in Northern California cited them. In spring 2014, *The Roar* published a special edition called "The Water Issue" about California's drought, raising awareness in the school community and urging students, "Stop using so much water."

Coral Gables Senior High School, Miami, Fla.

While some programs have moved aggressively toward convergence, others have staffed each platform separately. That is the case at Coral Gables Senior High – and it was a decision made by students themselves, said Melissa Nieves Gonzalez (personal communication, June 13, 2014), adviser for the school newspaper, *highlights*[1]. Both the paper and CavsConnect.com, the student-driven news portal, have won all-Florida honors from the Florida Scholastic Press Association.

"Many newspapers have now moved away from the print newspaper in favor of the online newspaper. Our school has a separate online news publication and staff in order to give the site the proper attention it needs to grow," Gonzalez said. "It has been suggested by journalism trends that 'print is dead' and that traditional print newspapers should shift to newsmagazines. The student staff, however, tends to prefer the more traditional newspaper design in favor of the trend toward news magazines, even though I have encouraged them to try adding one newsmagazine issue a year to ease the possible transition."

Gonzalez's students don't shy away from controversial subjects. A recent issue featured a special report headlined "[High] School: From the true effect of drugs on student life to their prevalence among the student body, highlights takes an honest look at teen drug use." It included a poll that found "72 percent of students have tried drugs" and "40 percent have come to school intoxicated and/or brought drugs to school." The opinion section of that issue tackled such hot topics as the U.S. embargo of Cuba and the restoration of felons' right to vote.

Meanwhile, CavsConnect offers continuous updates – even

---

1. The school uses a lower case h in the newspaper's name.

covering the 2014 World Cup soccer tournament in Brazil during the summer. The site offers its content in both English and Spanish.

As with many scholastic journalism programs, Gonzalez said, funding is a challenge. "We are a fully self-funded paper. Students are required to sell advertising in order to fund the printing and supplies needed. Fortunately for us, our community businesses are very supportive, and we earn enough to fund our printing with some money left over for regional, state, and national workshops." She said her principal also "is very supportive of all of our journalism programs, and he provides technology and resources when possible."

It can be grueling for students to generate both revenues and stories for student media, Gonzalez said, but the payoff is worth the effort.

"My students learn the obvious writing skills, but they also learn skills in rhetoric, argument, grammar and mechanics, and problem-solving. They also learn communication and social skills when they interview and write, as well as when they must work cooperatively with their peers and editors," she said. "As far as the school community, I feel they benefit from the simple joy of reading. They are learning about relevant issues to them and some issues that they would have never cared about. Either way, they may have just enjoyed reading something, which I hope will lead them to try reading something else."

Stellar programs pay it forward

As a teenager, Mark Newton, the head of the Journalism Education Association, attended Grand Junction High School in Grand Junction, Colo. He was on the staff of *The Orange & Black*, the school's award-winning newspaper. Its adviser then was Gary Cordray.

"I wanted to be my adviser in high school," Newton said (personal communications, June 13). He realized that dream: Before moving to Mountain Vista High School in 2008, Newton spent 18 years as a teacher and journalism adviser at Grand Junction High. One of his students then was Megan Fromm. Fromm (personal communication, April 18, 2014) credits Newton with inspiring her to become a journalist and then to shift into journalism education: She was a journalism adviser at the Charles E. Smith Jewish Day School in Rockville, Md.; has taught at several universities and is now an assistant professor of communication at Boise State; and was recently elected as JEA's professional support director.

That chain of connected individuals represents another common trait of successful scholastic journalism programs: They transmit their passion and excellence to the next generation.

"It is remarkable," Newton said (personal communications, June 13 and June 18, 2014). "It's cool to see that legacy. I think all teachers are honored that one – or two or three – students journey down a path similar if not the same as theirs. You enjoy seeing their joy."

This is why Fromm became a journalism teacher. "I felt that journalism education was so important – that it was beneficial and should be accessible to all types of students," she said (personal communication, April 18, 2014). Fromm has been the JEA's news literacy curriculum leader, teaching at conventions and workshops and partnering with organizations such as Poynter and the American Society of News Editors to promote news literacy via scholastic journalism.

Fromm said successful programs have advisers who aren't afraid to let students lead. "There is a sense of ownership; everyone's invested. The best adviser is able to convey a high level of responsibility. Students know there are real consequences for their work, positive and negative. You can't just put 30 students in a room and say, 'Go put out a newspaper.' It takes team-building and understanding students and priorities. A good adviser fosters a culture of accountability. Students must realize who they are accountable to and what their responsibilities are."

When that happens, young journalists blossom.

"High school students are looking for their place in the world. In practicing journalism, they must think beyond themselves. It forces them to engage in the wider world. They put their stamp – their name – on work that gets distributed and read throughout the community," Fromm said. That can be both exhilarating and scary. "In no other classroom or space is an adult telling them, 'You can do it – we trust you. Here are the tools. This is all you.'"

Students will make mistakes, said Fromm, who cringingly remembers misspelling a headline for her fifth-grade newspaper

("Earthquack strikes Japan!"). "But those are learning opportunities, too, for a developing young adult. It doesn't matter how hard you fall, it's whether you get up again."

She said every story is a learning opportunity. Journalism staff members become more informed and better connected through their work on scholastic publications. "Students who practice journalism are more aware of global, cultural and social issues. Journalism prepares students to be better citizens."

Chapter 9

Teaching High School Journalism in the 21st Century

 By: David Burns & Rebecca Tallent

Introduction: Not your grandfather's journalism

"Traditional" journalism is no longer traditional. The basic concepts are still there, but the physical format has changed radically. How radically? About as much as the change between former journalists Edgar Allen Poe and Mark Twain's forms of weekly narrative journalism and the current condensed bursts of information available 24/7.

But, just because the delivery platforms have changed does not mean that journalism is dead or dying. Good journalism is in even more demand because people want their news in multiple forms from a multitude of resources. Just as important, teaching journalism in the 21st century is more than teaching the 5Ws and H; it is teaching important components of core curriculum, including critical thinking, creativity, communication and cooperation.

The primary change for high school journalism teachers is they need to set aside the idea of printed broadsheets and look more toward digital formats, which are less expensive and more instantaneous. They should embrace the idea of embedding links and video plus consider multiple information placements online, in video sites and in social media.

Preparing to teach

Details are important in journalism, and in teaching those details, begin with the syllabus. A detailed syllabus helps the teacher stay on track and allows the students an immediate understanding of all they will be experiencing during the school year. This often includes information about what journalism is, and what it is not.

Too often, students will take a journalism class thinking they will have free rein to say what they want, how they want to say it. They are unaware of the limitations on journalism writing in terms of Associated Press (AP) style and the rigid requirements that each work must include news value. For broadcast students, they often believe they will be seen on screen, not realizing the majority of the work is done off-screen, behind-the-scenes; and it is work which must be precise in execution. Yearbook and magazine students also frequently suffer misconceptions about what types of projects they will be involved in while composing their work. They all need to see what lies ahead, with the understanding it will apply to them.

So that the syllabus is not book length, concise writing is essential. It is important to state in simple terms that every student will be editing and writing certain elements, learning certain broadcast techniques and/or practicing page design. It is also essential to have information explaining what AP style is and its importance to the industry for maintaining format consistency and continuity.

While writing a syllabus, look for the consistent teaching opportunities available from each medium. For news, the day-to-day events that always happen – club events, government meetings, police reports, official speeches, festivals/community events, sporting events, etc. – provide excellent and ongoing story prospects. However, one should also be prepared to cover breaking news, which may impact the school or community. These may include natural and man-made disasters, political events which impact education, or controversial community events which impact students and their families. Flexibility – the ability to bring newsworthy issues into the classroom for use as teachable moments – is critical in a journalism class. News is new, whatever is happening. How local people respond is also news and should be considered. It is easy to incorporate expected news into the class lesson; the trick is having the flexibility to include the unexpected. Often, the easiest way to broach the subject is to ask: "Why is this news?" and guide the discussion along the lines of news requirements and impact.

The basics

What is news? Many people do not understand that news has certain basic elements. The most ignored is timeliness. School administrators often want to delay the release of current information or expect something that happened months or even years ago to appear in the newspaper or broadcast. News is immediate, not delayed. While an issue might be important, it may not be *newsworthy*. With this in mind, here are the 11 basic elements of what Brad Phillips (2012) described as the elements which makes news:

- **Conflict** – Good stories have conflict, he said vs. she said; opposition.
- **Proximity** – It is something unique within the local community.
- **Incident** – Anything that has gone wrong. This can be man-made (car crash, school shooting) or natural (major storm, earthquake).
- **Prominence** – The people involved are well-known.
- **Immediacy** – It is happening right now (a building explodes; people need to avoid the area).
- **Timely and relevant** – There is a time frame around an event which makes it important that the information go out quickly to the people who need it (a bridge on a major highway is down; a hearing about a proposed city ordinance which will cost business owners clients).
- **Scandal** – Anything that smells of cover-up (a Congressional aide is accepting bribes to influence legislation; a teacher has married a student).
- **Significance** – It will affect a lot of people. For example: a plane crash in the community which kills 126 people, including a family of five on the ground.
- **Unique** – Stories with an unexpected hook. These are often scientific discoveries or an unusual circumstance: a home-

less man returns a valuable ring and the publicity helps him find his family.
- **Hypocrisy** – People getting caught going against what they say they believe (an animal shelter caught abusing animals).
- **Human Interest** – Stories which appeal to emotions, or stories designed to evoke a specific response; offbeat or interesting items.

Once the news elements are identified, reporters frequently use the 5Ws and H method of telling the story, starting with whichever of the elements is most important (Kershner, 2005):
- Who
- What
- When
- Where
- Why
- How

Young journalists often cram all the 5Ws and H into a lead. A general rule of thumb is to keep leads to no more than 25 words for brevity and clarity (Kershner, 2005). Leads should capture the attention of the reader while relaying the most important information first. It is up to the reporter to decide what the most important information is and how to structure the lead. The rest of the 5Ws and H can follow in subsequent paragraphs (Kershner, 2005).

For example: The student council decides that all school clubs must be registered through them, for accountability purposes. Depending on the point of view of the student reporter, any number of the 5Ws and H can be in the lead. There is no absolute right or wrong when determining the news point of view, although the news judgment does need to be valid based on what is newsworthy.

Changes in presentation platforms really do not change the basics of news writing (Brooks, Kennedy, Moen & Ranly, 2002). News writing is brief, concise and adheres to the above-mentioned elements. What makes something news can be written in any platform: microblogs, broadcast, online publications, print publications, magazines, 'zines, video bursts, and whatever will come in the future. The point is, news is news, and news takes good writing and reporting skills to effectively relay the information.

No matter what the format, all news begins with a lead, also known as lede (Kershner, 2005; Brooks, et. al, 2002; Weinberg, 1996). This is a short paragraph which initially gives the most important information about the news event. Additional information follows the lead, but the lead is intended to provide the gist of the news in case someone only reads the first paragraph.

Most young reporters write what is known as a "nut graph," which condenses the information about the story. More experienced writers use alternative forms of writing, including anecdotes, arresting images or a multiple paragraph lead to provide context or show action. In every case, the information needs to both convey information and the importance of the story (Kershner, 2005).

The rest of the news story is structured to provide information in descending order from most to least importance. This is traditionally known as the inverted pyramid method of writing. But, the body of the work is still structured and contains both attribution of facts and transitions between ideas and sections (Brooks, et. al, 2002). Each story must lead the reader through the story, not just provide random information. In longer stories – say an article for a traditional blog – the writer may use the inverted pyramid method for each section within the body, linking each with transitional statements. If the work is shorter, say for a microblog such as a Tweet, then only the most important element is identified, usually with a link to the longer story.

At this writing, Twitter is the undisputed king of microblog news, but that is changing. Vine, a social media platform that allows users to share six-second videos, is quickly catching hold, and faster platforms are on the horizon. The basic elements still remain the same, however: The most important information based on the elements of newsworthiness goes first. Secondary elements come later or are embedded in a link to be followed. This is, in essence, the same as traditional news writing: Bring out the important facts first.

Another key element to teaching is the use of AP style. While many news organizations have their own style formats, understanding AP certainly gives students a common grounding in style and how to use it. AP style varies from traditional English in its use of periods (one space after, not two); numbers; titles (Mr., Ms., Mrs. are almost never used); how certain places are stated (such as Vietnam, one word, not two); and abbreviations (state names are not abbreviated using the two-letter style used by the U.S. Postal Service) (Associated Press, 2014). AP style is absolutely necessary in terms of consistency, clarity and accuracy.

When going out to cover a story, students should be encouraged to get out of their comfort zones and cover people and issues with which they are not necessarily familiar. Diversity is a major part of life in the U.S. and students should learn to approach people and talk about a variety of issues. After all, reporters don't necessarily select their own assignments or the people they interview for an assignment. By interviewing the less-covered people (these may include clubs for ethnic groups, the human rights or environmental teams, the disability services office, religious groups, etc.), student reporters explore their own biases, learn about different cultures/concepts/points of view and give voice to a previously under-covered population in the media (Weinberg, 1996).

By getting outside of their comfort zones, students also learn to listen more attentively and focus their stories on that single point with supplemental details. It also encourages accuracy because they will have a different audience reading their work who, unlike their friends, may not be willing to say "it's fine" when there are errors. It also encourages the students to be more balanced in their reporting since it teaches them to set aside their own preconceived notions and give a fair reporting of the facts.

Writing for online/digital media

Don't let the platform be confusing: Writing for news is writing for news. The written word for an online publication, Facebook or Twitter, has exactly the same basic principles as writing a hard copy newsprint paper: news first, written concisely and accurately. By working with the people they are interviewing, students learn communication skills and collaboration. They also increase their critical and creative thinking skills when they develop their interview questions (what do they need to know?) and decide the framing of the story. Not only do these elements make good journalism, they also complement the common core required by most high schools.

Structuring the story is essentially the same:
- Make sure the story is newsworthy and that it contains something people need to know.

- Get the most accurate information, and this means research. Remember, the Internet is not always the best resource, so also check old newspaper files and other resources.
- Think about what people need to know when formulating the interview questions and write the questions out thoughtfully. Journalists ask hard questions, so they should not be afraid to ask if it pertains to the story. Make sure to interview more than one source.
- After writing the first draft, double-check to make sure everything is covered; if not, get more information and add, but keep everything concise.
- Revise the work so it is clear and understandable while making sure the news is at the top. Copy edit carefully for grammar, spelling, style and punctuation.

When writing the lead, get straight to the point – leads do not need an introduction, just state the facts. The lead not only tells the most important information, it also lets the reader know what the whole story is about. Effective leads contain active verbs and avoid clichés.

In the body, every story must have a clear structure which leads the reader from point to point, usually in an inverted pyramid style, moving from the most important through the least important facts. The story ends when the reporter runs out of facts; there is no need to "tie the end of the story with a bow" or have a concluding statement.

Essential to every story – whether in print or online – are direct quotes. Each direct quote gets its own paragraph with attribution. *A note here*: In journalism, it is she or he *said*, not explained, expressed, laughed, or according to. Spaces count in journalism, so the shortest, most concise words are always the best. When not using a direct quote, indirect quotes help to move the story along, and the alignment of giving attribution to the facts makes the story both more meaningful and builds credibility. No fact should ever be placed in a story without attribution.

Journalists today incorporate video into their stories whenever possible. Research shows that consumers click on video items more often than text-only items on a website. Videos also help provide context and a sense of "being there" for the consumer. Since online journalism allows for hyperlinks and video, keeping an eye out for ways to bring video into any story is essential (see Figure 1).

The same elements in print/online are also true for video, but video has a twist: there must be compelling elements that *show* action, not just describe it. It may sound counterintuitive but most video stories, like print and online stories, begin with a well-researched and edited written script. Some even have storyboards, which are visual scripts that substitute pictures for words.

Whereas print and online reporters write for the eye, visual reporters write for the ear. To understand this concept, imagine providing directions to a gas station to someone who stops in town. If a map is drawn for the person, like a print journalist might do in a traditional newspaper article, it would be a detailed map in which the driver can refer time and again until he or she reaches the destination. The approach would change significantly if the person is given directions orally. In this case, verbal directions could provide too much detail, as the person would not be able to digest the spoken information. For effective communication, the message would be simplified. For example, the verbal directions might say, "Go to the second light. Take a right," instead of, "Go 2.5 miles and turn right onto Meredith Street." Visual landmarks might also be used to serve as guideposts; "Turn left at the McDonald's." In both cases, the driver can find his/her destination by remembering the simple

---

A hyperlink is a reference to data within the text that a reader can click on, or hover over with their cursor and automatically be transported to the Internet reference/location.

For example:

Another new element to the investigation is an increasing number of drinking water wells along the Salt Fork that now contain so much salt that the wells can no longer be used.

Words and phrases highlighted in underlined type will take the reader to maps of the wells and the Salt Fork River.

Script courtesy of the Oklahoma Educational Television Authority.

Figure 1

directions and looking for visual cues. In this way, the directions are customized – one for the eye (a detailed map or written description) or the ear (memorable landmarks or simple guideposts).

Video scripts are written in a specific format. To create a video script, divide a page into two vertical columns. The left column lists visual information (the content of visual graphics, for example, or a director's production notes). The right column contains all audio information. The right column may include, the reporter's narration, verbatim quotes from interview segments or the natural sound from a scene (i.e., protesters chanting). (See figure 2.)

Today, all reporting tools are compact and mobile. Since reporters now record video on their cell phones, they need to under-

[***DICK***] <mosAbstract>GFX FISH KILL</mosAbstract itemSlug>FISH KILL SALT FORK-CAM-2</itemSlug></mos>] [Anchor:Dick] {***DICK***} [ReadRate:14]	{***DICK***} FOR THE SECOND TIME IN A MONTH, THOUSANDS OF FISH HAVE TURNED UP DEAD ALONG A SECTION OF THE SALT FORK RIVER IN NORTHERN OKLAHOMA. AS WITH PREVIOUS FISH KILLS, WHAT CAUSED THE LATEST ONE IS A MYSTERY, BUT THE KILL IS NOW SPREADING TO ONE OF THE STATES MAJOR WATERWAYS
[TAKE PKG OUTCUE: AND WERE ORDERED TO CLEAN UP THE MESS TO 6:02 DURATION: 6;02 {PKG} [CG AT 0:02:LOW3RD\Bob Sands – Reporter\Aaron Byrd – Photographer] [CG at 0:27:low3rd\Spencer Grace\Kay County Game Warden] CG at 0:59:low3rd\Rep. Steve Vaughan\ (R) Ponca City] [CG at 3:18:low3rd\Jack Klinger\Lives on the Salt Fork River]	{***BOB***} IT'S A FAMILIAR SCENE IN KAY COUNTY. THOUSANDS OF DEAD FISH LINING THE BANKS OF THE SAND BARS AND FLOATING IN THE MIDDLE OF THE SALT FORK OF THE ARKANSAS RIVER. IT HAPPENED TWICE IN AUGUST, THE SECOND TIME ON THE 22ND AND 23RD, FROM THE HIGHWAY 177 BRIDGE TO THE CONFLUENCE WITH THE ARKANSAS RIVER. BUT THIS TIME, WHATEVER IS KILLING THE FISH DID NOT STOP WHERE THE TWO RIVERS MEET. KAY COUNTY GAME WARDEN SPENCER GRACE.

Script courtesy of the Oklahoma Educational Television Authority

Figure 2

stand how to write news scripts and upload the video to their news outlet, whether it is intended for a YouTube channel, for traditional broadcast on a campus TV or radio station, or for posting on a campus website, Facebook page, or Twitter account.

Embedding links is as simple as placing the actual link into the story once the article is posted. The complete URL needs to be included so anyone can make the jump. In many cases, embedding video links is as simple as copying and pasting. With both the story draft and the embed material open in a browser, position the cursor in the story to the spot where the embedded material should go – say a YouTube video. Select the "Share" button then the "Embed" button. An embed HTML code is provided under the YouTube material. Simply copy the HTML code from the YouTube site then paste the HTML code into the HTML code of the story. Once the video has been uploaded to the home site (again, YouTube, a website, or social media site), the video can be seen by clicking.

Social media

Writing news for microblogs begins just as writing a news story: It is just much shorter. Social media such as Facebook, LinkedIn, Tumblr and Path allow for longer pieces, but the works should still be short – usually about 300 words or shorter. Abbreviated sites such as Twitter are limited to 140 characters, so the essence or burst of news followed by a link is best.

In the longer pieces, the stories should have a concise lead, and then the rest of the information is written very tightly – giving the essential information with a link to further information. Leave out the least important facts. In social media, people want their information quickly and accurately, which means the reporter must write well in a very limited amount of space. The key in all of this is to make sure the news is dominant, concise and brief.

Micro videos

If the idea of a microblog is to present textual news information in a short, concise way, micro videos are the visual version of a microblog. When producing these videos the key is to choose visuals as carefully as one would choose their words in microblogs. Instagram, for example, allows a creator to produce videos as long as 15 seconds. Users of Vine – called Viners – have only six seconds to tell their stories. Think of micro videos as the visual equivalent of a newspaper or online story headline. It has to be brief, powerful and inform the viewer. Here are a few tips for creating effective micro videos.

Use close-up shots

Visual storytellers use various shot types to convey messages to viewers. A wide shot presents a wide vista to show the viewer where the action is taking place. For example, a wall-to-wall shot of a filled to capacity cafeteria. A medium shot shows only a segment of that larger scene. For example, a medium shot might only show one tightly packed table of people in the cafeteria. A close-up provides detail to the viewer of things inside that cafeteria. Examples might include a single shot of a diner, the cafeteria server or monitor, a tray full of food, or a conveyor belt of used trays. In a traditional video story there are far more close-ups than either wide shots or medium shots because close-ups convey a single message to the viewer and they provide the texture and detail of any scene.

If one sentence in a microblog conveys a single idea, or one complete thought, consider that one picture or video shot equates to one sentence. A series of shots then is the equivalent of a visual paragraph. Consider the wide shot of the cafeteria, the medium shot of the table with diners and a close-up shot of a single diner eating; together they tell the story of an overcrowded lunch room. A series of shots is called a "sequence," and they are the building blocks of any good visual story.

Since micro videos are so brief (only 6-15 seconds in length) and since they are usually consumed on a small mobile phone screen, wide shots are not very effective as they do not provide story detail and therefore cannot convey much immediate meaning to the viewer. So, micro videos use some medium shots but predominantly close-ups to tell these brief stories as they allow the viewer to see up close what the video producer wants to show the viewer.

Pre planning is crucial

Someone might think micro videos just happen but, in fact, producers of micro videos carefully plan out what they are going to say and show. They do this by using "scripts" and "storyboards" so they can edit down the words and pictures to the most essential elements to effectively deliver the message.

Keep it simple

Micro videos are not meant to convey complex thoughts. Keep Vine or Instagram posts to one simple idea that is delivered simply and effectively. For example, to convey the idea of wasted food in a school's cafeteria using a six-second Vine, a simple well-composed medium shot or close-up of uneaten food being shoveled into an already filled trash bin can be effective. The video does not need to show the cafeteria staff serving the food and the students NOT eating the food, too.

Let it move

Video cameras have two advantages over still cameras – the ability to capture motion in the shot and the ability to record sound while something is happening. Students can use these two characteristics to their advantage when creating any video. Allow objects to move within the video frame (a basketball player running toward the camera for a slâm dunk, for example). For a few reasons, it is not advised to use camera movement in micro videos (such as camera pans, tilts or zooms). Since micro videos are so short, successfully executing a smooth and complete camera move in the allotted time is very difficult. Camera movements also reveal additional information (a pan to the crowd after the slam dunk), which is sometimes difficult for the viewer to see and understand before the video ends. Lastly, since mobile technology relies on inconsistent cell service, fluctuating network connections can cause camera movements to appear jumpy and jerky.

Let it speak

Utilizing the sound that is recorded on site provides a sense of "being there" to the viewer. Stay quiet while recording to capture the roar of the crowd as they react to the player's slam-dunk, in the above example. Try not to join in the excitement, as the videographer's mouth is usually closer to the microphone than the crowd is and any comments and reactions can dilute the experience for the viewer. Remember, the most effective videos feature audio and video elements that complement each other. For example, a close-up of a student preaching that smoking is evil from a free speech corner while a group of students counter in opposition. This allows the viewer to hear the click of the cigarette lighter as one protester lights a cigarette, which can help transition to the inflammatory idea of banning smoking. In this way, the total can truly be larger than the sum of its parts.

Edit, edit, edit

Micro video applications have editing functions that allow videographers to cut videos down to the required length. This is an opportunity to distill the message down to its core elements. Here, eliminate any non-essential pieces of video or extraneous audio that do not contribute to that single, simple message which is the point to be conveyed. It is tempting to want to show a student looking disgusted at the cafeteria food, but if the message is about wasted food (not food quality), it is best to eliminate that shot and stay "on message."

When editing, keep splices simple. Avoid fancy transitions like dissolves, wipes or fades. These special effects unnecessarily shift the viewer's attention away from the message (wasted food) and toward the production of the message (camera work). As mentioned before, slow network connections may also make visual transitions seem jumpy or jerky, diverting the viewer's attention from the message.

Keep it clear

Video producers must keep production values in mind. Make sure the shots are well lit. If recorded sound is used, make sure the viewer can clearly hear what is said on the recording and can understand the content after viewing it the first time. Make sure each shot captures the action, is in focus and is well composed. There is nothing more frustrating for a viewer than to watch a video that is out of focus, inaudible and captures only part of the action.

Like writing a good story or microblog, creating compelling micro videos requires the creator to distill the message down into its basic elements. When done effectively, it can convey important messages to viewers and expand the number of viewers. However, the audience's expectations are high and their time and attention limited, therefore, all these elements are essential to succeed in today's social media environment.

What's next in social media? Crystal balls are murky, but it is expected that writing will become even more condensed. Thus, understanding what news is will become even more important to both the reporter and the consumer. In 2014, the emerging platforms included TVTag (talk with others while watching TV or another broadcast), Hi5 (meeting new people/social entertainment), MyLife (social and business networking), PerfSpot (blogging and photo sharing), Xing (business and career networking) and Kaixin001 (a Twitter-like Chinese networking site with games).

Each of these emerging platforms has similarities to the more traditional Facebook and MySpace formats in that there are blog and opportunities to share news and other information. However, these groups tend to track toward younger audiences in their teens and early 20s (in 2014, Facebook was appealing to a 50+ age audience).

Added to the traditional social media, government websites make online data mining easier for journalists to do research into documents and trends, such as information from the U.S. Census Bureau. Data mining involves gathering information from a website using key words and filtering systems available on the site. This can be a complex process, and it would be a good idea to ask local news professionals to explain more fully how the process works. Because gaining interviews – especially for student journalists – can be difficult, data-driven journalism is often the alternative.

Summary

Everything is new and nothing is new. Today's social media technologies are simply extensions of old technologies. The key concepts of sound journalistic practices as presented in SPJ's Code of Ethics remain crucial for today's student journalist and tomorrow's professional journalist. Journalists must be fair, accurate, ethical and accountable. Whether writing for a traditional newspaper, an online blog or a 140-character Tweet, it's the writer's responsibility to not only seek and present the truth but to do it in a fair, accurate, and compassionate way so that the journalist and the people presented in the stories are held accountable for their actions.

Today's microblogs and micro videos take brevity to the extreme and push the envelope on contemporary storytelling concepts. But, the responsibility for accurately presenting what happened, how it happened, to whom it happened and even why it happened still squarely lies with the storyteller.

Access to information has never been greater for journalists and the general public. Online databases, directories and public records have made the job of the journalist easier than in the past. But access does not replace analysis. The journalist's job still requires old-fashioned research and analytical interpretation of those figures to discover trends, identify discrepancies and to generate informed conclusions from the data that are supported by experts and authorities.

Chapter 10

High School Journalism's Value Goes Well Beyond Training for Journalism Careers

By Adam Maksl & Tracy Anderson

Journalism Education Association President Mark Newton's Facebook profile picture clearly displays a message he's telling everyone who will listen: "Journalism is the 21st Century English."

Newton's organization – with more than 2,500 members, mostly high school journalism teachers – is focused on strengthening high school journalism. One of its primary goals: To make sure that people understand the relevance and importance of scholastic journalism, even in an era when the traditional, institutional press seems to be changing rapidly, even sometimes disappearing (Journalism Education Association, 2014a).

Newton and others in JEA say that journalism is a natural training ground for the skills and competencies that are the cornerstones of our current educational era, where the focus is on preparing students to operate and even innovate in an increasingly tech-oriented, interconnected and dynamic world.

To help spread this message, JEA has begun developing new curriculum materials, with some explicit ties to nationwide educational initiatives like the Common Core. For example, in a white paper discussing its new curriculum (Journalism Education Association, 2014b), JEA says that one English/Language Arts standard that says students must "produce clear and coherent writing in which the development, organization, and style are appropriate to task, purpose, and audience" is easily accomplished in journalism and publications classes.

The value of scholastic journalism goes well beyond its ties to English/Language Arts, where programs are housed in many schools (personal communication, March 4, 2014).

"I don't know that I'm creating journalists as much as I am creating citizens or people who, no matter what they end up doing, better understand a media-rich world and can better function in that media-rich world," said Newton, who in addition to leading JEA teaches high school journalism in Denver.

To better connect to valuable skills outside of journalism, Newton and others have started to tie JEA's curriculum to the framework developed by the Partnership for 21st Century Skills, or P21, a coalition of business, government and education organizations focused on reforming education so that it more closely centers on development of skills and competencies relevant in a modern world.

How scholastic journalism encourages development of 21st century skills

The P21 framework encourages educational outcomes that focus on life and career skills, learning and innovation skills, and media and technology skills, all the while focusing on core subjects, such as language arts, mathematics, social studies, sciences and more (Partnership for 21st Century Skills, 2009).

Newton said he thinks scholastic journalism can connect to various areas, the so-called "four Cs" of the learning and innovation skills, especially critical thinking, communication, collaboration and creativity.

"I think it's really interesting because they're just naturally embedded," Newton said. "I think that really says a lot about the content areas, for lack of a better word, for what we're teaching. They're naturally inherent to what we do."

Critical Thinking

The first skill in the four Cs – critical thinking – includes reasoning effectively, using systems thinking, making judgments and decisions, and solving problems, according to material on P21's website. For example, P21 material says that solving problems includes the skill to "identify and ask significant questions that clarify various points of view and lead to better solutions."

In journalism, that clarification aspect of critical thinking is central to the trust-but-verify routine of journalistic reporting practices, Newton said.

"Somebody tells you something and you verify that," he said. "Somebody says this, and you go, that's interesting and let me figure that out. And you just critically think your way through almost every story."

Newton said that even questions like "which story goes on the front page?" or "which photo should I use to best tell a story?" involve critical thinking. They emphasize thinking about problems from a system-wide perspective, or as written on the P21 website, "how parts of a whole interact with each other to produce overall outcomes in complex systems."

Communication

Communication, the second area of the P21 learning and innovation skills, includes the ability to convey meaning via oral, written and non-verbal methods; listening to infer meaning; using media and technology tools effectively for communications; communicating with diverse and different audiences; and understanding and tailoring messages depending on purpose.

Journalism teaches all those skills, Newton says. In fact, he says that communication is the very essence of journalism.

"That's journalism," he said. "That's what we do."

Newton says that in a rapidly changing technology environment, scholastic journalism increasingly teaches students how to use new technologies and tools to best tell stories. For example, he said his students will look at a story and decide which tool best will connect and engage with audiences. He said his students might use traditional tools like yearbooks and newspapers, but they might use social media and websites to share information.

"They can actually make things that resonate with an audience," he said.

Collaboration

Working respectfully with diverse groups of people, being willing to compromise to find shared solutions and valuing individual contributions as part of a larger collective goal are central to the collaborative goals of P21.

Scholastic journalism, Newton says, has always focused on developing these skills.

"Nothing we do is in isolation," he said. "It's all done in terms of collaborating; it's all done in terms of the idea that we're a team."

Newton used as an example the Maestro Concept, a technique developed by newsrooms to emphasize a team-based approach to reporting and storytelling in which all people working on a story – from the writer, to designer, to editor, to photographer – develop comprehensive journalism packages through collaborative discussions. The technique is used by many high school journalism teachers.

Even in a journalism era that focuses on one-man-bands, or so-called backpack journalists, Newton said it all comes back to working together.

"You look at the idea that nothing ever gets done in journalism in isolation, even though there's a little bit of a push to be the backpack journalist and those things," he said. "I think what we're doing still is we're coming back and we're seeing how all of our work integrates with the whole."

Newton said that even if his students don't go into journalism, they know they can use those tools in any field.

"They can work together and find solutions, create a product; they can do all different kinds of things because they know what it's like to be a part of a team," he said.

Creativity

Creativity, the fourth and final goal of the P21 framework, goes hand in hand with the concept of innovation. From developing incremental changes to radical solutions to problems, P21 skills emphasize the notion that 21st-century students must be creating new ideas that solve contemporary problems.

It's difficult to be in journalism without some focus on innovation, whether in how reporting is done, how stories are told, or how journalists interact with audiences. Newton said that innovation is integrated into everything that he encourages his students to do in their work.

"It's everything from design, and how we do that, to the creation of new ways of reaching people," he said. "You look at how does journalism use Twitter, how does journalism use Facebook, those types of things."

For Newton, this 21st-century skill is really about "creating creatively," with a focus on developing a real-world product that fulfills some real-world need.

"It's fascinating because one of the things we know about teaching and learning and student engagement is that the more engaged they are, the more real that education is," Newton said.

He says often so-called "innovative" approaches to education focus on this constructivist, experiential model that is ingrained into the DNA of scholastic journalism programs.

"They're empowering kids," Newton said. "It's the whole idea of finding something that's authentic and creating a product."

"Journalism kids do better"

By tying journalism curricula to P21 skills, Newton and others at JEA hope that educational decision-makers will continue to value the role journalism plays in many schools. The benefit of scholastic journalism, however, is not only anecdotal. Education research on student achievement helps further tell the story.

Jack Dvorak, a retired journalism professor at Indiana University, has studied the academic achievement of students involved in journalism. His research (Dvorak & Choi, 2009; Dvorak, Lain, & Dickson, 1994) shows that students who worked for newspapers and yearbooks in high school tended to get better grades in high school, earn higher scores on college entrance exams and get better grades in their first years at college.

For example, students involved in high school journalism had an average GPA of 2.8 during their freshman year in college versus 2.73 for those without high school journalism experience, according to a 2008 report by Dvorak (Newspaper Association of America Foundation, 2008). In freshman English classes, the difference was 3.05 (B-) for those with high school journalism experience versus 2.94 (C+) for those without.

Other research from Dvorak and Choi (2009) shows that the success of those involved in high school journalism continues later into college. For example, on the ACT CAAP Writing (Essay) Test, which colleges administer to sophomores to measure learning outcomes, the average test-taker who had been involved in high school journalism ranked in the 74th percentile versus the 66th percentile for those with no high school journalism experience.

One of Dvorak's early works on the link between high school journalism and academic success was called "Journalism Kids Do Better." That message is something that Newton wants to convey to others, a message that focuses on journalism classrooms being more of a training ground for citizens than one for future professional journalists.

"Whatever it is they are going to do, their participation in scholastic journalism put them further ahead," Newton said.

Journalism's path to other professions

Journalism to public affairs, university presidency and much more

With nearly 30 years of executive leadership experience in government and higher education, Kathleen Wilbur was named Central Michigan University's vice president of development and external affairs in 2011. In this position, she directs and manages the university's government relations program, leads the development and implementation of a comprehensive fundraising program, and oversees the office of alumni relations.

Wilbur had served as the university's vice president for government relations and public affairs since 2002. She also previously held the position of interim president for the university from July 2009 to March 2010 and was a special adviser on the establishment of CMU's College of Medicine.

A 2007 inductee into the Michigan Women's Hall of Fame, Wilbur's career over the years along with her community contributions have been significant. She believes some of her success can be attributed to the lifelong skills she developed as a student journalist at Michigan State University (personal communication, April 10, 2014).

Prior to joining CMU, Wilbur was the first woman to direct three different state departments, including Michigan's Department of Consumer and Industry Services, which she established and where she helped oversee a $567 million annual budget and the licensing of more than 1.5 million individuals and entities.

The skills she developed long ago in journalism helped guide some of her actions in many of these roles.

For example, "the 5 W's and H; who, what, when, where, why and how. It is very clear and direct," Wilbur asserted. "We use this in communication every day.

"A lot of it is asking questions. It's being curious. It's always asking, 'why are we doing it this way?'" Wilbur explained. "Critical thinking develops... You really learn to listen. Well, you better learn to listen or you're going to miss the story."

Wilbur referred back to the old saying, "you learn so much more from listening than talking."

"I think a curriculum like journalism forces you to build confidence," Wilbur said. "Because if you don't have the confidence, you don't get the story."

Journalism also teaches you to be resourceful, which is an important skill in any field. As a journalist, you often think, if I can't get the story this way, I will do it another way, she added. "It's about finding another way and that's a great life skill," she said. "There are many different ways to get the answers."

Journalism to law

Matt Casebolt, an attorney in Denver, has been in practice for the past decade, though his roots stem from journalism. In high school, he was co-editor of the school newspaper, *The Orange and Black*, along with Doris Truong, who now serves as a homepage editor at *The Washington Post*. Casebolt also worked on the college paper, *The Catalyst*, at Colorado College, a small liberal arts school.

Despite his love for journalism, Casebolt felt it made more economical sense to pursue a political science major and eventually law school (personal communication, April 3, 2014).

"There's actually quite a lot of carryover from studying journalism to law both in terms of drafting and in terms of layout of court exhibits and in marketing your own legal practice and things of that nature," Casebolt said.

Technology was the first advantage of his journalism studies – even more than 15 years ago.

"In high school we were exposed to the Apple Macintosh product, and that got us computing at a time when the Internet revolution had barely even scratched the surface," Casebolt explained, adding that this exposure put him ahead when entering college because he was much more seasoned than most of his peers.

"The daily use of technology was absolutely key to everything," he said. "Learning how to lay something out and understanding layout theory back then ... every single webpage that I see now follows the same theories as page layout and design that I learned in high school journalism."

Having that head start in new technologies gave Casebolt an advantage not only in his career but also during his undergrad years and during law school.

"I was sitting taking notes on my laptop at a time when it wasn't yet cool do that," he recalled. "Did it give me advantage? Yes, it did."

The writing and interviewing skills that Casebolt gained so early on also helped him to become a better attorney.

He referenced the value of the most traditional acronym of journalism: who, what, when, where, why and how.

"That transfers right into law," Casebolt said, adding that in law, writing also must provide immediate access to the data of an argument with concise and simple writing. "Those skills were drilled into us."

And of course, deadlines, deadlines and deadlines. In journalism, if you miss a deadline, your missing story leaves a hole in the paper and a headache for your editor and ultimately, is a disservice to readers. In law, if you miss a deadline, it can affect the outcome of your entire case, Casebolt concluded.

In a way, journalism inspired Casebolt to pursue a career in law.

"Journalism was my first exposure to the Bill of Rights, the First Amendment, the Constitution," he said. "That early exposure got me interested in law."

High school and college journalism gave him plenty of time to master key skills.

"In my day, in journalism, you had to put the paper to bed – or get it to press," Casebolt said. "Those deadlines were something you had to hit."

"Like journalism, what drives the law is facts, facts, facts," he said. "Just as the editor has to get the facts from the reporter, so does the attorney have to get the facts from the client to report to the court. And your interviewing skills with the client are very important."

Casebolt said he remains very thankful for the guidance he received from his mentors along the way.

"My high school advisor, Mark Newton,… he is responsible for all of this. I'm personally grateful for all he did," Casebolt said. "Mark never stopped being a student; he was just our leader, and he was a journalist to the core. I learned a lot from him."

Journalism to medicine

Jenna Singleton spent four years studying journalism and working on the paper, *The Update*, at H.H. Dow High School in Midland, Mich. (personal communication, May 23, 2014).

"I learned the concept of sharing ideas, more so than in nearly any other class I took," Singleton said. "To get a newspaper issue from blank pages to thoughtful, interesting articles and eye-catching designs took a team of people working together and valuing input from others."

She also learned the importance of fact checking.

"Even if it was just a high school distribution list as opposed to a newspaper with high volume, such as the *Times* or *WSJ* [*Wall Street Journal*], you knew that every word said in reference to a student or teacher could be misinterpreted and needed to be backed up," she said. "It taught me the importance of using words carefully and having full confidence in the facts before submitting them to be published."

Singleton is now a resident in emergency medicine at Beth Israel Deaconess Medical Center in Boston, Mass.

"Journalistic skills helped me… I work in emergency medicine, which is a fast-paced career requiring constant teamwork and communication," she said. "In that way, it reminds me of high school journalism deadlines, the week before the paper went to press, when every member of the team was working toward a common goal. I learned not only how to function in a high-stress environment, but I also now enjoy it."

Singleton also gives much credit to her high school journalism adviser, Betsy Rau.

"Betsy was one of my favorite teachers," Singleton said. "She gave us all an environment where we felt useful and welcomed. I'm not sure how much of that was the subject matter versus how much was the way she chose to run our journalism program, but it was a great four years, and I strongly considered pursuing journalism as a junior and senior in high school."

Communicating high school journalism's role in the 21st century

The four Cs – critical thinking, communication, collaboration, and creativity – were all important skills that Wilbur, Casebolt and Singleton said they learned through journalism education. These are skills that continue to help them in their non-journalism careers, from the critical thinking Casebolt uses when questioning a witness in court to the collaboration and communication skills Singleton uses in the ER.

The skills taught in journalism are used in many other contexts.

Showcasing the wide-ranging value of scholastic journalism as more than just a vocational training ground is one of Newton's top priorities as president of JEA. He said that one challenge, though, is that journalism – and particularly scholastic journalism – needs to be a little better at promoting itself.

"We need to start screaming a little bit about ourselves," Newton said. "We scream about everybody else. We tell everyone else's stories. Perhaps we need to start telling ours."

Newton said that one problem might be the word "journalism," which he said evokes some connotations of ink-on-paper traditionalism and an industry that is dead.

"It's not," he said. "It's evolving, and it's different, and it's still much needed, and it's still required for democracy, and it's all of those things."

But perhaps the word journalism – or even the state of the industry itself – is immaterial to the question of high school journalism's value. Newton said that he doesn't focus on creating journalists – although he's created quite a few and is still happy when students choose that path – but rather he focuses on creating citizens.

"I have no illusion that I'm creating journalists," Newton said. "I hope I do, but what I'm creating is people who can go out and understand and participate in a world because they have participated in high school journalism. They're going to set themselves apart as citizens. They're going to set themselves apart as knowledgeable. They're going to set themselves apart in whatever profession they decide."

Chapter 11

How Journalism Teaches Critical Thinking Beyond the Newsroom

 By Leticia Steffen

Critical thinking is one of those skills that nearly everyone in education and in the professional world feels is crucial for any successful student or employee. In the field of journalism, critical thinking skills are essential. Journalists must be able to ask the right questions, identify relevant sources, evaluate material from sources and organize information into articles that will help the public understand various issues. Teaching students how to become journalists is a natural way to teach students how to become critical thinkers.

The Foundation for Critical Thinking, in its web-based article "A Brief History of Critical Thinking" (2013), traces the roots of critical thinking back to the teachings of Socrates. Since then, the notion of critical thinking has evolved from something that was thought to be part of the nature of human beings to a fairly well-defined, somewhat complex concept that can be developed, refined, analyzed and assessed (Foundation for Critical Thinking, 2013).

The foundation presents the following as a definition: "Critical thinking is the art of analyzing and evaluating thinking with a view to improving it" (Foundation for Critical Thinking, 2013). In the foundation's publication *The Miniature Guide to Critical Thinking: Concepts and Tools* by Richard Paul and Linda Elder (2009), it states: "Critical thinking is, in short, self-directed, self-disciplined, self-monitored and self-corrective thinking. It requires rigorous standards of excellence and mindful command of their use. It entails effective communication and problem solving abilities and a commitment to overcoming our native egocentrism and sociocentrism."

Critical thinking is something an individual can demonstrate in a variety of ways. To help business and professional groups identify ways critical thinking is applied in practical settings, the foundation offers seminars in critical thinking with objectives that are directly applicable to teaching in the field of journalism (Foundation for Critical Thinking, 2013).

The first objective – Understanding the pervasive role of thinking in human life (Foundation for Critical Thinking, 2013) – connects to the field of journalism very clearly. Journalists must always have their thinking caps on when they're working, and students of journalism learn that thinking is, indeed, crucial to the profession – and, ultimately, to their lives. Sometimes it's challenging to convey this idea in a classroom setting; after all, anyone working in an educational setting assumes that students are doing some kind of thinking. But when the subject being taught is journalism, teachers have tangible ways to show how thinking plays a role in what journalists do: Why does a journalist choose a particular lead for a story? What sources should a journalist pursue when writing a story? What direct quotes should a journalist use and what information should a journalist paraphrase?

All of these questions must be addressed through very deliberate thinking on the part of the student journalist. In addition, students of journalism are encouraged to analyze the various ways people think about issues and to convey these different viewpoints in the articles they write, giving readers a broader perspective on the issue.

Objective No. 2 – Understand the importance of developing higher order thinking to replace lower order thinking in order to reason well through complex issues on the job (Foundation for Critical Thinking, 2013) – also connects directly to journalism. When a journalist is presented with a range of perspectives on a particular issue, that journalist must use reason to organize these perspectives in a story allowing the audience to develop their own perspectives on the issue. If students have the opportunity to begin practicing these skills in a high school classroom, they become much better at grappling with, and ultimately explaining, complex issues as they progress through their educational careers.

This practice also applies to objective No. 4 from the foundation – Understanding how to analyze thinking by focusing on its parts or elements, and how to apply understanding of the elements of reasoning to workplace decisions and problems (Foundation for Critical Thinking, 2013). Oftentimes, journalists and editors must work together to determine what stories to include in a publication or on a broadcast given space and time limitations. The process of reasoning through all the options helps professional journalists make well-thought-out decisions on news content. Failing to do so may lead to simplistic treatments of complex topics (or ignoring issues of relevance to the audience); this does not benefit readers in any way. In the high school classroom, teachers often help guide high school journalists in making these decisions. As the students become more skilled and comfortable at making these decisions on their own, teachers can step aside and allow the students to take control and responsibility.

The final two objectives from the foundation's seminars also have direct application to teaching journalism. Objective No. 10 – Using categories of questions as a tool for learning, (Foundation for Critical Thinking, 2013) is ingrained in the practice of journalism. Student journalists learn to develop lists of questions before interviewing sources to help them gather the most relevant information. Oftentimes, these questions can be categorized from simple to complex, allowing a journalist to progress through an interview and encourage the source to share information that will be crucial in the development of an understandable story.

Objective No. 11 – Beginning to understand how to ask high quality questions, (Foundation for Critical Thinking, 2013) is another key element in the field of journalism. If journalists fail to think through the different kinds of questions they need to ask sources, they will not gather the kind of information necessary to write a story that the audience will benefit from. And the skill of developing "high quality questions" is particularly important when a journalist is writing about a complex issue requiring the collection of information that leads to better public understanding of an issue. Imagine if a political reporter failed to delve into questions about the motivations behind a proposed law. What kind of understanding will the public develop about the issue if the journalist doesn't ask the high quality questions then thoroughly report on the answers to those questions?

One of the most beneficial aspects of high school journalism is helping students realize that the questions they ask sources have varying degrees of usefulness. Student journalists learn how to become skilled at asking questions that will provide insightful responses. These skills not only help make these students good journalists, they also help them become better students.

Importance of critical thinking in post-high school settings

In any business or profession, critical thinking skills can help workers become more thoughtful about the choices they make and the strategies carried out to perform a task or assignment. If high school graduates have already been exposed to the practice of critical thinking, their transition into the next phase of their life becomes a bit easier.

This also applies to military service, which some high school graduates choose to pursue after receiving their diplomas. In the 2013 *Military Review* article "Education for Critical Thinking," Col. Thomas M. Williams of the U.S. Army Reserve said a recent study of the Army's culture found "a strong desire to build a mission command culture of innovation and creativity, risk taking, and emphasis on flexibility and discretion" (Williams, 2013).

Williams recognizes that the "ability to think well takes training, and practice" (Williams, 2013), so he recommends that the Intermediate Level Education curriculum in the Army become more organized around critical thinking and not content, allowing students to "learn more about creating and sharing knowledge developed through problem solving" (Williams, 2013).

The article "How We Think: Thinking Critically and Creatively and How Military Professionals Can Do it Better," published Sept. 16, 2011, in the *Small Wars Journal*, recommends the use of critical and creative thinking to help identify incomplete or ill-considered ideas (McConnell, Lira, Long, Gerges & McCollum, 2011). The article's authors, Richard McConnell, Leonard L. Lira, Ken Long, Mark Gerges and Bill McCollum, conclude: "Better thinking helps us avoid disasters and accomplish missions better." They also note that better thinking "expands the military profession's thinking capacity to problems not normally considered within the profession's paradigm that leads to ill-considered actions; or better, it prevents those ideas from taking root in their organizations all together" (McConnell et al., 2011).

The Institute of Critical Thinking also adopts a practical application of critical thinking by conducting and sponsoring workshops and training that emphasize the need to help people address problems they face in life through a rational and philosophical approach (Institute of Critical Thinking, 2014).

In addition, critical thinking has long been recognized as a key component of a student's higher education experience. From May 2007 through April 2010, the Association of American Colleges and Universities embarked on an effort to create rubrics articulating criteria for 16 learning outcomes (Association of American Colleges and Universities, 2014). Among the 16 outcomes in the AAC&U's Valid Assessment of Learning in Undergraduate Education (VALUE) project is critical thinking.

The AAC&U defines critical thinking as "a habit of mind characterized by the comprehensive exploration of issues, ideas, artifacts and events before accepting or formulating an opinion or conclusion" (Association of American Colleges and Universities, 2014). Further the AAC&U notes that "research suggests that successful critical thinkers from all disciplines need to be able to apply those habits in various and changing situations encountered in all walks of life" (Association of American Colleges and Universities, 2014).

Critical thinking in state high school graduation requirements

Whether a student plans to jump straight from high school into college, to immediately join the work force, or to enlist in a branch of military service, high school graduates are expected to have some level of critical thinking ability. In fact, critical thinking is a key component of the K-12 educational philosophy. Education groups including the National Education Association and the Journalism Education Association have identified four "C's" that are imperative to prepare students: critical thinking, communication, collaboration and creativity. In Chapter 10 of this book (High School Journalism's Value Goes Well Beyond Training for Journalism Careers), the role of critical thinking in the JEA's philosophical framework was discussed in greater depth (Journalism Education Association, 2014b).

Although critical thinking has been identified as a key component of learning at nearly every level of education, when reviewing high school graduation requirements articulated by individual states, it is difficult to determine where critical thinking fits into the menu of graduation requirements.

Most states define graduation requirements in terms of credits or years of exposure to specific subject areas. For example, states require that students complete a certain number of English, math, science, social studies/history and elective courses or credits. Within each state, students can meet the requirements through a variety of specific course offerings.

In Colorado, a set of guiding beliefs of high school graduates was developed by the Colorado Department of Education and adopted by the State Board of Education in May 2013. Among those beliefs is the idea that "(p)ost secondary and workforce readiness requires content knowledge, the ability to apply content and skills in a problem solving context" (Colorado State Board of Education, 2013). Problem solving is a key component of the critical thinking definitions mentioned earlier in this chapter.

In Florida, the general requirements for high school graduation as articulated in the K-12 Education Code of the 2012 Florida Statutes specify the importance of developing the ability of "reading for information" in English courses (Florida Statutes, 2013). Florida also recognizes the importance of developing in students the skills of "creativity, interpretation and imagination" (Florida Statutes, 2013). The inclusion of creativity and interpretation also ties closely to the definition of critical thinking.

In Maine, the state Department of Education's requirements stipulate that to demonstrate high school graduation preparedness, students must show "D. How to identify relevant information; and E. How to evaluate, interpret, paraphrase, and organize the information for use" (Maine Department of Education, 2002). Many critical thinking scholars recognize that the ability to evaluate information is key in the development of critical thinking skills.

The Oregon Department of Education stipulates that high school graduates in that state must demonstrate career-related knowledge and skills in the following areas: personal management, problem solving, communication, teamwork, employment foundations and career development (Oregon Department of Education, 2005). Again, problem-solving skills are part of nearly every definition of critical thinking.

While some state high school graduation requirements articulate specific skills related to critical thinking, including problem solving, creativity, interpretation and evaluation, the majority of state high school graduation requirements focus on the completion of coursework in the main areas of English, math, science, social studies/history and electives. Fortunately, within many high school English departments, students still are able to fulfill graduation requirements by enrolling in a journalism course or participating in the writing and production of student media. Through these journalism experiences, students can develop clear critical thinking skills.

How critical thinking skills are incorporated into the practice of journalism

Through these high school journalism opportunities, students often gain a richer development of critical thinking skills. Looking at the AAC&U critical thinking VALUE rubric (Association of American Colleges and Universities, 2014), it becomes clear that the practice of journalism corresponds directly to several higher-level critical thinking skills.

The ability to explain issues clearly and comprehensively demonstrates students have achieved the "capstone," or highest, level of critical thinking (Association of American Colleges and Universities, 2014). In the field of journalism, students are taught the importance of clarity to aid in readers' comprehension of sometimes complex issues. Thorough reporting also allows high school journalists to help readers develop an understanding of issues, which relates to the AAC&U's "milestones," or mid-level of explanation of ideas, which states that the "(i)ssue/problem to be considered critically is stated, described, and clarified so that understanding is not seriously impeded by omissions." (Association of American Colleges and Universities, 2014).

Another component of the AAC&U critical thinking VALUE rubric is "Evidence – Selecting and using information to investigate a point of view or conclusion" (Association of American Colleges and Universities, 2014). At the capstone level of this component is the development of "comprehensive analysis or synthesis," where "viewpoints of experts are questioned thoroughly" (Association of American Colleges and Universities, 2014). Again, when students are practicing journalism, they are encouraged and taught to question the information they receive from all sources to determine what information is most reliable.

In the "Influence of context and assumptions" component of the AAC&U critical thinking VALUE rubric, an individual at the capstone level is expected to carefully evaluate the "relevance of contexts when presenting a position" (Association of American Colleges and Universities, 2014). Again, students learning journalism are taught the importance of examining the relevance of different sources' positions as they relate to the context of the story.

Finally, in the "Conclusions and related outcomes (implications and consequences)" component of the AAC&U critical thinking VALUE rubric, students at the capstone level are expected to "place evidence and perspectives discussed in priority order" (Association of American Colleges and Universities, 2014). Any student who has learned the inverted pyramid style of journalism is familiar with the importance of organizing and prioritizing information based on what's most important or relevant to the reader.

Even if a high school student doesn't fully attain the capstone level of these components, by practicing journalism, they are naturally exposed to the importance of these skills. In other types of writing, these capstone level skills may be addressed but they may not be as crucial to the success of the students' writing. When student journalists achieve the capstone levels of critical thinking in their work, they also learn that they are fulfilling an important role to their audience and the public. In fact, when journalists (at any level) do not write with clarity, thoroughness, analysis or organization, and when they select sources that aren't clearly aligned to the context of their stories, journalists will often receive public criticism for their work.

The fact that the work of a journalist exists in such a public forum requires aspiring journalists to take extreme care in learning the profession if they want to have any success professionally. Critical thinking is ingrained in the field, and failure to critically think when you are a journalist will limit your career options.

As mentioned earlier in this chapter, the practice of high school journalism also has clear ties to the objectives developed by the Foundation for Critical Thinking. These skills include analyzing ways of thinking, developing categories of questions and learning how to ask high quality questions (Foundation for Critical Thinking, 2013).

The kinds of articles high school journalists choose to write often demand critical thinking skills. In a recent informal analysis of online high school newspapers published across the United States through School Newspapers Online (SNO Sites), the most popular stories covered in early 2014 (not including the usual event and sports coverage) included:

- the prevalence of assessment testing in high schools
- the impact of recent bad winter weather on high school schedules
- the effects of limited sleep on high school students
- the reasoning behind nontraditional high school class schedules (including year-round and block schedules)
- how to effectively plan for college
- dangers of alcohol
- bullying in high school
- dress codes in high school
- increased dependence high school students have on technology
- negative health habits of high school students

None of these topics can be addressed with simple explanations. The need for analysis and thoughtful treatment of these sensitive topics is clear, especially in high school, when students are beginning to take their first steps into the responsibilities and decision-making of adulthood.

Insights on critical thinking skills from students, teachers and professionals

"Doing" journalism at the high school level clearly is key to teaching young learners about the complexities of critical thinking. Lucy Chen, a high school journalist in Maryland, wrote about the importance of critical thinking in high school journalism (Chen, 2010). In her article, "Critical Thinking About Journalism: A High School Student's View," which was published in summer 2010 by *Nieman Reports*, Chen explained how she completed a news literacy project in a government class that featured speakers working in a variety of professional media organizations, including Time magazine, ABC News and *USA Today* (Chen, 2010). She said she quickly learned that "a journalist's job is to find the information they need, decipher it, and convey a story coherently" (Chen, 2010). In addition, Chen said, "I grew more skeptical about the facts I read or hear, especially those I find online, where anyone can post information about anything" (Chen, 2010).

After taking the government course, Chen created a quiz with questions she used to help judge how a person selects "credible sources and reliable information," and she joined the staff of her high school newspaper, recognizing that she could readily use her newfound critical thinking skills in the process of daily newsgathering (Chen, 2010). For Chen, a high school journalism experience provided the opportunity for her to move from understanding and recognizing what critical thinking is to actually practicing critical thinking.

Jesse Gainer (2012), an associate professor at Texas State University, San Marcos, explains the connection between understanding critical thinking and applying it, and the important role this plays in a democratic society: "Teaching students to use critical thinking to analyze and discuss ways that new literacies support democratic movements throughout the world, and then applying this knowledge to their own writing of digital texts, is to teach the principles of democracy."

In high school journalism courses, students have the opportunity to write stories and create content for public distribution, much like the process Gainer (2012) describes of writing digital texts. This allows students to apply their critical thinking knowledge in an open forum.

Students of journalism in the United States learn that they play an important role in maintaining a democratic society. By having a direct connection to a very public responsibility, the need for critical thinking in their journalistic pursuits becomes more meaningful than merely another lesson to be learned in school or another writing assignment to be read only by the English teacher.

The practice of journalism moves students into the more advanced stages of critical thinking: stating clearly, describing comprehensively, thoroughly questioning viewpoints of experts, evaluating relevance of contexts when presenting positions, placing evidence and perspectives in priority order.

In her article "Teaching Students to Be Global Citizens," Deborah Hoeflinger (2012), an adjunct professor of history at the County College of Morris and a retired high school teacher, recognizes the importance of introducing students to the news and, thus, increasing students' awareness of current events and their critical thinking skills. "Students' awareness can also be increased by including the study of current events in the classroom," Hoeflinger (2012) writes for *The Delta Kappa Gamma Bulletin*. "Reading the newspaper keeps students informed and enhances critical thinking skills, and school personnel should help students develop the habit of reading the paper."

High school journalism courses require students to be aware of current events and to explore the potential impact current events may have on their audiences. And as the creators of news content, student journalists again realize the important role they, as journalists, play in society. High schools that support the publication of a student newspaper, whether in print format or online, are encouraging all students to become better informed and better critical thinkers.

In the *Editor & Publisher* article "Critical Thinking," posted March 11, 2014, writer Nu Yang provides perspectives on the importance of critical thinking skills in the profession of journalism.

Yang quotes Rex Smith, editor of the *Albany (N.Y.) Times Union*, who says he agrees with Mel Mencher, professor emeritus of

Columbia University. Mencher taught Smith that journalists should be the smartest people in any room and that they should always display intelligence, energy and curiosity (Yang, 2014). Smith concludes (Yang, 2014), "The most important task for a j-school – or, for that matter whatever path a young person follows into the newsroom – is to teach smart students how to think like a journalist."

Clearly, thinking like a journalist means thinking critically.

Chapter 12

The Use of High School Workshops

By Jimmy McCollum & June Nicholson

The national survey conducted as a basis for this book revealed that workshops play an integral role in the development of scholastic media. Ninety-six percent of high school advisers who responded to the survey reported that they had attended at least one workshop since becoming an adviser or instructor, and almost half said that they had attended more than 10. One-third responded that university journalism programs had contributed to their media through workshop sessions, and 21 percent said that working professionals had contributed through workshops.

A study of high school workshops finds that they take on a variety of functions and shapes – from the more formal-sounding "conventions" and "conferences" to the more informal-sounding "camps" and "boot camps." This chapter examines the history of workshops, provides snapshots of several current workshops and describes challenges that workshops face and the benefits they provide.

History

Workshops evolved from journalism organizations that began springing up in the first three decades of the 20th century. Laurence R. Campbell, who dedicated a half-century to improving high school journalism and was called "Mr. High School Journalism" in one 1987 obituary (Konkle, 2003), wrote that "[a]mong the unheralded heroes of American journalism are the founders of high school press associations" (Campbell, 1967, p. 1). Campbell noted that high school newspapers started coming alive after World War I, and their advisers began seeking guidance. "They looked in vain to English departments and organizations of English teachers. They looked in vain to schools of education and state departments of public instruction. They looked in vain to local newspapers. Still in their infancy, schools and departments of journalism recognized this opportunity." (pp. 4-5). In the second and third decades of the 20th century, these state and regional associations began:

- Oklahoma Interscholastic Press Association, 1916
- Central Interscholastic Press Association, 1921 (changed to NSPA in 1928)
- Oregon Scholastic Press, 1921
- Minnesota High School Press, 1921
- Michigan Interscholastic Press Association, 1921
- Iowa High School Press Association, 1921
- Northern Interscholastic Press Association, 1922
- Indiana High School Press Association, 1922
- South Dakota High School Press Association, 1922
- Missouri Interscholastic Press Association, 1923
- Montana Interscholastic Press Association, 1923
- Texas High School Press Association, 1923
- Illinois State High School Press Association, 1924
- Southern Interscholastic Press Association, 1925

With the establishment of these associations, not far behind were conferences and conventions. In 1913, Oklahoma University hired H. H. Herbert to teach in the brand new School of Journalism. From the one-story, three-room, wooden journalism building, Herbert oversaw the beginning of the Oklahoma Interscholastic Press Association in 1916. OIPA held its first convention that year on the Norman campus, and it remains the oldest state organization in the country (Burke, 2013).

The Journalism Education Association was founded in 1924 as the American Association of Teachers of Journalistic Writing in Secondary Schools (Konkle, 2013). The first convention became the annual national high school journalism convention and took place in 1921 at the Palmer House in Chicago.

"When I tell people this, they're always a little bit surprised by it," said Kelly Furnas, executive director of JEA. "It used to be, every single year it was over Thanksgiving break. If you can picture that, it was a formal awards dinner where students would dress up and have Thanksgiving dinner with students from around the country" (personal interview with K. Furnas, May 21, 2014).

Willard G. Bleyer, who had helped start the American Association of Teachers of Journalism in 1912, organized the Central Scholastic Press Association in 1921 at Wisconsin. He and its director, E. Marion Johnson, coordinated its move to the University of Minnesota as it took on a national scope as the National Scholastic Press Association. Since 1921 the organization has served its members by offering national workshops, contests, scholarships and critiques (Konkle, 2013).

In 1921, Detroit-area high schools unveiled a plan for an organization to improve publications. The "High School Editors Conference" was held on May 22, 1922. The University of Michigan's chapter of Sigma Delta Chi, a journalism honor society, sponsored the conference. It drew 100 editors and advisers and used the theme "A Better Press for a Better World." The conference grew into the Michigan Interscholastic Press Association (MIPA, 2004).

To the south in that year, Franklin (Ind.) College students Bill Bridges and Ray Blackwell noted the struggles that Indiana schools had in publishing newspapers and yearbooks, with very little journalism education to be found. They brainstormed the idea for a gathering during which publication staffs could discuss and solve their problems. With encouragement from Franklin College and assistance from *The Franklin Evening Star* publisher and co-owner Eugene C. Pulliam, they started the Indiana High School Press Association. Its first convention was Oct. 29, 1922. Four decades later, Pulliam – who had helped found Sigma Delta Chi – and his wife gave Franklin College stock from their Central Newspaper Inc., and that gift was converted to a $30 million endowment to the school's journalism department and the Indiana High School Press Association which he had helped start (Jacobs, 1997).

Also in 1922 was the first conference of the Central Interscholastic Press Association, which six years later would become the

National Scholastic Press Association. The conference took place at the University of Wisconsin and drew 574 delegates from 16 states. The registration fee was $1.25 per delegate, which included a banquet, ball and carnival. Lodging in Madison was free for up to six delegates per school. The conference offered publication ratings for 238 newspapers, 103 annuals and 48 magazines. All American ratings went to 14 newspapers, 14 annuals and nine magazines.

The Columbia Scholastic Press Association's first convention was in 1925. CSPA traces its history to Joseph M. Murphy. In February 1924, Murphy enrolled in the Teachers College at Columbia University. In the fall, Columbia administrators approved Murphy's plan for an annual convention and contest in the spring (Hines, 1982).

Murphy created the Columbia Scholastic Press Association and began planning its first convention. He set the contest entry fee (doubling as the membership fee) at $1 per publication, with a deadline in late February. The fee for attending the two-day convention was $1.50 per person. Boys stayed overnight on campus, while the girls stayed in hotels with advisers.

"They only advertised it that first year to states east of the Mississippi," said Edmund Sullivan, the third and current director of CSPA. "We still can't understand why. Murphy didn't understand why, either, even years later. But when he was asked by the university to start this up, I guess this was what they picked. Maybe they just didn't think people would come from farther away" (personal interview with E. Sullivan, May 22, 2014).

One-hour "sectional meetings" were offered during the two days: "What Is News?"; "Editorial Writing" (offered twice); "Humor" (offered twice); "The Faculty Adviser and the Newspaper"; "Verse"; "How to Write Sport News"; "The Faculty Adviser and the Magazine"; "Advertising"; "The Short Story; "The School Paper and School Publicity"; and "Business Management" (Hines, 1982).

On Friday night, the convention featured a banquet and then a bus tour of New York including visits to *The New York Times* and the *New York World*. The convention ended on Saturday with a business meeting and an awards ceremony and then a Columbia College Varsity Show at the Waldorf-Astoria Ballroom.

One month later, Murphy created *The School Press Review*, which included articles and highlights of the convention and contests. CSPA's second convention, in March 1926, was advertised to schools throughout the country. It drew 747 people. For many years, Murphy recruited prominent speakers to close the convention, such as U.S. Sen. Hubert Humphrey, D-Minn.; First Lady Eleanor Roosevelt; President Harry Truman; President Dwight D. Eisenhower; Edward R. Murrow and Fred Friendly (Joseph M. Murphy, personal communication, January 15, 2014). CSPA added a fall conference in 1940 and a summer workshop in 1981.

The University Interscholastic League, an extension program at the University of Texas, had been formed in 1913 with the merger of the Debating League of Texas and the Interscholastic Athletic Association (University Scholastic League, 2014). The UIL's second director was Roy Bedichek, who had been a reporter for the *Fort Worth Record*. In December 1922, his first year as director, he encouraged schools in the state to mail their newspapers to the UIL. They listened.

"Here they come, all sorts, sizes, complexions, but uniformly rectangular in shape," Bedichek wrote. "They all possess this one common feature – and none other – rectangularity. They are not all even printed, one comes in mimeographed." Bedichek then encouraged Lloyd Gregory, a journalism professor at UT, and the university's chapter of the journalism honor society, Sigma Delta Chi, to start a high-school journalism competition In May 1925, delegates from throughout the state traveled by train to Austin for the first conference. *The Dallas News*, the *Beaumont Enterprise*, the *Houston Chronicle* and the *San Antonio Light* paid for the train tickets (Hawthorne, 2009). The UIL's first conference under DeWitt Reddick's direction – the Interscholastic League Press Conference – was in May 1928 (Komandosky, 1981).

"Reddick was and remains to this day the most important figure in the evolution of the League's journalism efforts," said Bobby Hawthorne, who served as UIL director of journalism from 1979 to 1989. For two decades, Reddick directed UIL conferences and meetings, authored the 1949 book *Journalism and the School Paper* and distributed pamphlets for high schools across the state. The UIL's journalism program has grown into one of the largest scholastic press associations in the country. Its purpose, according to Hawthorne, "is not and never has been to crank out fledgling reporters but rather to encourage young people to read newspapers, to think freely and deeply about timely issues, to write clearly and precisely and to understand the news business well enough to know whether 'fair and balanced' is a principle or a slogan" (Hawthorne, 2009).

The first summer workshop was offered by Northwestern University in 1934 as a division of the National High School Institute, which itself started in 1931 and offered programs in debate and theater. The first journalism program attracted 38 students, equally divided between males and females and from 22 states. Most of them came from schools that had participated in the Medill Press Conference, an annual editing and writing competition. At that conference, an unfolding news story would be acted out, and the students would have to cover it. When the Journalism Division began, its classes were modeled in part on those "staged stories." The students who attended Northwestern's institute were known as "cherubs," a nickname that survives to this day. As for that label, Roger Boye, who started working at the journalism program in 1971 and became director in 1985, had one explanation.

"One story has it that back in the '30s, the president of the university was looking out over his window, and his wife was standing next to him. And his wife says, 'Oh, look at all those youngsters out over there. They look just like a group of cherubs.' And the president of the university turns to her and says, 'Cherubs, they ain't'" (Yoon-Hendricks & Rodriguez, 2013).

The program was discontinued from 1946 and 1950 because of post-World War II needs.

"There were so many veterans on campus," Boye said. "They just used up all of the existing dorm space, plus there were little temporary huts around campus for the veterans to stay in, so it just was too much to have additional high school kids on campus."

In 1951 the program was re-started and extended to five weeks. The Journalism Division reached 100 for the first time in 1958, and the highest enrollment was 113 the following year and in 1967. In those years, "it was just a matter of renting a few more typewriters" (personal interview with R. Boye, May 21, 2014).

In a 1947 *School Activities* article, Laurence Campbell wrote that now that World War II was in the past, high school publications could blossom with the boost of universities. He promoted 10 ways that colleges could contribute, half of them dealing with workshops and similar offerings, among them:

- Cooperate with local, state, regional and national school press associations in their educational programs.
- Sponsor school press conferences and tournaments, stressing educational rather than promotional objectives.
- Provide speakers and critics for school press conventions, school press banquets, school assemblies and vocational conferences.
- Sponsor clinics and critical services organized to improve student publications, stressing functional rather than technical rating.
- Offer special workshops, demonstration classes, or institutes on school press problems during the summer with intensive training supervised by experts in the school press. (Campbell, 1947)

L. J. Hortin (1949) described in a *Journalism Quarterly* article the 1948 workshop at the University of Ohio, the third that it hosted. Some 100 editors and 15 advisers representing 28 high schools in Ohio and Pennsylvania attended. They were divided into three groups: newspaper editors, yearbook editors and business managers, with each group overseen by a university faculty member. In addition to discussing news style, front-page design, editorials and similar topics, the newspaper group spent a good deal of time on newsworthiness. Some student conclusions about the gossip column were:
- Scandal should never be permitted in a high school paper.
- Chatty, good-natured columns are permissible.
- Items such as "Who was seen at the roadhouse last night?" should be handled with caution.
- Newsy items are better than pure gossip.
- The writer of this kind of column must be a student of sound judgment and keen news sense. Most judging committees apparently frown on the gossip column.

The yearbook group worked on copy, layout, art, typography, covers and staff organization. Those in the business manager group discussed advertising problems, circulation and bookkeeping. Challenges for the workshop included finding instructors, supervision ("Recreation must be provided, for high school youngsters come to the workshops to play as well as work," Hortin wrote), getting the students to speak up, cramming enough practical work into a one-week session, and communicating to both the young students and advisers.

"In reality, however, therein lies the most valuable part of the workshop procedure: it permits a joint approach to the problem of editing a newspaper or yearbook," Hortin wrote. "With teacher and pupil both present, the participating school is certain to get much more out of the discussion." Hortin made these conclusions about the summer workshop:

- It permits student editors and advisers to meet others in their profession.
- It gives them a taste of university life.
- It permits them to seek solutions of their individual problems.
- It tends to broaden the horizon of student editors.
- It permits the fundamentals of journalism to be instilled early in the lives of the students.
- It raises the standards of the participating newspapers and yearbooks.
- It has the informality and freedom of a convention and at the same time it has the teaching function of the schoolroom.

In a national survey conducted by Benz (1959), 19 universities responded that they hosted summer workshops. June was the most popular month with 10 colleges hosting workshops then. Girls outnumbered boys by an average of 74 percent to 26 percent. Most workshops lasted a week. The workshop at the State College of Washington was four weeks, and Northwestern's institute was five weeks. The largest workshop by number of students was at Ohio University, which hosted 1,324 in 1958. The cost ranged from $21.85 for a one-week session to $250 for Northwestern's five-week workshop. Several schools offered special classes, including (numbers in parenthesis represent the number of schools offering the courses): letterpress and offset newspapers (18); yearbooks (16); mimeographed and duplicated newspapers (15); magazines (14); photography (13); school pages in community newspapers (9); and newspaper business management (9).

All of the universities presented some kind of recognition to the students at the end of the workshop, including diplomas/cer-tificates (16), contest awards (6), and college scholarships (4). All of the workshops reported offering a good deal of recreation and entertainment, including a first-night mixer (16); swimming, tennis, bowling or other sports (16); a "dress-up" banquet with speaker and/or entertainment (14); campus tours (13); a tour of a professional newspaper or printing plant (10); and a half-day-or-longer outing to a nearby city, state park, river or lake (5).

Attendance at Ohio University's workshop made it the largest one by mid-century. Attendance grew from 67 in its first year, 1946, to 943 from 11 states in 1955. Advisers from 81 schools attended that year. As a *School Activities* article put it, "If he wants to, the student may swim in the university's Olympic-size swimming nata-torium, play tennis, softball volleyball, softball, or take part in other group games. Free movies, picnics, and dances round out the spare-time activities. The week is climaxed by a 'graduation ceremony,' preceded by an all-workshop banquet" (Turnbull and Baird, 1956, p. 300).

William Click was the third director of the workshop, following George Starr Lasher and Loren J. Hortin. In his first year, 1965, the workshop had 1,899 in attendance, and it peaked with 2,221 in 1967.

"In the early years I was there, we got people because we had tennis courts and a golf course they could play on – free, I think – and an indoor swimming pool," Click said. "As more and more people got those in their neighborhoods and in their backyards, at-tendance started going down" (personal interview with W. Click, May 19, 2014).

With so many students arriving from so many places, work-shops have their share of drama, and Click's time at Ohio was no exception. One year, he had a student from Pittsburgh whose parents got a phone call from a man saying he had kidnapped her. They frantically called Click, wanting to know where she was. Fortunate-ly, a dorm supervisor had seen her 15 minutes earlier, and she was tracked down at the bookstore.

"We got her on the phone with her parents," Click said. "But of course, they still wanted her to come home because they were afraid she was going to be kidnapped. The police who got involved in that said, 'It's probably some local guy who knows she's gone and just wanted to scare the hell out of her parents.' She refused to go home, so I guess it all ended OK. But that wasn't funny at the time at all, especially since the dean of a nearby school of journalism was there viewing us that day. He was thinking of starting a journalism workshop, and he thought I was unusually busy, going from one phone to the next to make the calls."

Louis Ingelhart created the landmark Ball State University Summer High School Journalism Workshops in 1966 after sending out a survey to journalism teachers in the state. He structured it as two weeks of newspaper instruction and two weeks of yearbook. Photography was taught all four weeks. That first summer, 159 students from Indiana and Kentucky attended. Three years later, students were coming from as far away as New York and Nebraska (Jounalism Education Association, 2014c).

After the workshop placed more emphasis on photography – offering it during all four weeks – attendance boomed, passing 1,000 in 1978. By the early 1980s, 300 to 400 students were on Ball State's campus each week for a summer with attendance nearing 1,500. Two factors made Ball State's workshops stand out, said Brian Hayes, who directs the workshop now.

"Number one, the options students had to attend our workshops were enormous at that time," Hayes said. "Students could pick what week they wanted to attend and if they wanted to come multiple weeks. There were some students that even stayed all four weeks. The students appreciated having that flexibility" (personal interview with B. Hayes, May 27, 2014).

The other reason was the presence of nationally known faculty.

"We hired people like H. L. Hall, Casey Nichols, Linda Kane and many other names that are widely known and synonymous with journalism education," Hayes said. "We weren't too concerned about just sticking with local teachers. We really tried to branch out and find the educators that we believed were doing the best work and were innovative in the classroom."

Hall brought students to the yearbook and newspaper workshops and also led them.

"First, I directed the yearbook workshop, and then I moved over and directed the newspaper workshop for several years, and then I started teaching the advisers portions of the workshop," said Hall, who taught at the workshop for 20 years – one year, for all four weeks. "It was my home away from home during the summer.

It was considered the premiere workshop in the country" (personal interview with H. Hall, May 22, 2014).

At the national convention level, the two associations representing teachers and publications partnered in 1970.

In April of that year the Journalism Education Association and the National Scholastic Press Association held their first joint convention in Anaheim, Calif. What had been only one convention in some form since 1921 – the National High School Journalism Convention –became the Fall National High School Journalism Convention and the National High School Journalism Convention.

Kelly Furnas, JEA executive director, said that in the early 1970s, it looked more like two conventions that happened to be occurring at the same time.

"JEA was responsible for most of the programing aimed at teachers, and NSPA was responsible for most of the programing aimed at students," Furnas said. "Teachers would go to the JEA sessions and students would go to the NSPA sessions, and yet they were in the same hotel at the same time. That line over the past 40 years has really blurred because so many of the teachers want to learn the skills that the students are learning. So we really don't distinguish as much anymore. It became a natural marriage" (personal interview with K. Furnas, May 21, 2014).

In January 2013, officials with both organizations signed a long-term joint operating agreement to operate the fall and spring conventions. JEA's President Mark Newton said that it's a 50-50 partnership, with JEA handling the programming and NSPA the logistics.

"We focus on programming a convention for all of these skills, curriculum initiatives, certification, press right. We focus on making great journalism teachers and making great students," Newton said. "NSPA focuses on making sure they get a lot of people there to take advantage of that – setting up the trade show, exposing students to the colleges and the yearbook companies" (personal interview with M. Newton, May 19, 2014).

Diana Mitsu Klos, NSPA executive director, said the partnership made sense 40 years ago and certainly does now in journalism's volatile economic environment.

"It's foolish to take this go-it-alone type of attitude," Klos said. "We maintain independent identities – technically, we serve different constituents – but these are constituents and members who work day-to-day together, in classrooms, in clubs, in lunchrooms, on weekends. It makes complete sense from everyone's point of view in terms of these national conferences" (personal interview with D. Mitsu Klos, May 29, 2014).

Attendance at the conventions has risen from the 100s in the early 1970s to highs of 5,367 for San Francisco in 2001 and 6,353 for Washington, D.C., in 2009 (Journalism Education Association, 2014c).

Dow Jones News Fund workshops

The 1968 Kerner Commission report was a trigger for the summer minority urban journalism programs sponsored by the Dow Jones News Fund. The workshops began with a pilot the same year Kerner was released. By 1970 the number of workshops grew to 12 (Kenney, 2009). Today, some two dozen workshops operate throughout the country, with eligibility focused on students facing barriers entering journalism – including coming from a community or school that offers limited opportunities for journalism training (Dow Jones News Fund, 2014).

Linda Shockley, long-time deputy director of the Dow Jones News Fund and now managing director, said that in the early planning in 1968, success meant about 10 percent of participants became journalists.

"At this point, roughly 13,000 people have participated in the workshops, so if only 1,300 became journalists by those standards, that would have been significant," she said (personal interview with L. Shockley, Sept. 2, 2014).

Shockley said the workshops "furthered journalism as a career in the eyes of minorities just as Kerner had envisioned."

The workshops helped make "scholastic journalism an important activity in urban high schools and helped integrate students of color into high school media in other communities," Shockley said.

Shockley noted that some of the workshop participants went on to win a Pulitzer Prize:

- Ernest Tollerson, a 1968 American University workshop participant. He is interim CEO at the Nathan Cummings

Foundation. Tollerson was a reporter, editorial writer and editor at *Newsday, The New York Times* and *The Philadelphia Inquirer.*

- Angelo Henderson, who participated in the 1980 University of Kentucky workshop, wrote features for *The Wall Street Journal.*
- Jose Antonio Vargas, a participant in the 1998 San Francisco State University workshop, was a member of the *Washington Post* team of reporters who covered the Virginia Tech shootings.
- Ann Scales attended the 1977 University of Missouri workshop and is a former *Boston Globe* journalist

Shockley said the workshops also elevated the value of scholastic journalism for the teachers. As many as 240 teachers attended the workshops each year with support from the News Fund. The National High School Journalism Teacher of the Year competition grew out of the workshops and resulted in honors for more than 300 high school journalism teachers.

"Several of these teachers have distinguished themselves as leaders in scholastic journalism, on the college level and in the media industry," Shockley said.

Alumni of the teacher programs include Mario Garcia, the famed media design consultant; Nancy Green, former media executive and current director of communications for a large community college system; and Randy Stano, a design professor at the University of Miami.

Shockley said journalism faces challenges with young people. She noted that young people make career decisions earlier and that journalism salaries are not highly competitive.

The journalism job market is unstable, she said:

Youth are still choosing journalism as a career because of their interest in communicating and sharing news. Their embrace of technology and storytelling seems to have continued unabated.

(But) the media industry's struggle to identify realistic profit levels and methods for making money from a digital future underscore the uncertainty of careers in the business."

Shockley said concerning career choices, "especially in communities with limited resources, parents often discourage students from pursuing low-paying fields. The waves of layoffs and downsizing and general industry hand-wringing are also a deterrent."

But she remains optimistic. "Journalism schools' movement to teaching students to be entrepreneurial, innovative and to use mobile technology may lead to developing the new leaders with solutions," she said.

Money and community support continue as challenges, Shockley said. She noted that there are excellent, well-backed programs where outstanding media teachers have been honored by the fund as teachers of the year at schools such as Palo Alto (Calif.) High School, Amos Alonzo Stagg High School (Stockton, Calif.), Iowa City High School, Carmel (Ind.) High School, Indianapolis Central High School, Harrisonburg (Va.) High School, Prince George (Va.) High School and Annandale (Va.) High School.

Shockley was less hopeful about any significant improvement in numbers of people of color, including managers, in newsrooms and media companies.

"I honestly don't know what will change the dynamic," she said. "The business imperative hasn't been convincing; the common good has not worked. I'm at a loss."

Other news industry or industry-related workshops for high school students also have had an impact in drawing young people to journalism, Shockley said. Several news organizations operate programs within their newsrooms.

Of particular significance is the apprenticeship program operated by the *Detroit Free Press,* with scholarship support from the Ford Motor Co. During the school year, as many as 24 high school newspapers receive a page in the *Free Press* to cover their schools. Through the years, many students have received scholarships to attend the School of Journalism at the University of Missouri and several of these students are award-winning practicing journalists.

As for the future of high school journalism, Shockley had this to say:

> The future is definitely challenging for all of the media and particularly for diverse voices. As we move ever more quickly toward a digital, mobile-oriented 'mass' media, people of color and those with limited resources are in danger of being excluded or marginalized yet again. Some elements of social media have been used effectively to communicate, to create niche media and to capitalize on

tech savvy sectors but the pace needs to be accelerated if students of color are to be competitive in the job market and as entrepreneurs.

Current workshops

The authors counted more than 170 workshops and conferences offered year-round by colleges, state press associations and other organizations [See Table 1, page 176. For a complete listing of the 170 workshops and conferences, go to http://www.newforums.com/resources/ebooks/]. Here is a look at several of them.

Advisers Institute

The Journalism Education Association started the Advisers Institute in 2012 to help teachers with training and with finances.

"When you bring kids to a convention, like in the fall and the spring, often the school's going to pay for it because you're with kids," Mark Newton said. "A lot of times in the summer when you're flying solo, your professional development is on your own dime. So one of the reasons why we picked Las Vegas in the middle of July was because it's pretty cheap to get to Las Vegas in the middle of July, hotel rooms are fairly cheap in the middle of July, and Las Vegas is fairly cheap. There are certainly better places in people's minds to have a workshop, but in terms of the cost factor, that seems like a very reasonable three or four days of professional development's worth for $155, plus all your other expenses" (personal interview with M. Newton, May 19, 2014).

Newton said that in 2012, JEA hoped to attract 25 and 50 participated. Then in 2013 it hoped for 50 and 100 attended.

Newton said another reason for the institute was the ability to focus just on the teachers.

"When you have a convention in the spring and the fall, you have to have kid entertainment," he said. "When you have a workshop in the summer with adults, you don't have to worry about what they do at five o'clock; they're on their own."

Sessions in 2014 included "The past, present and future of online newspapers"; "Making grading your last priority"; "'App'solutely spectacular"; "Teaching news literacy"; "Beyond analytics: It's about user engagement"; "Journalism as 21st century education"; and "My iPhone does what?" (Journalism Education Association, 2014d).

Table 1. Workshops and Conferences Offerd by Colleges

State	Sponsor	Workshop Name	Month	Location	City	Website
Alabama	Alabama Scholastic Press Association	The Long Weekend	June	University of Alabama	Tuscaloosa, Ala.	http://aspa1.ua.edu/2014/02/the-long-weekend-2014/
Alabama	Alabama Scholastic Press Association	State Convention	February-March	University of Alabama	Tuscaloosa, Ala.	http://www.aspa.ua.edu
Alabama	Alabama Scholastic Press Association	Fall Regionals	September	Various locations	Mobile, Tuscaloosa, Huntsville, Ala.	http://www.aspa.ua.edu
Alabama	Alabama Scholastic Press Association	Multicultural Journalism Workshop*	June	University of Alabama	Tuscaloosa, Ala.	http://www.aspa.ua.edu
Arizona	Arizona Interscholastic Press Association	Arizona Interscholastic Press Association's Summer Workshop	July	Walter Cronkite School of Journalism and Mass Communication	Phoenix, Ariz.	http://www.azaipa.org/628/for-advisers/register-now-for-aipas-summer-workshop/
Arizona	Arizona Interscholastic Press Association	Arizona Interscholastic Press Association's Fall Convention	October	Arizona State University's Memorial Union	Tempe, Ariz.	http://www.azaipa.org/565/for-advisers/date-set-for-fall-convention/
Arizona	University of Arizona School of Journalism	Journalism Diversity Workshop for Arizona High School Students*	June	University of Arizona	Tuscon, Ariz.	http://journalism.arizona.edu/node/637
Arizona	University of Arizona School of Journalism, Investigative Reporters and Editors, Border Journalism Network	Watchdog Workshop	April	University of Arizona	Tuscon, Ariz.	http://journalism.arizona.edu/news/watchdog-reporting-focus-april-12-13-workshop-university-arizona

NOTE: For a complete listing of the 170 workshops and conferences, go to http://www.newforums.com/resources/ebooks/

Medill-Northwestern Journalism Institute

At Northwestern, organizers recently decided to distance the program from the terms "High School" and "National" that had been part of the name since 1934 and the Medill-Northwestern Journalism Institute.

"We felt that the students we were trying to reach, these highly successful academically, journalistic students, weren't interested so much in high school, they're interested in thinking about college," said Roger Boye, director.

"As they say, 'Who reads *Seventeen* magazine?' It's not 17-year-olds. Seventeen is the wish book for the 14- and 15-year-olds. By the time they're 17, they're reading *Cosmo*. So we wanted to put the focus on Northwestern and Medill."

In the past two years, Cherubs have come from Guam, Canada, France, China, El Salvador, Indonesia, Taiwan, South Korea and Greece. As Boye said, "'national' in the name wasn't really telling the folks out there in the world that we were international, not national" (personal interview with R. Boye, May 21, 2014).

Based on space in dorms and computer labs, the institute now limits enrollment to 84 each year, receiving almost two applications for each opening. Most Cherubs are rising seniors, former or incoming editors-in-chief, and one-third have done some journalism outside of school. The duration of the institute, five weeks, is another distinction. (The 2014 fee was $5,200.) Boye said that the faculty and students are able to bond during the five weeks.

"A number of lifelong friendships have evolved from this program," he said. "One or two weeks, people get to know one another, but in five weeks, much more deeper friendships develop."

Finally, the Northwestern institute emphasizes professional journalism rather than scholastic journalism.

"The focus of our program is not to make your high school newspaper or yearbook better," Boye said. "There are a lot of programs out there that do that. We try to take a focus on journalism as it's done professionally out there in the real world. Now, you can apply the principles of solid journalism as done in the real world to your high school publications."

High School Journalism Institute

The High School Journalism Institute, housed at Indiana University, has had only four directors since its beginning in 1946: Gretchen Kemp, Mary Benedict, Jack Dvorak and Teresa White, who began as director in August 2008. The institute has evolved from two weeks to three five-day sessions to two five-day sessions (in 2012). The first session offers workshops in yearbook, digital photography, graphic design and newspaper. The second offers workshops in yearbook, digital photography, graphic design, television news, multimedia and documentary filmmaking. Added in 2014 at both sessions was the Communication Team option for students who had previously attended the institute. This team arrives a day early and serves as the institute's communication office staff, reporting on the other students using http://www.hsji.org and social media accounts (personal interview with T. White, May 15, 2014).

"They get beats, and they do backpack journalism," White said. "They're here when people are checking in. They're taking pictures, reporting, tweeting, live-tweeting events, posting on Facebook and trying to engage people, writing and posting stories on the web, sending out a press release, sharing photos with people."

On one of the five days, they get to go shadow a communications staffer on the Indiana campus.

White said one reason she created the Communication Team was interest in public relations at the college level: almost 40 percent of IU's undergraduate population takes the PR track.

"Number two, I want somebody to go around and take pictures of all of these things and write stories about them," White said. "One summer I tried to hire a college student to do it, and the college student couldn't even keep up with it all because there's too many places to be and too many things to cover. So I thought, 'Why not just put the students in charge of doing it themselves?'"

The year 2014 marked the third year for the HSJI's Converged Newsroom workshops, offered during the second week. It reinforces "soft skills" such as teamwork and meeting deadlines that help determine a staff's success, White said.

"I found we had a lot of students who came from weak programs or who had never been on a publications staff who didn't know how a newsroom felt like," White said. "They didn't know that rush, they didn't know that energy. We could call it 'stress,' but face it: most people who like journalism enjoy that little rush. So I wanted to simulate that. I thought it would be beneficial to them and allow them to practice backpack journalism."

Whereas the typical workshop session offers a bit of hands-on training but mostly instruction, the Converged Newsroom is the opposite: the teachers coach, and the students choose one of two newsrooms: Sports Journalism or Arts and Entertainment. The teachers select team leaders on the first day. On the second day, the students attend an assignment meeting for various news teams followed by a skills session.

"We have a buffet of three or four skills that we think they may need," White said. "They're an intensive workshop for an hour and a half – writing for the Web, digital photography, collecting and editing audio, shooting and editing video – and the students pick the ones they want to go to." After lunch, the students venture out into the field while the advisers stay back at the newsroom. The goal each day for each team is to publish something on http://www.hsji. org by 9 p.m.

Each year the Converged Workshop has a new theme. In in 2013 it was "Hoosier Sports and Film."

The students in both newsrooms watched the movie *Hoosiers* and did a Q&A with its screenwriter, interviewed a former sports editor and an Indiana basketball player, watched the movie *Breaking Away,* based on UI's Little 500 bicycle track and toured the race's track and museum, and interviewed the race director, riders and coaches. The producers of *Hoop Dreams and Harp Dreams* (about an international harp competition at IU) also talked with the students.

"We put something in place for them to cover every day that they can spin off and come up with other things," White said. "One kid called four Big 10 athletic directors and interviewed them about the expense of certain sports.

"We just 'journalism geek out' during the week. We all just feed off of each other."

The cost for the workshop is $399 per five-day session.

Carolina Sports Journalism Camp

The Carolina Sports Journalism Camp celebrated its third year in June 2014. The School of Journalism and Mass Communication at the University of North Carolina hosts the four-day residential workshop, which accepts 40 students from throughout the U.S. each year. It offers sessions in sports play-by-play, photography and writing.

"We are very fortunate to be in a place with a wonderful supply of writing instructors and also a place that has such a wonderful ACC basketball history," said Monica Hill, director of the North Carolina Scholastic Media Association (personal interview with M. Hill, May 20, 2014).

In the mornings, students attend a college-level sports journalism course taught by Tim Crothers, former senior writer at Sports Illustrated and collaborator with UNC coach Roy Williams' autobiography "Hard Work: A Life On and Off the Court." Crothers is an adjunct teacher at UNC and is the lead instructor at the camp. Guest speakers have included Michael Lee, who covers the Washington Wizards and the NBA for the Washington Post and who serves on the camp's advisory board, and Carolina Panthers play-by-play announcer Mick Mixon. Other features of the camp include covering and reporting on a press conference and touring UNC's sports media facilities.

The registration fee is $500 for in-state students and $750 for out-of-state students.

"We formed an advisory council when we began to think about developing this, and that has been the key to the success of the camp," Hill said, adding that the council has included the Post's Lee, the associate athletic director at UNC, the beat writer at *The News and Observer* and the dean of the summer school, as the summer college class is tied to the camp.

"Everyone from the start agreed to contribute to the camp on a pro bono basis; they continue to do so, and all proceeds go to the North Carolina Scholastic Media Association."

"Niche" workshops

A current trend is the so-called "niche workshop" – a group of teachers getting together and doing some workshop instruction for one day or a few days that is specific to what they want for their students.

"In Colorado that's how we started our program reTHINK," Newton said. "A bunch of advisers got together and said, 'We really need to help our kids get this, but let's invite everybody else as well'" (personal interview with M. Newton, May 19, 2014).

reTHINK is a four-day program with an accompanying Summer Adviser Workshop held in June at Rock Canyon High School in Highlands Ranch, Colo. It celebrated its ninth year in 2014 and has drawn students from more than 40 Colorado high schools. The charge is $150.

Newton's Mountain Vista High School student Taylor R. Blatchford was named JEA's 2014 Journalist of the Year.

For Aaron Manfull, journalism adviser at Francis Howell North High School in St. Charles, Mo., starting a summer workshop was a family idea.

Manfull had often taken his students to nearby workshops at Ball State and the University of Iowa.

"They both have great summer workshops, but the timing on some of those didn't work for my students," Manfull said. "We have registration here on July 24, and that's when a lot of workshops happen, so I wanted something close that was in June" (personal interview with A. Manfull, May 21, 2014).

He said the University of Missouri's summer workshop had started to dwindle, and it was cancelled for the summer of 2014.

Meanwhile, his wife, Kate, had worked in advertising with Save-A-Lot and eventually as an account executive with Weber Shandwick public relations firm. In 2007, she began her own marketing/graphic design business.

"So we talk a lot of shop at home," he said. "She's very supportive of me in my job, probably one of the most supportive spouses anywhere, and she did like to help out with the program here. She believes in giving. If the kids want to get educated on something, she wants to help them. She's endless energy.

"And so in some sick, twisted way, we thought this would be a fun little hobby for us – run a camp for a few days and bring some great minds in from all over the place."

At first, Manfull simply wanted to do something local that his students could attend.

"And then I thought, 'Well, heck, let's just open it up to whoever.'"

So in January 2011 the Manfulls decided they wanted to do a workshop. They just needed a home. So they sent an email to Lindenwood University, four miles away from Francis Howell North High School.

"We said, 'Hey, we've got this idea for a camp. We'd like to run it. We need a place for it,'" Manfull said.

Lindenwood agreed to partner with the Manfulls. In the first Media Now STL workshop, in June 2011, almost 50 students attended – 25-30 were from Francis Howell. In 2013 the workshop reached 100. In 2014, more than 150 registered and took the following courses: Web Development – Intro; Web Development – Advanced; Mobile (Smartphone/Tablet) Journalism; Broadcast/Video Essentials; Photography Essentials; Broadcast/Video In-Studio; Writing; Design: Newspaper; Yearbook; Photography – Feature; Editorial Leadership – Editors-in-Chief; Editorial Leadership – Section Editors; and Advising Publications (advisers only).

Manfull, a veteran workshop speaker himself, said that workshops are having to rethink their length because of the many different directions students and teachers get pulled in the summer.

"What's too much to have a kid commit to, and what's not enough where they're not really getting anything out of it?" he said. "Finding that, then what are the skills and things that kids need today to keep up?"

The price of this workshop is $280.

A "micro" workshop that's noteworthy for its location is the CUE Final Cut Pro X Camp, designed for teachers. This four-day camp is based on the aircraft carrier USS Hornet, moored at Alameda Point on San Francisco Bay.

The camp is hosted by Computer-Using Educators Inc., a California-based non-profit organization. The cost of $690 for CUE members or $730 for non-members includes food and lodging on the ship. It offers three levels of instructions: beginner, intermediate (10 projects or fewer) and "BADASS" (CUE Final Cut Pro X Camp, 2014).

Newsroom by the Bay

When Paul Kandell decided to become a partner of the three-decades-old Newspaper by the Bay program, he knew the first edit he and co-director Beatrice Motamedi would make.

"The first thing that we changed was we got rid of 'paper,'" said Kandell, who advises two award-winning publications at Palo Alto High School and was the 2009 Dow Jones News Fund National Journalism Teacher of the Year. "It became 'Newsroom by the Bay,' and we were committed to a digital focus" (personal interview with P. Kandell, May 23, 2014).

The workshop gives an iPad to every student for the week and divides the students into teams of 10-12, assigning each team a website along with a team leader, typically a college journalism student.

"We say, 'You are now a news organization, you've got to determine what you want your focus to be for the week and go out and fulfill that focus,'" Kandell said.

The program, which costs $2,195 for boarders and $1,095 for commuters, takes approximately 70 students each June. One third of them are from California. The rest come from 25 states and a half-dozen countries. Furthermore, the program designates the students as Year 1 and Year 2.

"There were some students who already came in with enough journalistic skills that they didn't need to do the basics even with the iPad," Kandell said. "We wanted to provide a structure for students to maintain if they came back the second year. The Year 2 program focuses more on building your own brand and pursuing your own ideas," such as pitching and placing stories in the professional world. These Year 2 students – Counselors-in-Training – get to meet the guest speakers and take their own field trips. They are considered the "eyes and ears" for the program. They also organize activities and report undertakings for the Year 1 students. Students can even come back a third year and become a team leader.

Students get classes in the morning ranging from traditional journalistic writing to using the Web to tell a story and using the iPad as a multimedia production tool.

In the afternoons, student teams have free reign on Stanford University. As the week progresses they take field trips in San Francisco. Year 2 students can get a Silicon Valley tour.

Newsroom by the Bay pays close attention each June to the Supreme Court, whose last rulings of the year tend to coincide with the workshop. In 2012 came the "Obamacare" ruling, which was made the focus of reporting that day. And in 2013 came the "Defense of

Marriage Act" decision – on the same day as the workshop's San Francisco field trip. Organizers built the website http://1day1story. newsroombythebay.com overnight, and the Year 2 team stayed back and operated it as if it were a home-base newsroom.

"We had 15 reporters on the ground in San Francisco for pretty much the most exciting day that city had seen in a long time," Kandell said. "There were street celebrations – hundreds, thousands of people on the streets – and everybody wanted to talk. Our students would take the iPad up to them and interview them. One student called it 'journalism heaven.' It was the easiest reporting ever."

Kandell suggested that professional news organizations would have been envious.

"Nobody else had this experience on the ground at that moment," he said.

Another feature of the program is sports strands that the students can pursue, including trips to San Francisco Giants games at AT&T Park. In 2013 and 2014, Stanford Stadium hosted the annual California Clasico, pitting Major League Soccer rivals the LA Galaxy and San Jose Earthquakes.

"We get students in to see the practice, which is pretty cool," Kandell said. "Some of them have gone into the press box during the game. There was a media event last year where a player went to the local children's hospital and spoke with the kids there. It was an amazing reporting experience."

Challenges

Nearly all of the summer workshop directors that the authors interviewed noted a decline in attendance over the last decade. This can be attributed to a number of factors. First is the growth in the number of workshops offered across the country.

"In the past 20 years you've certainly seen an increase in the number of workshops being offered, to the point I might argue that there's an abundance; there might almost be too many to sustain themselves right now," Furnas said. "More and more journalism programs without a lot of means need a regional workshop to go to. They can't fly to a national workshop or a national convention, so they want something regional. Obviously 'within driving distance' means you have to pop up a lot more workshops, so you'll see a lot of states or regions within states take on some workshops" (personal interview with K. Furnas, May 21, 2014).

That 170 number does not include workshops offered by yearbook companies. At least 175 such workshops were offered by these companies during the summer and fall of 2014. Jostens Inc. held its eighth Adviser University in July, its three-day National Workshop in Scottsdale, Ariz., in July-August and 56 regional workshops in 34 states and two Canadian provinces (Jostens, 2014).

Herff Jones held 48 workshops in 22 states from May to September (Herff Jones, 2014). Commonwealth Brands Inc. (Balfour) hosted 39 summer workshops in 16 states from June through September (Balfour Yearbooks, 2014). Walsworth Publishing Company held 30 workshops from March to October in 20 states (Walsworth Yearbooks, 2014). Lifetouch Inc. offered three summer workshops, in Tennessee, California and Connecticut (Lifetouch yearbook, 2014).

"In the mid-'70s is when I really saw a big surge in yearbook company workshops," said Laura Schaub, national creative design and media consultant with Lifetouch and former Jostens consultant and executive director of the Oklahoma Interscholastic Press Association. "A lot of times they started as a one-day workshop in the fall, and then they expanded to a three-day workshop" (personal interview with L. Shaub, May 19, 2014).

Newton said that since the 1970s yearbook companies started to realize the value of the workshops as an opportunity to meet the needs of customers and train their clients, and as a way to improve the quality of journalism.

"They look at it as a two-way street," Newton said. "One is, 'Hey, let's make sure our clients – our advisers and editors – are up to speed on some of the things that we offer,' and two, 'Let's help them create a meaningful, well-rounded, journalistic product'" (personal interview with M. Newton, May 19, 2014).

Newton said another yearbook company trend is direct, intense adviser instruction.

"As a yearbook person myself, I can go to a workshop with my students and work on some things, but I also have some opportunities to go by myself and do some very specific things that are directed to the adviser and the teacher," he said. "They see it as an educational component along with helping their clients finish the book."

A shrewd tactic by the companies was embedding workshops into the contracting process, Furnas said.

"As a high-school teacher you see the value in that," Furnas said. "I can essentially embed into the price of the book training for my staff. That's a really, really nice and easy way to get a lot of extra education without having to write a separate check for sending students to a workshop" (personal interview with K. Furnas, May 21, 2014).

The Columbia Scholastic Press Association's Summer Journalism Workshop used to offer yearbook sessions but dropped them in the last five years.

"Yearbook printing companies bury the workshop cost in the printing contract," said Edmund Sullivan, executive director of CSPA. "So whatever the school is paying, or whatever all those students or parents are paying for the books, is helping to pay for the real cost of bringing five to 10 staff members to the workshop. And of course the other difference with the company workshop is the company is going to basically train you how to do the work with them and for them to prep your book. Each of the companies has its own set of plug-ins for Adobe InDesign. They used to have their own software, but most of them have standardized on the Adobe software, which most all of the schools use" (personal interview with E. Sullivan, May 22, 2014).

Another factor in attendance is summer academic schedules students' face.

"Today's students are busy, busy, busy," said Vanessa Shelton, executive director of Quill and Scroll International Honorary Society for High School Journalists and former director of the Iowa High School Press Association and the UI Summer Journalism Workshops. "You'd think with summers, they wouldn't be quite so busy, but they're working. They're participating in extracurricular activities like cheerleading or football and have summer practices. They're participating in international exchange programs or other educational programs...and then there's the usual family vacations" (personal interview with V. Shelton, May 22, 2014).

"Bless their hearts, they're so ambitious, they like to do it all," she said, adding that some of the students who do make the workshops may come late or leave early.

The mindset of the advisers has changed, too, said Karen Flowers, director of the Southern Interscholastic Press Association and the South Carolina Scholastic Press Association.

Summer journalistic training does not seem to be as mandatory across the board as cheerleading or band camps. Plus, advisers are busy, too.

"When I was an adviser, it was relatively easy for me to come and bring a lot of students to the summer workshop because I had maybe at least two months off in the summer," Flowers said. "But now, so many of the students need to work. The advisers are burned out. They don't want to look at another thing called 'work' in the summer" (personal interview with K. Flowers, May 13, 2014).

Joe Dennis, director of diversity and high school outreach at the University of Georgia, is concerned about the families that ask, "Do we really want to invest this much money in our child going to a camp representing an industry that is closing newspapers and laying off reporters?"

"Especially in this time where the consensus among people not in the industry is, 'Oh, journalism, that's a dying art. We don't want to go down that road,'" Dennis said. "It's more critical than ever to expose these kids to journalism to show them the opportunities there. We need to give them the skills that apply whether they pursue journalism or any other avenue. And for teachers, again, same benefit. For instance, a lot of them don't have that initial journalism experience" (personal interview with J. Dennis, May 13, 2014).

At the national level, Newton has seen decreasing attendance at the JEA/NSPA spring convention. For example, the highest year of attendance was back in 2009, with 6,353 in Washington, D.C.

"We think that the window of opportunity on some of those days is closing because school districts and states are not letting kids leave in the spring because of all that state testing," Newton said. "It's also the prom season, it's also the end of the year, and so a lot of the advisers see the spring convention as, 'Why take them if there is only one or two issues left, or the yearbook's over'" (personal interview with M. Newton, May 19, 2014).

He said school districts also are pushing back on spring convention attendance because of the travel costs.

"Advisers are told, 'You can go out of state once, but you can't go twice in a school year,' and so advisers have to make a choice,"

Newton said. "Or, 'You can't go out of state at all anymore unless there is some kind of competition.'"

This leads to perhaps the largest challenge to workshops today: finances.

"The economy is certainly hurting because there simply isn't money," Flowers said. "I hear that over and over: 'We can't afford it'" (personal interview with K. Flowers, May 13, 2014).

The High School Journalism Institute has surveyed its students through the years, asking who paid for their trip.

"It used to be 'the school,' 'the school,' 'the school' or 'the school and my parents,' but now it's more 'my savings and my parents' as the bulk of the answer," said Executive Director Teresa White. "Some of the high school publications might have received some funding from the school itself, but most likely that's dried up or it's being put to use elsewhere" (personal interview with T. White, May 14, 2014).

"Just like everyone else, print advertising is down. You think it's down for professional media, what do you think it is for scholastic media?" White said. "They're in the same boat; their advertising revenues are down, too, and that's a lot of what they use to pay for their extras – their conferences and workshops and conventions."

White said that she was also interested in seeing whether the recession was causing fewer schools to attend or causing students to fund fewer students; she found the latter.

"We only lost one or two schools along the way who regularly sent people," she said. "Instead of sending 15 people, they were sending 10 or eight; or, instead of sending 10, they were sending only five."

Financial issues feed into another problem – what is happening to extracurricular activities and non-core subjects in high school curricula.

"As more and more emphasis is put on standardized testing of core subjects and on AP tests and on dual-credit and on anything else that has to do with getting into college and getting a certain test score or providing data for some department of education somewhere, then less time is spent on fine arts, less time is spent on electives, and those things are being crunched out of the curricula of high schools," White said.

Some examples that she provided: offering only one section

of Beginning Journalism; compressing one term of Photojournalism and Design and another term of Writing and Reporting into one term; moving the Beginning Journalism class in with the Publication Production class and letting them meet simultaneously; and pushing out the Production class and making it extracurricular.

Alongside the emphasis on core subjects, college prep and standardized testing is the shifting of the money to go toward more teachers to focus on those subjects. And shrinking state budgets particularly affect public schools, which are the ones that send the bulk of their students to workshops.

"Schools get money to pay for remediation for math and English," White said. "They'll put money toward AP courses. So it's really important we keep convincing people – and we're slowly getting there in some states – that journalism is 21st century English."

She said media literacy is needed more than ever now because of the majority of content produced by non-professional journalists.

"In a media-saturated world, journalism is important," she said. "It can teach critical thinking, communication skills, media literacy – all the things that people say they want their students to learn, but they seem to think they're going to learn it sitting in a traditional classroom in straight rows reading out of a book…and it's not going to happen. Businesses say, 'I want people who can work in teams and can think critically and solve problems and who are self-directed and who can communicate well and can use technology.' Journalism does all of that, but (school systems) are not rewarding it."

That's where journalism workshops and conventions can help, Newton said. There, teachers first of all learn – and learn to promote – that journalism is 21st century English.

"And two, we want to make sure that they're really great instructors so that their students are learning and creating great products that are authentic and the community is going, 'Wow! We just can't get rid of this because it's so amazing,'" Newton said. "The better instructors we have, the fewer problems we have in terms of legal issues, ethical issues, any of the journalistic mistakes that happen because of ignorance or poor training. The better educated the instructor is, the better prepared the instructor is, the better the product will end up, and then it's the one thing you can't cut because it's so darn good" (personal interview with M. Newton, May 19, 2014).

Newton said a lot of instruction in the JEA's summer Advisers

Institute and at other workshops and conventions is driven to ensure that teachers are outstanding and not so much stressed out about creating the product as they are creating the skills necessary to create the product – "the hard skills and the soft skills," as he put it.

"Every time you can do that, what you see is a super bounce," he said. "There are pockets of excellence in journalism throughout the country, and one of the reasons for that is either a formal workshop or training or an informal one where those advisers are motivated either by collaboration or by, 'I'm really going to work hard to help that person down the street.'

"You see that in the workshop model. You have the 25-year adviser sharing, and then you have the emerging adviser who's been in it five, 10, 15 years, and you put those two together in a workshop setting and you get this vibrant energy, you get this cool past knowledge, and it comes together and the kids see how it works and the advisers see how it works. And they see somebody who's like them or somebody that they can aspire to be, and it's really powerful."

Finally, the balancing act of programming is a challenge.

Shelton said curriculum changes are evolving faster than she has ever seen to allow students to keep up in the digital world.

"Before, there was tweaking of your curriculum that addressed things like the types of equipment you were using or software you were using, and that would come about once every few years," Shelton said. "But now there seems to be some changes every year – social media, mobile journalism, software, creating apps" (personal interview with V. Shelton, May 22, 2014).

At the same time, as Joe Dennis with the University of Georgia emphasized, workshops must not abandon key principles of storytelling.

"We need to stop using siloes – 'Well, this is broadcasting, and this is journalistic writing,'" Dennis said. "Combine them and say, 'We're going to learn a little bit about writing, we're going to learn a little bit about shooting and editing.' The core of it is journalism, reporting, researching, getting a good interview. Whatever the medium is, we need to stop focusing on the medium and focus on the core principles of journalism" (personal interview with J. Dennis, May 13, 2014).

Benefits

Despite the challenges that workshops face, those who have planned and attended workshops are quick to point out a variety of benefits, 10 of which are outlined in the following paragraphs.

First, of course, are the ideas that students can glean – and the excitement that they get from workshops. H. L. Hall, whose yearbook and newspaper at Kirkwood High School in Missouri were consistent recipients of the Associated Collegiate Press Pacemaker and Columbia Scholastic Press Association Crown awards, does not doubt his students excelled because of the training they received at workshops.

"I remember sometimes my students would call me from a summer workshop and say, 'We just came up with this idea; what about it?'" Hall said. "And I'd say, 'If you're excited about it, go for it.' There's no doubt that you just can't grow on your own; you need to learn from others" (personal interview with H. Hall, May 22, 2014).

Others agree.

"A lot of this is literally Journalism 101 because these kids are rank beginners, so it's equipping them," said Edmund Sullivan. "But in most cases it's unlocking the enthusiasm, it's revving up the motivation – helping them find their motivation – and it sends them out with a lot of confidence in their ability to tackle this. I often hear from teachers that the ride home on the bus or the train or the plane is just amazing. The kids are still so hyped about the event, they're so energized by it, and the ideas that come out of them…it's as if they get a whole second wind. And, they're more thoughtful about it and more reflectively thoughtful about it because they do have a perspective on it now that they didn't have" (personal interview with E. Sullivan, May 22, 2014).

Furnas said the ideas don't even have to be new to be helpful.

"Teachers will send their students to a workshop, and the students will be told something that the teacher has already said in the classroom, but the students just now started taking it seriously because they heard it at a workshop," Furnas said. "It's a sense of frustration for a lot of teachers, but it really does make sense from an educational perspective: the idea of reinforcement, of differentiation and of targeted, intense training is such an incredibly great model for education. The workshop/conference model where you're going to spend 40 hours straight thinking about journalism…incredibly powerful" (personal interview with K. Furnas, May 21, 2014).

A second benefit from a workshop is the bonding experience that takes place within a staff.

"They get along better, they drop a lot of the distance with one another, they figure out how to solve the intra-group dynamics," Sullivan said. "This takes them out of the school, out of their ordinary setting, and they have to work with one another and rely on one another to understand all this, and then suddenly as a group they have to interact with other groups who are doing the same thing as they are: 'Oh, wow!' So it solidifies the group, and at the same time it opens them up to a whole lot of other ideas. They're inspired by something they see somebody else do and then go create something entirely different. I've had advisers who've said, 'The next couple of months the kids are just feeding off the enthusiasm'" (personal interview with E. Sullivan, May 22, 2014).

Third, students benefit from the exposure to students from other schools. As Sullivan put it, students discover that they're not alone.

"I've heard students say that coming to a workshop – and the summer workshop is actually even a better example than the school-year conferences because it's generally more of an immersion environment, particularly if they're staying overnight – often opens the mind of a student editor to the fact that other people at other schools go through the same experiences they do," Sullivan said. "One student once said to me, 'I really always thought that I was a sort of lonely and only, because there was only, like, a half-dozen of us on our school paper staff. All the athletes in the school have one another, and there's a band and two choral groups, even the foreign language clubs do something together as an event during the year. We're just always off by ourselves.'

"So when a group like that comes to one of our events, or any of these summer events, they look around the room and they see all these other kids from all these other schools even in other states who are doing the same thing, and they start in a sense talking shop with one another. They start introducing themselves to one another: 'How did you do that?' 'Oh, really…that happens to you, too?' 'Oh, yeah, here's what we do.' And suddenly, there's this blossoming of confidence and interest in what they're doing, and there's a whole new motivation."

White said that for some students who attend workshops, journalism might not be a big deal at their school.

"But they get here and find out that it is a big deal at this college, and it's a big deal with a lot of other high school students," White said. "They meet friends that they stay in touch with the rest of their lives in some cases, especially now with social media. They go back and they're leaders. It strengthens the programs. Even if the teacher is not strong with experience, if you've got a fired-up editor, it can really grow the staff and develop the program" (personal interview with T. White, May 15, 2014).

Furnas said he hears a lot about people wanting to move to online or downloadable modules.

"I don't want to neglect that that's an important way of learning," he said. "But I would really, really lament the day when people from 10s or 20s or 100s of different high schools stop getting together in a room to talk about the way they teach or learn journalism because there's such a value to that that can't necessarily be changed into a written or an online format" (personal interview with K. Furnas, May 21, 2014).

Fourth, students at workshops can bond not just with other students but also with college students and professionals. White calls it "the trifecta" (personal interview with T. White, May 15, 2014).

"There's a triangle there," White said. "High school students love to talk to current college students who have similar interests, and they love to talk to alumni. And alumni, if they had a good experience in college, love to give back. They love coming back to campus, being invited to speak and meeting young journalists who aren't jaded in any way and are still excited and eager about what they're doing. They love to meet with current (college) students. Current students look up to them. They all look up to each other. They either look back or look up. And they feed off of each other; they get so excited.

"Imagine: you're a high school student, you just finished your freshman year, and you're sitting here talking to an editor of the *Tampa Bay Times* who's a Pulitzer Prize winner. And he says, 'So you are the columnist of your newspaper? Here's my business card. Why don't you send me some columns and I'll give you feedback?' How often is that going to happen to the average high-school student?"

The confidence that emerges from interactions with peers and professionals leads to a fifth benefit – giving staffs the ammunition to stand up to the administration.

"When you have kids creating a voice, you have kids talking about things that sometimes could be uncomfortable," Newton said. "It can be very concerning to a principal to have a kid push back or decide that their voice is contrary to what everybody else thinks" (personal interview with M. Newton, May 19, 2014).

Newton continued:

> Part of our job is teaching kids and advisers how to deal with that, but also it is teaching it so well that that doesn't become an issue. And I think that one of the ways that you look at a workshop is that ability to have some very dedicated time, when you're entirely focused on just one thing and make some really good decisions for the quality of your book, website, broadcast, magazine or newspaper.
>
> What we're really trying to do every time we have a workshop, most people are saying to their teachers is, "We want you to be really great at this so that you can push back a little bit if your school decides to cut scholastic journalism, or at least you can make some really solid arguments about why to keep it or how to converge programs so that you can still maintain a yearbook and a newspaper when money might be tight and they want to get rid of one of those." Whether that's the state level or the national level or the local level, I think that the workshop model really supports that.

Sixth, workshops give all students – whether they pursue journalism or not – valuable life lessons, Flowers said.

"Through these workshops, we are helping the students see journalism as a possible career choice, but more importantly, even those who do not go into journalism are going to have skills that other students in high school simply don't get – communications, technology, team-building, ethical thinking, interviewing process, current events," Flowers said. "They are such better citizens by having gone through the workshop and from their journalism programs" (personal interview with K. Flowers, May 13, 2014).

Newton said that journalism in general, and workshops in particular, offer "everything that they want education to be – 'they' being the political and educational leaders – it's collaboration, it's critical thinking, it's creating, it's communication skills. All those things come together very well" (personal interview with M. Newton, May 19, 2014).

A seventh benefit for workshops is allowing students to get exposed to college, and vice versa.

"Having the chance to get away from home, living a pseudo-college-student existence by staying in a dorm, in close quarters with people you don't really know, having to walk to class across campus, trying to manage your time and trying to balance your socializing with your classroom, trying new things, being exposed to new ideas, having somebody push you and immerse you in a subject matter and have high expectations for you when you're away from home and learning how to take care of yourself is a good thing for everyone," White said. "You get a little test drive of college life, albeit with curfew and bed-check and close supervision" (personal interview with T. White, May 15, 2014).

Of course, colleges get mileage from workshops, too.

"Anybody who knows anything about recruiting college students knows that, if you can get them to stay on your campus, that's half the battle," White said. "Once they stay overnight on your campus, they're going to have a good idea that they like it or not."

One thing Click said he learned early on is that most workshop students will not pursue a future in journalism.

"Those are the brightest kids, and they're going to go into medicine and law and teaching and all kinds of other fields," Click said. "Some, of course, do go into journalism – from my figures from 20 years ago, no more than 20 percent. But, after all, you want bright students, and you're glad to have them" (personal interview with B. Click, May 19, 2014).

As for journalism majors at Ohio University, Click would survey them and ask why they had enrolled there.

"As I recall, the number one reason they came to OU was that they visited the campus," he said. "The number two reason was that their high-school journalism teacher had been there and highly recommended it. And the number three reason was that a friend of theirs in high school had been there for a workshop and thought it was a neat place and highly recommended it. So the college gets that benefit."

Eighth, advisers benefit from workshops – from short-term best practices to long-term survival.

"Nothing else prepares journalism advisers for the things they will face," Flowers said. "Today more than ever, so many advisers are just being thrown into the classroom – no background at all. They probably are English teachers because they have to be. I was a high school English teacher, but I did not know what a byline was" (personal interview with K. Flowers, May 13, 2014).

Flowers, who at her workshop has created a "Staff Management" session by combining the editorial leadership session for students with a class for advisers, cited a South Carolina teacher who has produced an award-winning yearbook for years but who faced having it taken away from her because she didn't have an English degree.

"So one of the things we are working with is trying to help our advisers see how they can get around this," Flowers said. "We're going to have to do some work with the principals and with the state: Wouldn't it be better to have a history teacher who knows what she's doing rather than throw an English teacher in there who has no clue what she's doing?"

Speaking of advisers, a ninth benefit of workshops can be the kickoff for the next year that they provide.

"When I talk to advisers and try to convince them of coming, I say, 'This is the way to *begin* your year," Flowers said. "Yes, I know it's at the end, and yes I know you're tired from all you're doing, but if you can get your staff for the next year together at your summer workshop, you can start your plans.' We know in journalism it's a year-round bang; you can't quit in May and pick it back up in September. Having the workshops in June, they can get together and bond with their staffs."

These nine benefits certainly apply to national conferences as well. Klos attributed a final benefit to the national gatherings: boosting cohesion in the host communities.

"We see that in city after city and regionally as well," Klos said. "There's always a local committee of volunteers – by their working together, when the conference is done – boy, you have a group of people who've really learned a lot of aspects that help their teaching and help them get networked, and they have a group of students who are really excited and really keyed up about what they do. You get this collegial environment, and that is a good legacy of having these conferences together. Each place we go, we help either build or energize and expand a core group of people that are there" (personal interview with D. Mitsu Klos, May 29, 2014).

Chapter 13

The Relationship Between Working Journalists and High School Programs

By: Rebecca Tallent, Tracy Anderson & Mac McKerral

In the 1974 work *Captive Voices: High School Journalism in America*, Jack Nelson describes the isolation of high school journalism:

> The commission's survey and staff studies found little evidence that professional journalists are aware of high school journalists' legal rights or are concerned about their problems. In fact, high school media is so isolated that in most cases professional journalists are not even aware that problems exist. (Nelson, 1974, p. 197)

Not much has changed during the intervening years.

In the 2014 survey of high school teachers (Chapter 3), 56 percent of the responding teachers said they receive no support from their local professional news media. Where teachers said they do receive support is through local professionals speaking to their classes with fewer numbers reporting help with workshops or providing internships.

Colleges and universities fared nearly as poorly as working

professionals with 53 percent of the teacher respondents saying they receive no contributions from higher education; of those receiving assistance, most (34 percent) said they receive workshop assistance and nearly a quarter of the teachers said colleges and universities will provide guest speakers.

During the writing of this book, the SPJ Journalism Education Committee was frequently questioned about whether high school journalism still exists beyond being a public relations tool for the school.

The 2014 survey shows high school journalism is still alive – and viable – in many communities across America. Why are they being ignored?

The answers are not simple, although the solutions may be.

Looking back

Nelson said in 1974 that few editors reported giving little if any thought about high school journalism prior to the survey. When questioned, several editors said they would like to know more.

Back in 1994, David Hawpe, then of *The (Louisville) Courier-Journal*, said not nearly enough was being done to promote the importance of high school journalism as a career entry point. With Hawpe's guidance, his newspaper had taken over the journalism instruction and production at a local girl's school and supervised three Urban Journalism Workshops each year. However, "Death by Cheeseburger" only identified nine other programs where local news organizations (including the Poynter Institute for Media Studies) were actively working with local school journalism programs.

In 2014, several of the lauded programs were gone, including ones with the *Louisville Courier-Journal*, the *Seattle Times*, the *Detroit Free-Press* and the Freedom Forum Rainbow Institute.

"Captive Voices" suggested local newspapers adopt local school papers. In the wake of *Hazelwood School District v. Kuhlmeier*, "Death by Cheeseburger" recommended local news media provide "vigorous moral and support material for the practice and teaching of journalism" in secondary education and independent youth programs. Specifically, "Death by Cheeseburger" said:

Every newspaper should take responsibility for the existence – and well-being – of school newspapers in its community. State press associations and other groups at the national level, should develop plans to support scholastic journalism, whether this is initiated through individual schools, school systems or scholastic journalism associations. (Freedom Forum, 1994)

Nelson made an excellent point in "Captive Voices" when he said one of the main problems facing local media is they are unaware of the legal restrictions which limit high school journalism. While most have heard of the *Hazelwood* ruling, they may not understand it or how schools today actually employ the powers granted by the decision. Unfortunately, most news organizations neither take the time to find out nor ask how they can help local secondary school programs.

As a result, most professional contact with high school media is when the students take a tour of the local newsroom or the sporadic speaking engagement by a reporter or editor. The number of workshops sponsored by local news organizations for secondary students has dropped from a reported 46 percent in 1974 to 19 percent in 2014.

Couple this with the *Detroit Free-Press* abruptly dropping its 29-year-old high school journalism program in July 2014. Lauded in "Death by Cheeseburger" as an outstanding program in 1994, the Gannett-owned paper said in 2014 there was no longer a financial interest in the program, which allowed high school students to work alongside professionals in the newsroom. After the announcement, program alumni expressed concern that students, in particular black students, would be shut-off from a potential career in journalism, as the program was a pipeline for minority students to enter the field.

In 1994, the Freedom Forum's *Death by Cheeseburger* praised 10 specific newspaper programs for their work with high school newspapers. But by 2014, only four of the 10 were still in operation (the *Sarasota Herald-Tribune* in Florida, the *Ft. Lauderdale Sun-Sentinel* and the *Virginian-Pilot* in Virginia, all of which have an altered format, and the Poynter Institute for Media Studies, although the *St. Petersburg Times* has been renamed the *Tampa Bay Times*).

What is heartening is that although several news organizations have eliminated their support of scholastic programs, others have joined. In 2014, some of the news organizations holding seminars or workshops with financial support from the Dow Jones News Fund were the California Chicano News Media Association, Connecticut

Health Investigative Team Reporting Workshop/C-HIT Investigative Summer Reporting Workshop, National Association of Black Journalists J-SHOP, New England High School Journalism Collaborative (co-sponsored by the Boston Globe), Write On Sports in New Jersey, and the Urban Journalism Workshop in New York. These are in addition to the multitude of workshops offered by colleges and universities (see Chapter 12).

Today

Most journalists got their start in the field by participating in high school journalism programs. Nelson said in 1974 that substantive contacts do help students, teachers and the professionals willing to reach out. It not only helps students who may go into journalism, it also provides media literacy and critical/creative thinking skills for students who choose another field.

By 1994, the Freedom Forum reported a survey by the American Society of Newspaper Editors where of 234 responding newspapers, 14 percent said they offered mentoring programs, 25 percent provided high school student internships, 18 percent said they provided financial aid, 30 percent said they helped student newspapers, 24 percent said they offered minority student scholarships and 41 percent offered high school journalism seminars. That is a far cry from the 2014 survey where of 244 responding high school teachers 56 percent said professionals made no contributions. Of the media organizations that did contribute, guest speakers (54 percent) were at the top of the contributions, followed by workshop sessions (20 percent), internships (19 percent), funds for materials (6 percent), scholarships (5 percent) and other (8 percent). (For more information, see Chapter 3.)

Around the time of "Death by Cheeseburger," many news organizations began adopting high school journalism programs, but many editors said that practice ended when newsrooms began layoffs in the early 21st Century as the industry began shifting from print to electronic (Internet) media. Student-centered programs such as VOX at *The (Spokane) Spokesman-Review* disappeared. However, other news organizations are picking up new programs.

CNN now has CNN Student, where middle and high school students can learn about news while blogging and posting stories. CNN allows iReports from students and encourages teachers to use the news in their various classes. Students can also email the editors, comment on podcasts and are encouraged to send in news reports for broadcast.

The Virginian-Pilot shifted its program from recruiting teen correspondents to a two week workshop, the annual *Virginian-Pilot* High School Diversity Journalism Workshop, where during the last two weeks of June students work in the newsroom, go to editorial meetings, work with photographers to learn about photography and assign photos to go with stories, and conduct interviews and write stories around workshop classes on journalism. At the end of the workshop, the newspaper publishes the student-produced four-page paper. Workshop organizer Denise Watson said the newspaper actively begins advertising for the workshop's eight open slots (primarily targeting high school juniors) around the end of February or the beginning of March (personal interview with D. Watson on Aug. 14, 2014). "We take students from any local school – public, private or home schooled," Watson said. "We have even accepted a couple of students because they wanted to start or re-start a newspaper at their high school." More information about the workshop can be found at http://pilotonline.com.

At Poynter, the one-week workshop for area high school students teaches the basics of news with help from the *Tampa Bay Times*, which also has a student publication, *TBTwo*, and local TV station WTSP-TV. Like the *Virginian-Pilot* workshop, the Poynter program delves into news basics – including how to tell a story online and with video, ethics, photography, typography, and social media. "Poynter's high school program would not be nearly as robust or impactful without involvement of local journalists and newsrooms," said workshop coordinator Wendy Wallace. "The Gannett Foundation even supports the program with a $5,000 grant" (personal interview with W. Wallace on Aug. 13, 2014). Information about the Poynter program can be found at http://www.poynter.org/.

Another newspaper which has significantly altered its high school program is the *Sun-Sentinel* in Florida. In 1994, the Ft. Lauderdale newspaper recruited 126 high school students to craft the pages of its high school news page. Those students contributed as writers, photographers and artists. Today, Monica Wesoloski, *Sun-Sentinel* marketing manager, said the paper has a website called TeenLink (http://www.sun-sentinel.com/teenlink/) which replaced the former high school news page (personal interview with M. We-soloski on Aug. 14, 2014).

"*Teenlink South Florida* is an online and quarterly print news-paper," said Jennifer Jhon, *Teenlink* editor (email interview with J. Jhon on Aug. 15, 2014). "We cover entertainment news and features online and college information in print. We have a staff of 35-40 students from high schools throughout South Florida. We also run a Teen Voices column in the editorial section of the *Sun-Sentinel* on Fridays. These are opinion columns reprinted from local high school newspapers as well as columns provided by the *Teenlink* staff. Fi-nally we have the annual High School Journalism Awards program presented by the *Sun-Sentinel*, Forum Publishing and *Teenlink*. We invite every high school newspaper in Broward County to enter, and we have print and online categories. Several Broward County high school newspapers are national award winners, including Cypress Bay (*The Circuit*), Cooper City (*The Lariat*) and Coral Glades (*The Prowl*) so the competition can be intense."

The newspaper also has a News in Education page (http://sub-scribers.sun-sentinel.com/services/newspaper/education/nie/) that provides newspaper lessons online for teachers, students, parents and sponsors. *The Union-Tribune San Diego* offers an annual Young Latino Journalism Scholars Program each summer and literally pulls high school students into the day-to-day operations of the daily newspaper. During the summer of 2013, 10 Latino high school stu-dents throughout the county were selected to work at *U-T San Diego* alongside the mentorship and guidance of professional journalists.

The program, which runs for several weeks and is in its third year, is designed to provide young people with practical experience both in print and digital media. At the end of the program, the stu-dent team produces a special section that is published in the *Sunday U-T San Diego* print and online editions. The package includes rich profiles of San Diegans who have made a difference in their com-munity and includes stories, photos and videos (*San Diego Union-Tribune*, Personal communication, Aug. 28, 2013).

The program is funded by San Diego Gas & Electric and clear-ly leaves a lasting impression. The students, identified as potential leaders of the future, were chosen from dozens of applicants.

"I enjoyed being able to shadow professionals and experience what it is like in the field," said Francisca Martinez from Orange

Glen High School (personal interview with F. Martinez on Aug. 28, 2013). "I also loved learning about the integration of print and digital media. The hands-on experience in journalistic writing and video production was amazing."

Stories the students covered included a professor who preserves and presents black world history in Old Town San Diego, a volunteer who oversees the serving of 4,000 meals a day to the homeless, and a feature on the first female director of the San Diego LGBTQ Community Center and her nationwide travels to advocate the importance of pride and acceptance.

Katrina Roybal of Castle Park High School noted that the experience was very fulfilling.

"Being able to shadow professionals and report on what they do gives the program hands-on learning," she said (personal interview with K. Roybal on Aug. 28, 2013).

Rashid Binnur from Mar Vista High School had a similar reaction. "I was able to observe the importance of being a persistent reporter and accurate interviewer, and the necessity of having integrity in your work," he said (personal interview with R. Binnur on Aug. 28, 2013).

When professional journalists interact with high school journalism programs, the impact can be extremely valuable.

William Love has been teaching high school journalism in Sandpoint, Idaho, for the past six years.

Love said he realizes that journalists are very busy, so any time they can come into the classroom it is helpful from a teacher's perspective as well. A mentor program or internship opportunity can really be a benefit for the right students, he added (personal interview with W. Love on Sept. 5, 2014). Love's journalism program is part of Idaho's Professional-Technical Education Division (CTE in other states), and receives additional funding to provide professional equipment for students to use. One of the requirements of PTE is that programs have a committee of professionals to serve as a link between the school and industry. Professional journalists can obviously help high school programs meet that requirement.

The publisher of the local newspaper in Sandpoint, Idaho, has visited Love's students a handful of times to provide a critique of a recently published program and offer students encouragement in what they are doing.

Love said he sees value in both sides: for the professional journalists and the students. "Creating a connection could benefit both the program and the journalist. For students, it provides a connection with someone who they can read regularly in print or see on the evening news," he said. "That can mean a lot to students. On the other hand, the journalist has the opportunity to open the world of journalism to students who might not have considered it as a profession."

One of Love's students, a former editor-in-chief, recently completed a summer internship at the local daily newspaper, *The Bonner County Daily Bee*. There were several positives on both ends. Love and the publisher of the paper have even discussed expanding the summer internship into two next summer – one on the editorial side, the other on the business side.

"My student received validation of what he was doing in my class and for his decision to study journalism at Ball State University. The student also put together some quality clippings from a professional setting that offered him some great opportunities as soon as he reached campus," Love explained. "Finally, during the internship, he also had the opportunity to see the business side of the newspaper. It really opened his eyes to a side of journalism that he didn't get to see with the school paper."

Love added that a young, fresh perspective adds another layer of benefits to newspapers.

"For the paper, they received quality work and some fresh ideas from a teenager that looks at the world differently," he said.

Finding ways to work with pros

Mark Newton, president of the Journalism Education Association, teaches at Mountain Vista High School in Highlands Ranch, Colo. He teaches a variety of journalism classes and advises the school's news magazine, yearbook and television station.

Newton said that an assessment of a weakening presence of professional journalism outreach to high schools would be a "pretty accurate statement" (personal interview with M. Newton on Sept. 3, 2014). Factors causing that include budget cuts, reductions in staff at news outlets and journalists who have survived budget cuts having much more to do. He used a Journalism Day for high school students sponsored by a Denver TV station as an example.

"It just doesn't happen anymore," he said.

He also said the diminished emphasis on journalism in school curriculums makes things worse. If a school announces a cut in a football program, parents "go berserk."

"I get it," Newton said. "It's football. But when we have programs of excellence in journalism, no one seems to care. Those are programs we should cultivate."

And Newton said that in many cases, teachers assigned to student media advising and journalism classes have little or no interest in it. That reduces the advocacy role teachers should play.

"I am a journalism teacher and a media adviser – not someone assigned to do it," Newton said. "That makes it easier for me to say, 'I see (the value). I get it.'"

Newton said the most effective programs bring the students to the professionals – workshops and conferences. But getting journalists into the schools to work with students and advisers comes with a lot of value, too, he said. Unfortunately, it comes with a lot of hurdles – everything from school time schedules to principals who do not hold journalism or journalists in high regard.

But Newton said the biggest problem is the intense focus in schools on instructional time – teaching to the tests – and the ability of working journalists to teach effectively once they're in the classroom. "They are professional journalists, not necessarily professional speakers or good teachers," Newton said.

Entering a classroom to teach requires skills and preparation, Newton said. It is not the same as telling stories – even good ones – to a class full of journalism students. "You are talking about the difference between a Career Day and an educational experience," he said. And so the JEA model for keeping the journalism fire alive in high schools seems the most effective, he said.

Kelly Furnas, JEA executive director, shared "the highlights" of the organization's scholastic journalism efforts (email interview with K. Furnas on Sept. 22, 2014).

- JEA hosts two national conventions a year, which draw 4,000 to 6,000 journalism students and teachers. Training is offered on nearly every aspect of media production.
- JEA offers a certification program for teachers that combines credentialing and testing that leads to "Certified Jour-

nalism Educator" or "Master Journalism Educator" status through the JEA.

- JEA provides teachers what they need most, curriculum. "We developed over a hundred lesson plans spanning 11 content areas in journalism as a benefit to our members," he said.
- JEA produces a quarterly magazine that provides articles and handouts on the finer points of journalism education. JEA also offers a website, http://www.jeadigitalmedia.org, devoted to the teaching of technology.
- JEA uses a 2,000-member email distribution list that allows teachers to interact virtually for mentoring and support.

"We have tons of awards and contests – some in conjunction with our conventions, but others are recognition for career – or academic career (achievement) in the case of our High School Journalist of the Year contests," he said.

Michael Koretzky, an SPJ board member representing Region 3, the Southeast, described SPJ Florida's high school outreach efforts as "failed and feeble" (personal interview with M. Koretzky on Oct. 1, 2014.

Nevertheless, he forges on.

SPJ Region 3 tried to formalize a relationship with the Florida Scholastic Press Association's District 7, which holds an annual fall workshop for nearly 2,000 students, Koretzky said.

"We provide as many speakers as they need and have even hosted a massive First Amendment Free Food Festival," said Koretzky, who serves as content director and editor-in-chief for HSD Holdings.

But the challenges that came with that effort are ones common to any partnership effort, he said.

- Sometimes national organizations are not well organized at the regional and local level.
- Changes in leadership at a partner organization can stop momentum or worse, end the partnership.

"Those new directors have scant few hours to dedicate to just the basics of hosting an annual workshop, so they have little time to embrace novel efforts," Koretzky said.

The lesson he has learned: "Scholastic press groups in general are isolated from other journalism groups because major journalism groups prefer to work with college students, who can pay dues on their own and are one step from becoming pros."

Koretzky makes a personal effort to get into schools to teach – "critique their paper and sit down to review whatever they want," he said.

"Problem is, this is a sporadic and uncoordinated effort. And while some of those teachers stay in touch via email to pose questions and seek help, I seldom visit twice. Other SPJ Florida board members have attempted the same, but the fact is, most can't ditch work at 2 p.m. on a Tuesday to visit the class, and students today are so packed with activities, they can't meet after school without their parents revamping their entire lives."

Koretzky wants to shift his and SPJ's efforts to partnering with JEA, he said.

"Because I'm a manager with more flexible hours, and my company encourages philanthropy, I'll choose one school within a reasonable distance to mentor via visits, email, Skype and other tools," he said. "JEA's imprimatur will lend 'cred' to the teachers and also help us develop literature to convince pro-journalist bosses to let their employees donate a few hours per school year."

Koretzky offered two keys to successful in-school programs: make sure the instruction is multiplatform, "not just teaching how to write a news story," and create programs that meet school district standards for continuing education hours for teachers.

The more creative the programs the better, Koretzky said.

"What I know about principals – the way to get them involved – is to do something they can write a press release about," Koretzky said.

John Ensslin, a past president of SPJ and longtime reporter at the *Bergen (N.J.) Record, The Rocky Mountain News,* and *The Colorado Springs Gazette,* among others, began a push during his SPJ presidency to elevate the organization's involvement in high school journalism.

He called the decision to do that "personal" (personal interview with J. Ensslin on Oct. 2, 2014).

"My decision to become a journalist was sparked very early when Mrs. McDonough, my fourth grade teacher at St. Michael's elementary school in Union City, N.J, came down with a cold," he said.

The substitute teacher, Mr. McDonough, talked to Ensslin's

class that day about his job as night sports editor at *The Hudson Dispatch*, Ensslin's hometown newspaper at the time.

"I was hooked," Ensslin said. "Get paid to follow baseball games and stay up late. Sign me up, I figured. I wonder how many young people in high school might also have a life-shaping experience if they were to be exposed to journalism as a classroom topic."

Ensslin said school administrators who shun journalism and journalists overlook the transferable skill set that a journalism curriculum brings.

He acknowledged the media's news coverage of its own problems plays into the thinking of school officials – industry-wide layoffs and news outlets shutting down, such as the *Rocky Mountain News* in Denver, where Ensslin once worked.

"So it's understandable, but misguided," he said. "Because as we all know there is a new wave of jobs being created that call for a different set of social media skills that were not a requirement when I started out.

"Also we need to drive home the point that no other craft forces a student to learn critical thinking skills (better) than journalism. Even if a student never walks into a newsroom, there is something to be gained by learning how to boil down a complex set of facts into a clear and concise story."

Ensslin emphasized the need for in-school programs and workshops to:

- Involve real-world reporting and creating stories from that reporting.
- Teach students how to take a story apart and put it back together again, which is a great way to learn story structure.
- Go beyond a "traditional journalism" approach and include shooting and editing a video, Tweeting and exploring other formats of storytelling.

"Kids pick up on this stuff a lot faster than older folks," he said.

Ensslin said Jim Roberts, formerly a reporter for Reuters and *The New York Times* and now Mashable's executive editor and chief content officer, paid a visit to the *Bergen Record* newsroom to give a pep talk to the survivors of the "newspaper industry apocalypse."

Mashable, an online source for news and information, drew

34 million monthly unique visitors and had 14 million followers in 2014.

"(Roberts) turned from a traditional journalist to a Tweeting maniac working online all day," Ensslin said.

"(People like Roberts) are in every community. They can talk about the exact opposite of what high school administrators believe about journalism."

Ensslin said he is concerned about the difficulty of building standard programs for the schools that could earn teachers continuing education credit.

"In Bergen County alone there are 70 school districts, all very different," he said. "But if you can find one willing to listen, and get some coverage for it, then you can start the ball rolling."

So, principals do like programs that help them generate press releases?

"That's not a stretch," Ensslin said.

Section IV

Conclusions

Profile 5

ADRIENNE FORGETTE

Martha's Vineyard Regional High School (750 students, public)
Oak Bluffs, Mass.
Yearbook (club)

Yearbook adviser Adrienne Forgette said she's feeling optimistic these days. She just landed a job in Georgia as a high school publications director, and recently attended an exciting JEA conference in San Diego.

"They revealed the new curriculum initiative that is aligned to Common Core," Forgette said, which she said could help make media studies more viable in schools and much more attractive to administrators.

Forgette, 34, has been a teacher for 11 years at four different schools. She got her start as a publications adviser for Northern High School at Owings, Md., seven years ago when she took over for an outgoing yearbook teacher.

"It was a Crown Award (CSPA) publication; there was a long-standing tradition – it was a big job," she said. "The program was highly respected and well-supported. There was a level of excellence; they traveled and competed throughout the country."

And although Forgette had no professional publications experience at the time, and she was assigned this position, she drew from knowledge she gained as the editor-in-chief of her high school yearbook and as a reporter for the school's newspaper. She said she also took advantage of professional development opportunities offered through the yearbook company. And this year she said she gained even more experience working through a local newspaper and as a blogger for CNN.

"I was chosen as one of seven members of CNN Fit Nation's triathlon team," she said, "and part of the requirements was blogging about my experience training for my first triathlon. It was a segment on 'Sanjay Gupta MD.' "

Forgette said she has enjoyed advising yearbook, an extracurricular activity at her current high school, Martha's Vineyard Regional High School (MVRHS) in Oak Bluffs, Mass., but misses being a journalism adviser. "I'm a National Board Certified English teacher, but I feel like a journalism teacher first," she said. "Here, there's no infrastructure, and no kids want to be part of it."

MVRHS, with a community of 750 students, currently has a one-page printed newspaper and no online presence. There's no dedicated physical space for publications, and publications advisers "roam" from classroom to classroom as they teach additional English classes, she said.

That's why Forgette's eager to move on next year to Darlington School in Rome, Ga., where she said she will be designing curriculum for publication classes and advising yearbook and the online newspaper. She'll move from a public high school to a private one, and is excited to focus solely on journalism, she said.

"As I look forward, the issues will most likely be First Amendment issues, prior review, and how much administration will trust and foster a free press," Forgette said. "First Amendment rights get tricky at independent schools, but I am determined to build a journalistically sound program that the administration trusts."

Forgette said she understands, however, what it's like being watched closely by administration.

"We were under prior review at my previous school in Maryland," she said. "They looked at everything we published.

"We ran a great picture of a kid at a basketball game, a huge goose egg on his forehead, with the caption saying something like: 'I'm so glad I didn't get hurt and was able to finish the game.' It was funny, but when administration saw it they said, 'Print this and the coach will lose his job.' They were concerned the kid might have had a concussion, and shouldn't have continued playing," Forgette said.

"They also had an issue with our club hockey team, which was not school sponsored, and didn't want it to appear in the same section with other sports teams. We ran it anyway, and didn't hear anything."

Forgette said that most administrators she's worked with have been "lacking" when it comes to student press law.

"My first gift to them is the *Principal's Guide to Scholastic Journalism,* she said. "Many of them have been clueless – they don't want kids to cover any real issues. I guess it's a PR thing."

Chapter 14

Conclusions: What Needs to be Done

By *Rebecca Tallent & Lee Anne Peck*

In an age where lobbyists and public relations practitioners out-number journalists in the U.S. and state capitals and corporate executives spend company dollars supporting political candidates, the need for diligent public watchdogs may be more critical than ever. Add to the above that today's elementary and high school students have never seen a truly free press in action – only a wartime press established in the 1990s that is hobbled by free press restrictions, such as media pools and limited access to information – and it is easy to see the need for incubating press-press, free-thinking people with strong, all-around communication skills at all levels of education.

High school journalism still exists in the United States, but its survival depends on solving several problems. Unfortunately, as the previous chapters have stressed, many of these problems have never been solved – they are the same as they were four decades ago. These include the following:

- **Training for high school journalism teachers.** Colleges and universities – especially traditional teacher colleges – need to re-invent their programs to teach English (and other) majors how to teach journalism. The 2014 study showed how few teachers are actually well-trained to teach the subject; colleges and universities – especially ones that offered these types of courses in the past – should again offer courses in scholastic journalism. Teachers who are or were not able to take scholastic journalism courses in college should be encouraged to complete the JEA certification.

- **Consistent curriculum design among high school teachers on the state and national level**. Schools should be encouraged to include the latest technology to aid in student learning. Journalism courses should be recognized as fulfilling Common Core requirements.
- **Higher education should also become more involved with local scholastic journalism**. It is not just a recruiting tool; it is an extension of the university's purpose (especially for land grant and many private universities). Offering expertise in teaching, editing, writing, photography, script writing and many other elements of the field can cement relationships and provide encouragement to talented young people.
- **Colleges and universities should offer more workshops for teachers as continuing education credits.** Professional media outlets that sponsor workshops should also make sure instruction for teachers is included in the workshop. This can assist those English teachers and librarians who have had the advising of the student media thrust upon them with no background on the subject or laws pertaining to student media.
- **Professional media involvement**. Many professional journalists began their careers in high school classrooms, and it would be their gift to future journalists to provide moral and material support to scholastic programs and their teachers. Funding college scholarships or offering internships for highly motivated high school students need to become priorities again.
- **Education of school administrators.** Professionals should help high school administrators understand what journalism really teaches: the JEA-identified critical thinking, creativity, collaboration and communication skills, all of which are valuable tools no matter what field a person eventually enters.
- **Lobbying school districts**. Professional news organizations such as the Society of Professional Journalists should lobby school districts for improved funding for scholastic journalism programs. Programs should be adequately funded, so students can learn the important skills offered in journalism classes.
- **Enthusiasm and participation from high school students.** More than one-fourth of the respondents said they believed their

students had a lack of interest in participating in journalism courses or student media. A 2014 study by the Knight Foundation, "The Future of the First Amendment," found that high school students showed for the first time in a decade "a greater overall appreciation for the First Amendment than do adults." The study points out that students want the right to speak out. Journalism ties into this desire. (Knight Foundation, 2014)

From the current SPJ study, who needs the most help? The answer seems to be the schools that currently receive no help from local professional news organizations or college and universities. These are schools of all sizes, and there is no distinction between public or private. Without a school media outlet, these students may never become efficient news consumers or be able to fully grasp the skills taught through journalism classes.

Some teachers responding to the study said they sometimes feel lonely and isolated in their teaching. If JEA-affiliated members can feel this way, the non-affiliated teachers could be completely overwhelmed. The results of this study also strongly encourage non-affiliated teachers to find and participate in their state scholastic journalism association, so they no longer feel alone.

Professional groups, such as SPJ, should encourage high school journalism through scholastic membership – which provides information on writing/reporting, diversity, Freedom of Information and other vital issues – and openly, actively support the Student Press Law Center. Thanks to the results of this survey, SPJ in 2014 resolved to further help scholastic journalism with outreach by chapters (both professional and college) and is working in conjunction with the JEA and SPLC to find new avenues to assist high school programs.

Journalism as a whole is not dead or dying: It is simply changing delivery platforms. Scholastic journalism is in the same boat, but in many cases it cannot change platforms or adjust to changing delivery systems due to a lack of funds and/or support from administrators, local professionals, parents and fellow teachers. This prevents students from receiving training that will help them throughout the rest of their lives whether they become working journalists or not. This training will assist in their professional status, citizenship skills and other vital aspects of living in a 21st century democracy.

Today's high school students are neither less smart nor less in need of the skills that can be provided by journalism courses. It is incumbent on the whole of the journalism community – higher education and professionals – to help find ways to support and encourage budding journalists and their scholastic teachers.

Chapter 15

High School Journalism in the United States

References & Annotated Bibliography

Abbott, A. (1910). High school journalism. *The School Review, 18*(10), 657-666.

Abbott examines the status of high school journalism in 1910 when school newspapers were coming into fashion and journalism was being accepted into the curriculum. He makes a compelling argument that journalism is a vital force within the curriculum. The author tends to consider female students as more inclined toward the artistic while giving male students the authority for news; he also tends to see the newspaper as a cheerleader for the school, especially for alumni.

Abrams, M. (1977). Tinkering around with high school journalism. *Photolith ScM, 17*(5), 14-16.

The author explains how a game using Tinker Toys can be used to promote a sense of staff cohesiveness, which is essential to the operation of school journalism departments.

Amster, S.A. (2006). *Seeds of cynicism: The undermining of journalistic education.* **Boulder, CO: University Press of America.**

This book is a cynical yet fairly comprehensive look at the state of high school journalism in three Southern California high schools shortly after the events of 9/11. The author gathered her information and opinions through a series of observations and interactions with the students, teachers and administrators of the unnamed schools. The work takes a look at the history of high school journalism in the United States and is followed by serious looks at how students in the three schools determined what would be the news of each edition, why some students resisted using actual news and why news has become less important to the generation. There is some discussion about the differences between the prestige schools and a 78 percent Latino school.

Andrew, R. (1995.). Book review: Death by cheeseburger: High school journalism in the 1990s and beyond. *Contemporary Education, 66*(2), 123.

The reviewer states he believes the Freedom Forum report on the status of high school journalism provides insights for anyone concerned with issues of press freedom; he also believes the book would make an excellent handbook for journalism educators.

Anonymous. (1971, November 15). Letter to Mr. Wayne Brasler, University of Chicago. Copy in possession of Central Interscholastic Press Assoiation.

This letter by an anonymous author provides facts about the first Central Interscholastic Press Association convention in 1922. CIPA was started at the University of Wisconsin, Madison, in 1921.

Anonymous. (1977). 1977 High school journalism workshops. *Photolith ScM, 26*(7), 16-22.

Describes high school summer journalism workshops for students in 18 states.

Anonymous. (1986). Twisted Times editor still shouts dispute not moot. *Student Press Law Center Report, 7*(2) 6-7.

This is a follow-up report to the Bryan High School suspension for the *Twisted Times* alternative newspaper, which came while student Karl Evans appeals his suspension. Additionally, ACLU attorney James Harrington challenges that Evans' free speech rights had been violated, arguing that no justification for "prior restraint" has been demonstrated by the state.

Arnold, M. (Ed.). (1996). *The full palette diversity guide for high school journalism.* **Manhattan, KS: Kansas State University.**

This booklet presents 12 activities to help high school journalism teachers and staff members balance the content of their publications and the staff makeup, so all groups of students in the school are represented. The first 11 activities in the booklet are classroom activities designed for teachers and students. The final activity is intended primarily for advisers and includes suggestions for recruiting minority staff members and step-by-step plans for forming a local press association. Included with each activity in the booklet are a goal for each activity and strategies for attaining that goal; an approximate time line for the activity; ways of getting started and wrapping up each activity; a list of materials needed; worksheets; and a list of sources and resources.

Associated Press, (2014). *The Associated Press stylebook and briefing on media law*. Cambridge, MA: Perseus Publishing.

This is a style guide and media law book used by journalists, public relations professionals and others who write in news style.

Associated Press. (2010). **Kansas pulls fund from high school journalism: State education officials say they want curriculum to reflect future job market.** *Education Week, 30*(4), p. 5.

Kansas journalism teachers are worried that changes in the way the state finances high school programs could mean the end for student newspapers and yearbooks.

Associated Press (1986, December 19). Bryan injunction extended. *The Victoria Advocate*, p. 5C.

This wire service article covers a Bryan High School student's suspension for publishing the alternative newspaper *Twisted Times.* Although publication was allowed as the result of a judge's extension of an injunction, questions of First Amendment rights of students are raised in this court case.

Association for Education in Journalism and Mass Communication. (2014). AEJMC history. Retrieved from http://www.aejmc.org/home/about/aejmc-history/

The Association for Education in Journalism and Mass Communication began in 1912 as the American Association of Teachers of Journalism. Willard G. Bleyer of the University of Wisconsin was the chief organizer. The association's purpose had two goals: to hold an annual conference for those interested in the teaching of journalism, and to collect statistics relating to journalism courses and teaching. The AEJMC history site is regularly updated.

Association of American Colleges and Universities. (2014). *VALUE: Valid assessment of learning in undergraduate education.* Retrieved from http://www.aacu.org/value/index.cfm

This is an explanation of the Value Assessment of Learning in Undergraduate Education initiative supported with a grant from Bill and Melinda Gates Foundation. Proposed deliverables and a rubric for classroom use are described. It also explains the nine-state pilot test of the VALUE system.

Balazs, E.E. (1970, December). **High school journalism is dead! Dead! Dead!** *The English Journal, 59*(9), 1283-1284.

A former high school principal complains the newspaper format for high school journalism is dead and schools should switch to a TV format. Balazs states the problem with newspaper formats is they are too static; the news is too old by the time it reaches the consumer. Schools should instead invest in TV news studios, so the information can be more relevant and timely.

Balfour Yearbooks. (2014). Yearbook workshops and training events. Retrieved from http://www.balfour.com/educators/yearbook-advisers/events/
Balfour hosted 39 yearbook summer workshops for advisers and their staffs in 16 states from June through September 2014. Additional workshops are added regularly, including during the school year.

Ball State University Journalism Workshops. (2014). *History.* Retrieved from http://bsujournalismworkshops.com/contact/history/
This article from Ball State University describes the history of its summer workshop, which began in 1966 and has been one of the nation's elite.

Benz, L. G. (1959). Summer journalism workshops for high school students. *Journalism and Mass Communication Quarterly*, 36(1), 53-56.
This article covers "one of the significant developments in journalism education" in the 1950s – the rapid growth of summer journalism workshops. It is a survey of 19 such programs operated in 1958. The article reports the second summer workshop came 16 years after Northwestern's began in 1930; however, it should be noted that a number of states, such as Alabama and North Carolina, hosted workshops before 1946. The article does convey interesting facts and statistics about the 19 workshops and their demographics, offerings, cost, recruiting and recreation.

Bethel School District v. Fraser. (1986). 478 U.S. 675. Supreme Court of the United States. Retrieved from *LexisNexis Academic* at http://www.lexis-nexis.com/hottopics/lnacademic/
This case, appealed from the 9th U.S. Circuit, gave authority to school officials to sanction a student for giving a lewd speech at a school assembly in which he nominated a fellow student for office using explicit sexual metaphors. The court determined the First Amendment offered no protection for such speech when weighed against the educational mission of school regarding public civility.

Bowen, J. (1976). *Captive voices: Another look*. La Crosse, WI: Journalism Education Association.
Bowen's research sought to re-evaluate findings from a 1974 Kennedy Commission report regarding the state of high school journalism. Bowen concluded the initial report was at fault for making oversimplified conclusions about censorship and the prioritization of high school journalism. Ultimately, Bowen recommended further inquiry in the areas of censorship and funding in the high school press.

Boyd, J.A. (1960). High school journalism instruction in Indiana. *Journalism & Mass Communication Quarterly*, 37(4), 586-587. Retrieved from http://search.proquest.com/docview/1290728870?accountid=14214
Investigating questions regarding Indiana's high school newspaper advisers, Boyd's 1960 research yielded some important findings regarding adviser turnover and qualifications. Ultimately, recommendations included more rigorous requirements and better training for advisers.

Brooks, B.S., Kennedy, G., Moen, D.R. & Ranly, D. (2002). *News reporting and writing*. (7th ed). Boston, MA: Bedford/St, Martin's Press.

This is a college text on the basics of news reporting, including the nature of news, interviewing, gathering information, reporting with numbers, the inverted pyramid, beyond the inverted pyramid, writing the story, beat reporting, investigative reporting, writing for specific media and writing for online media. Media law and ethics are included.

Brown, W.M. (1988). Certification of the high school journalism teacher. *NASSP Bulletin, 72*(511), 27.

To help secondary schools find qualified journalism teachers and improve the quality of journalism instruction, the Journalism Education Association has designated a commission to establish certification requirements for such teachers. Individuals with teaching credentials and college majors or minors in journalism are considered.

Buller, T. (2011). Subtle censorship: The problem of retaliation against high school journalism advisers and three ways to stop it. *Journal of Law and Education, 40*(4), 609-658.

The article explores whether the problem of retaliation against high school journalism advisers is best addressed through courts, local school boards or state legislatures. Advisers are under fire, and students' speech is being "chilled." This article argues the best path to ending retaliation against journalism advisers is through state legislatures adopting statutes that prohibit adviser-retaliation, grant students a cause of action, and require local school districts to adopt consistent policies protecting student publications.

Burke, B. (2013). OU journalism: The first century. *Sooner Magazine*. Retrieved from https://www.oufoundation.org/SM2/Summer2013/story/OU_Journalism_The_FIRST_CENTURY

The first journalism class was taught at the University of Oklahoma in 1908. In 1913, the Oklahoma Interscholastic Press Association was formed on the campus; it remains the oldest scholastic state press association in the country.

Burch v. Barker. (1988). 861 F.2d 1149. 9th U.S. Circuit Court of Appeals. Retrieved from *LexisNexis Academic* at http://www.lexisnexis.com/hot-topics/lnacademic/

The court found that censuring students because they failed to follow a school district policy of prior review before distributing a non-school newspaper was a violation of their First Amendment rights. The court concluded that no one could have mistakenly assumed the school approved of the newspaper.

Callahan, C. (1998). Race and participation in high school journalism. *Newspaper Research Journal, 19*(1), 45-53.

This study researches minority participation in high school journalism. The author finds race is an indicator of whether a school has a newspaper and which students are leaders of the publications.

Campbell, A.S. & Reeves, J. (1985). Why teach high school journalism? *C.S.P.A.A. Bulletin, 43*(4).

The authors present a rationale for a comprehensive journalism program, consistent with the current "search for excellence in education," which provides students laboratory projects on both the school newspaper and the yearbook.

Campbell, L. R. (1940). *The teacher of journalistic activities in the American public high school* (Doctoral dissertation). Evanston, IL: Northwestern University.

In this dissertation, the author explores via a survey of high school teachers of journalism what activities students do in journalism courses or in student newsrooms.

Campbell, L.R. (1940). "Educational backgrounds of journalism teachers." School & Society, 51(1308), 86-90.

Six hundred and thirteen high school teachers of journalism in 48 states answered an 8-page questionnaire dealing with their work and experience. The author of the study laments many of the respondents did not have any journalistic experience. Says the author: "All too frequently principals in supposedly modern secondary schools thrust the task of sponsoring publications upon any one who happens to be an innocent bystander."

In general, the author laments school administrators don't understand that teachers of journalism need to have the same depth of instruction as those who teach English and other high school subjects.

Campbell, L.R. (1942). High school journalism and the war. *The High School Journal, 25*(5), 219-220.

This short article by a Northwestern University professor is about high school newspapers and how U.S. student journalists can help the World War II effort. It includes resolutions created by the Los Angeles Journalism Teachers Association.

Campbell, L. R. (1947, March). Schools of journalism help the school press. *School Activities, 19*(7), 215.

The author lists 10 ways college journalism programs can help high schools. The tips included cooperating with local, state, regional and national scholastic press associations and hosting workshops, clinics, contests and conferences.

Campbell, L. R. (1967). *The role, beginnings, membership and services of the high school press associations.* Iowa City, IA: Quill and Scroll Society.

The author uses a nationwide survey to analyze the policies and programs of high school press associations. The study also provides the year of origin, membership figures and activities of the associations.

Chastain, S. (1984, December 27). Student papers as a barometer of the times. *Philadelphia Inquirer.* Retrieved from http://search.proquest.com/docvi ew/293785390?accountid=14214

Chastain's article examines slick, well-produced high school newspapers and takes a look at the history of student journalism in the United States from the optimistic post-war 1940s through the socially conscious 1960s and 1970s. While great strides have been made to produce a more professional product, Chastain notes, ideologically, there's a shift to a more conservative tone. In addition, Chastain discusses the possible stifling of First Amendment rights and censorship by school administrators.

Chen, L. (2010, Summer). Critical thinking about journalism: A high school student's view. *Nieman Reports*. Retrieved from http://www.thenewsliteracyproject.org/
A high school student from Bethesda, Md., who works on the school newspaper The Black and White, discusses interacting with professional journalists via the News Literacy Project in which she participated through her Advanced Placement U.S. government course.

Cherub Application Booklet. (2014). *Journalism*. Retrieved from http://cherubs.medill.northwestern.edu/2014/about/
This is the application booklet for Northwestern University's Medill-Northwestern Journalism Institute.

Childers, J. P. (2012). *The evolving citizen: American youth and the changing norms of democratic engagement*. University Park, PA: The Pennsylvania State University Press.
Childers' book of essays focuses on the complaint that young people have no interest in U.S. democracy. He challenges this so-called decline. He examines seven high school newspapers and says he believes high school students are just as involved in civic life as ever; they just demonstrate this fact differently.

Clark, L.S. & Monserrate, R. (2011). High school journalism and the making of young citizens. *Journalism, 12*(4) 417-432.
The authors examine how high school journalism classes contribute to the socialization of young adults into citizens and how the classes contribute to the development of a collective sensibility. The study interviewed 45 high school journalists from 19 different schools and highlights how the high school students view citizenship and their role as a journalist in development of citizens. The study also looks at how some high school journalists come to view the costs of citizenship and active engagement through negative interactions with school administrations.

Click, J.W. & Kopenhaver, L.L. (1988, Summer). Principals favor discipline more than a free press. *Journalism Educator, 43*(2) 48-51.
The article reports on the authors' 1988 study looking at censorship and the importance of a free press in high schools following the Hazelwood decision. The study found high school principals and advisers strongly favored a review of all copy prior to publishing; that two thirds of all principals believed administrators should prohibit publication of articles they deem harmful even if the articles are

not obscene, libelous or disruptive; and that one-fourth of the principals surveyed do not believe that prior review should be considered censorship.

This 1988 article sets the groundwork for the authors' 2001 review of the same topic and sets the baseline for the later study, plus it shows the attitudes of administrators do not vary much between the two studies. This study does show significantly more disagreement between administrators and advisers than the 2001 study.

Cohen, E.D. (2004, Summer). Philosophy with teeth: The be wedding of philosophical and psychological practices. *International Journal of Philosophical Practice, 2(2).* **Retrieved from** http://www.instituteofcriticalthinking.com/about%20LBT.htm

In this paper, Cohen outlines how philosophical therapies such as his own Logic-Based modality, and psychological therapies, especially Rational-Emotional Behavior Therapy (REBT), work together synergistically. Cohen holds that the American Philosophical Practitioner's Association's bifurcation of psychological from philosophical practice is artificial, impractical and self-defeating.

Cohen, S. (1985, July 20). Paper has all the news that's fit for teens. *Orlando Sentinel,* **p. A5.**

Cohen profiles the monthly student newspaper New Expression, notable for its large readership and bold investigative journalism. Run by a nun operating out of a downtown Chicago office, the paper has often scooped professional journalists.

Colorado State Board of Education. (2013, May). *Colorado's High School Graduation Guidelines.* **Retrieved from** http://www.cde.state.co.us/sites/default/files/adoptedgraduationguidelines2013.pdf

This document outlines Colorado high school graduation guidelines, which were adopted by the state in May 2013.

Columbia Scholastic Press Association. (2014). *Biography of Col. Joseph M. Murphy* **[Adobe Digital Editons Verions]. Retrieved from** http://cspa.columbia.edu/who-we-are/history/joseph-m-murphy

This article from the Columbia Scholastic Press Association profiles Joseph M. Murphy, who built CSPA "into the nation's largest school press association" as the director of the association from 1924 to 1969.

Columbus North High School (2014). About Us. *CNHSMedia.* **Retrieved from** http://cnhsmedia.com/about-us/

This is the high school website from Columbus, Ind., North High School, which is an example of forward-thinking secondary-school journalism. It operates as a partnership with all other student media, including print and broadcast. It "serves as a hub of information for all that is Columbus North Student Media." The site is regularly updated.

Cornelius v. NAACP Legal Defense & Education Fund. (1985). 473 U.S. 788. Supreme Court of the United States. Retrieved from *LexisNexis Academic* http://www.lexisnexis.com/hottopics/lnacademic/

The court concluded a presidential order that prohibited legal defense and political advocacy groups from participating in the Combined Federal Campaign (an annual charity fundraising drive to benefit members and their families) did not violate the First Amendment. The government's reasons for doing so were viewpoint neutral and designed to eliminate disruptions to the workplace and ensure the success of the campaign.

Cutsinger, J. & M. Herron. (1996). History worth repeating. Minneapolis, MN: Josten's.

This 80-page book chronicles the history of yearbooks from their beginnings to the 1990s.

Dean v. Utica Community Schools. (2004). 345 F. Supp. 2d 799. U.S. District Court for Eastern District of Michigan, Southern Division. Retrieved from *LexisNexis Academic* http://www.lexisnexis.com/hottopics/lnacademic/

The court ruled that a student newspaper article about a pending lawsuit against the school district was illegally censored because it didn't take the school district's side. The article was censored because of its viewpoint, not any potential disruption to the school's educational mission.

Dickson, T. (2001.) Trends in university support of scholastic education. *Journalism and Mass Communication Educator, 56(1)*, 74-85.

The author discusses the role higher education plays in scholastic journalism. The author's findings show slightly fewer colleges/universities were involved in activities related to preparing future journalism teachers.

Dow Jones News Fund. (2014). DJNF high school journalism workshops [Web log post]. Retrieved from https://www.newsfund.org/PageText/Prg_HomePages.aspx?Page_ID=Prg_DJNFHighSchool

Dvorak, J. (1992). *Secondary school journalism in the United States.* **Bloomington, IN: Indiana High School Journalism Institute.**

The author conducted a survey of 834 educators and found that 94 percent of high schools have some type of student media; he also investigated additional media-related activities.

Dvorak, J. & Choi, C. (2009). High school journalism, academic performance correlate. *Newspaper Research Journal, 30(3)* 75-89.

In this study, the main independent variable included students on the staff of a school newspaper or yearbook without examining whether staff membership was connected with an academic course in journalism or as a stand-alone curricular or extra-curricular activity. The study found that on ACT standardized tests and college courses/tests, journalism students had significantly higher scores in 14 of 17 academic comparisons.

Dvorak, J., Lain, L. B., & Dickson, T. V. (1994). *Journalism kids do better: What research tells us about high school journalism.* Bloomington, IN: ERIC Clearinghouse on Reading, English, and Communication.

This classic piece of research was the first to show a correlation between involvement in high school journalism and performance on standardized tests and college academic performance. Additionally, this book highlighted a variety of issues in high school journalism, including censorship, and discussed the differing roles of high school journalism in American schools.

Fawcett, V. E. (1924). A unique project in high-school journalism. *The English Journal, 13*(4), 276-279.

This 1924 article describes a country newspaper edited by the students of a rural high school (under the direction of the English department). A "modern" project, the Elmsdale, Kan., paper is the only newspaper published in town and includes both community and school news. The paper serves students, the school and the community—which is a win-win situation for all involved.

Florida Statutes. (2013). *Requirements for high school graduation, revised.* Title XLVIII, K-20 Education Code, Chapter 1003, Public k-12 Education, Chapter 1003.428.

This statute outlines the general requirements for high school graduation in the state of Florida as determined by the 2013 Florida Statutes.

Foley, A. (2014, July 16). After 29 years, FREEP is indefinitely halting its high school journalism program. *Columbia Journalism Review.* Retrieved from http://www.cjr.org/behind_the_news/freep_ending_apprentice_progra.php

This is an updated article detailing the Detroit Free Press' reasons for closing its long-established high school journalism program as well as opponents' comments.

Former high school journalism students speak. (1984). *Communication: Journalism Education Today, 17*(4), 9-15.

Graduates from four high schools across the United States report on their high school journalism experiences and discuss the significance of those experiences in their professional lives.

Forrester, M.A. (1985). High school journalism influences professionals. *Communication: Journalism Education Today, 19*(1), 12-14.

A questionnaire asked professional journalists how high school journalism classes influenced them to choose their newspaper careers.

Foundation for Critical Thinking. (2013). Professional Development Workshops. Retrieved from http://www.criticalthinking.org/pages/business-and-professional-groups/1015/

The Foundation for Critical Thinking's website includes a section targeted toward business and professional groups, which describes professional development workshops and seminars designed to enhance critical thinking in organizational settings. The workshops and seminars mentioned on this site are all organized by the Foundation for Critical Thinking.

Freedom Forum (2015, January 14). *What is the public forum doctrine?* **Retrieved from** http://www.firstamendmentschools.org/freedoms/faq.aspx?id=13012

This document explains the types of fora and gives example of each. Determining the type of forum that exists provides guidance to courts in determining whether restricting speech in that setting is constitutional. The Freedom Forum is a nonpartisan foundation that supports the First Amendment to protect democracy. It operates the Newseum in Washington, D.C., and The First Amendment Center in Nashville, Tenn.

Freedom Forum. (1994). *Death by cheeseburger: High school journalism in the 1990s and beyond.* **Arlington, VA: The Freedom Forum.**

The 1988 Supreme Court decision in Hazelwood School District vs. Kuhlmeier reversed the way school officials saw the student press. With that concern in mind, the Freedom Forum's report provided recent research about high school journalism, did a content analysis of 233 school newspapers and reported on several interviews with people involved in or who have been involved with high school journalism. Many of the findings mirrored those found in Captive Voices, a similar study by the Robert F. Kennedy Foundation published in 1974.

Gainer, J. (2012). Critical thinking: Foundations for digital literacies and Democracy. *Journal of Adolescent & Adult Literacy, 56*(1), 14-17.

Gainer's column is the first of four published in Volume 56 of the Journal of Adolescent & Adult Literacy addressing digital literacies and popular culture. The columns explore critical perspectives on teaching and learning new literacies with specific attention to how race, class, gender and linguistic diversity are related.

Gallup, G. H. (1928). What shall we do about high school journalism? *Journalism Quarterly, 5(*2), 33-36.

The researcher explores the problems and solutions regarding journalism, which "has found a place in the high school curriculum," he writes. "It is there to stay." With teachers who are well-trained and who teach concise, forceful writing, newspapers can provide an important service to high schools, Gallup states.

Granberg, G.G. (1932). *The present status, trends, and objectives of the high school annual* **(Master's thesis). Greeley, CO: Colorado State Teaching College (now University of Northern Colorado)**

The purpose of this master's thesis was to determine the status of the high school annual, or yearbook—especially its "position in the schools of today." The author also makes suggestions on how to make the yearbook more "worthwhile."

Grumette, J. (1938) Training for citizenship: High school journalism. *The Education Digest 4(3)*, 42-43.

High school students, in short, need to learn "read between the lines" of a newspaper if one is to read it intelligently; therefore, the author explains, journalism should be taught to high school students in a social context. Why does one newspaper place a story on the front page while another paper buries that same story on page 36? If students learn what goes on behind the scenes at newspapers, they will have "merely prepared oneself for intelligent citizenship."

Gustafson, P. (1986, March 12). Fridley case may set precedent on student rights. *Minneapolis Star and Tribune.* **Retrieved from** http://search.proquest.com/docview/417639282?accountid=14214

The article covers Fridley High School's satirical underground newsletter, *Tour De Farce*, and a contentious battle over freedom of speech, following the student publishers' suspension from school. The Fridley School District's policy of requiring approval before publication was later struck down by a District Court judge on the grounds that the policy violated students' First Amendment rights.

Gustafson, P. (1986, July 10). High court ruling may help Fridley win school case. *Minneapolis Star and Tribune.* **Retrieved from** http://search.proquest.com/docview/417714700?accountid=14214

The article reports on a U.S. Supreme Court free speech case relating to an earlier piece, "Tour De Farce." Here, the Supreme Court ruling, in favor of school officials in Bethel, Wash., is cited as potentially aiding the Fridley School District officials in their case at the Court of Appeals, a potential blow for students' free speech rights.

Hall, L. (1984, Summer). Is high school journalism worth keeping? *Communication: Journalism Education Today, 17*(4) 5-7.

The author explores the role of the certification of journalism instructors in improving the quality of journalism education and of high school publications. The article also discusses the relationship of journalism to the English curriculum.

Hague v. Committee for Industrial Organization. 307 U.S. 496 (1939).

The court upheld the rights of people in Jersey City, New Jersey, to distribute labor union information and to speak freely on the streets and in city parks without being required to get a permit per city code. Allowing one city officer the authority to deny a permit based on his own opinion of the activity violated the First Amendment.

Hawthorne, B. (2009). Reporting for duty. In *University Interscholastic League: An illustrated history of 100 years of service.* **Marceline, MO: Walsworth Printing Co.**

This chapter from the centennial commemorative book about the history of the University Interscholastic League discusses Dewitt Reddick, "the most important figure in the evolution of the League's journalism efforts." Reddick spearheaded the UIL's first state journalism conference in May 1929.

Hazelwood School District v. Kuhlmeier. 484 U.S. 260 (1988).

The court determined a school district is legally entitled to exercise authority over school-sponsored productions, including the student newspaper, and especially when the production may disrupt the educational mission of the school.

Herff Jones. (2014). Events calendar: Herff Jones Workshops. Re-trieved from https://www.yearbooks.biz/?event=Calendar.Gallery&category=1
Herff Jones held 48 workshops in 22 states from May 2014 to September in 2014.

Hernandez, D. G. (1994). State of high school journalism: Poor. *Editor & Publisher,* *127(*14), 14.
In her review of the Freedom Forum's 1990s "Death by Cheeseburger" report, Hernandez explains the typical high school journalism teacher is actually an English teacher who has been given the additional responsibility of the school newspaper. As a result, she states, teachers are not certified and unable to teach the subject well. Her article also outlines many of the key points in the Cheeseburger report.

Hines, B. B. (1982). A history of the Columbia Scholastic Press Associa-tion. *The School Press Review,* *57,* 40-72.
This article, excerpted from Barbara Hines' dissertation, details the first six decades (1924-1981) of the Columbia Scholastic Press Association, started by Joseph M. Murphy.

Hoeflinger, D., (2012). Teaching students to be global citizens. *Delta Kappa Gamma Bulletin,* *79*(1), 15-20.
In this article, Hoeflinger highlights the problems related to students' deficiencies in knowledge about the global community and provides strategies for expanding student understanding of the world.

Hortin, L. J. (1949). A workshop for high school editors and advisers. *Journalism Quarterly,* *26*(3), 323-325.
Written by a former director of the Ohio University journalism workshops, the article describes OU's third such workshop in 1948. Students were divided into three groups: newspaper editors, yearbook editors and business managers. Hortin states the challenges for hosting a workshop include staffing, programming and supervising; advantages include letting students and advisers meet their peers and giving students a taste of college life.

Hosty v. Carter. (2001). Case No. 01-C-500. U.S. District Court for the Northern District of Illinois, Eastern Division. Retrieved from *LexisNexis Academic* http://www.lexisnexis.com/hottopics/lnacademic/
The court determined a university administrator was not entitled to qualified immunity for civil damages for telling the printer of the campus newspaper to stop the press run because she didn't like the content of the Governors State University campus newspaper.

Hosty v. Carter. (2003). 325 F. 3d 945. 7th **U.S. Circuit Court of Ap-peals. Retrieved from** *LexisNexis Academic* http://www.lexisnexis.com/hottop-ics/lnacademic/
The court determined the university administrator, Patricia Carter, was not

entitled to qualified immunity because the authority in Hazelwood v. Kuhlmeier did not apply to a university newspaper.

Hosty v. Carter. (2005). 412 F. 3d 731. 7ᵗʰ U.S. Circuit Court of Appeals. Retrieved from *LexisNexis Academic* http://www.lexisnexis.com/hottopics/lnacademic/
This en banc ruling, which means the case was reargued in front of all the appellate court judges, determined Hazelwood v. Kuhlmeier did apply to universities where the student media are subsidized by the university. Further, the law on whether Carter had the legal right to interfere by stopping the press was unclear; she was entitled to qualified immunity from civil damages.

Hosty v. Carter. (2006). 546 U.S. 1169. Supreme Court of the United States. Retrieved from *LexisNexis Academic* http://www.lexisnexis.com/hottopics/lnacademic/
The justices denied the petition to hear the case on appeal, which meant the 2005 opinion became the law of the land and prompted many state legislatures to pass "public forum" laws, which declared college and university campus media subject to First Amendment protection and closed that loophole from Hazelwood v. Kuhlmeier.

Hudson, W.M. (2010, June 12). Roy Bedicheck. *Handbook of Texas Online.* **Retrieved from** http://www.tshaonline.org/handbook/online/articles/fbe21
This article from the Texas State Historical Association profiles Roy Bedichek, the second director of the University Interscholastic League. He encouraged a journalism professor at the University of Texas to begin a high school journalism competition.

Institute of Critical Thinking. (2014). Retrieved from http://www.instituteofcriticalthinking.com
This website, home of the Institute of Critical Thinking and National Center for Logic-Based Therapy, includes information on upcoming workshops designed for practitioners in mental health, teaching, nursing, management, and related fields.

Jacobs, H. C. (1997). The beginning: Franklin College students turn dream into reality. In *Indiana High School Press Association: 75 years of service to scholastic journalism.* **Franklin, IN: Franklin College. Retrieved from** http://ihspa.files.wordpress.com/2013/02/click-here2.pdf.
This 75ᵗʰ anniversary commemorative book provides the history of the Indiana High School Press Association, based at Franklin College.

Jett, B. (2014, Spring). Top 9 tips from 9 top teachers. *Quill & Scroll, 88*(2), 13-15.
This includes best practices tips for classroom teachers in high school student media programs.

Jostens. (2014). *Inspire and educate with Jostens.* Retrieved from http://www.jostens.com/yearbooks/ybk_cp_workshop.html
In 2014, Jostens held its eighth Adviser University in July; its three-day National Workshop in July-August; and 56 regional workshops in 34 states and two Canadian provinces.

Journalism Education Association. (2013, January 22). *Officials sign long-term joint operating agreement with NSPA.* Retrieved from http://jea.org/blog/2013/01/22/officials-sign-long-term-joint-operating-agreement-with-nspa/
The Journalism Education Association and the National Scholastic Press Association signed a joint operating agreement in 2013 for their spring and fall conventions.

Journalism Education Association. (2014a). *Welcome to the Journalism Education Association.* Retrieved from http://www.jea.org/
The welcome page of the Journalism Education Association's website explains its mission statement which is to provide training for high school journalism educators through conferences, workshops, and various print and digital resources.

Journalism Education Association. (2014b). *Journalism curriculum white paper.* Retrieved from http://curriculum.jea.org/journalism-curriculum-white-paper/
This is a white paper in which Journalism Education Association leaders discuss the organization's curriculum initiative, including how the curriculum is designed to tie into Common Core standards and the Partnership for 21st Century Skills framework.

Journalism Education Association. (2014c). *National conventions.* Retrieved from http://jea.org/home/news-events/national-conventions/
This page provides attendance figures for each spring and fall JEA/NSPA workshop since 1990. The biggest spring convention was 5,367 in 2001 in San Francisco, and the biggest fall convention was 6,353 in 2009 in Washington, D.C.

Journalism Education Association (2014d). 2014 *Advisers Institute.* Retrieved from http://jea.org/wp-content/uploads/2014/05/ai-program-2014.pdf
This is the program of sessions held at the Journalism Education Association's 2014 Advisers Institute.

Journalism Education Association's Commission on the Role of Journalism in Secondary Education. (1987). *High school journalism confronts critical deadline.* Blue Springs, MO; Journalism Education Association.
This publication reports on a two-year study on the status of high school journalism and, in particular, the benefits of journalism classes for students compared with students who do not take journalism courses. More than 19,000 students in their freshman year of college were questioned and followed; the results

show students who were involved in high school journalism and/or yearbook scored higher than their counterparts on standardized testing.

Kenney, R. (2009). *COPY! The first 50 years of the Dow Jones Newspaper Fund.* **Princeton, NJ: Dow Jones News Fund.**

Written by Rick Kenney, Scripps Howard Endowed Professor of Journalism at Hampton University, the book outlines the vision of the people who created the Newspaper Fund. The history was published to mark the 50th anniversary of the Fund, which was founded in 1958. It began operation in 1959 and has touched the lives of hundreds of thousands of high school and college students, many of whom went on to distinguished careers in journalism.

Kershner, J.W. (2005). *The elements of news writing.* **Boston, MA: Pierson/Allyn & Bacon Press.**

The college textbook includes the author's five rules of good journalism; how to use the AP stylebook; rules of good grammar; what news is (and is not); active vs. passive voice writing; writing a quality news story; structure of a news story; interview techniques; how to cover a variety of events including speeches, meetings, courts, disasters and obituaries; and how to write feature stories.

Kincaid v. Gibson. (2001). 236 F. 3d 342. 6th U.S. Circuit Court of Appeals. Retrieved from *LexisNexis Academic* http://www.lexisnexis.com/hottopics/lnacademic/

The appellate court's opinion said the Kentucky State University yearbook was a limited public forum, and the administrators' confiscation of it – because they didn't like the content – was a violation of the First Amendment.

Kios, D.M. (2001, Spring). Sparking a passion for journalism in high school. *Nieman Reports,* **55(1), 52-53.**

The author reports on a new ASNE high school journalism project involving collaborative efforts with universities and established media. ASNE launched three multi-year programs to train teachers, nurture aspiring journalists and share information on the Web in an effort to jump-start and revitalize scholastic journalism.

Knight Foundation (2014, August 1). Future of the first amendment survey [Online forum]. Retrived from http://www.knightfoundation.org/future-first-amendment-survey/

Komandosky, S. W. (1981). *The Interscholastic League Press conference: A history,* **1924-1980 (Master's thesis). Denton, TX: North Texas State University.**

Konkle, B. E. (1995, Spring). Critique of death by cheeseburger. *Student Press Review,* **70(3), 31.**

The author critiques the Freedom Forum's report on the status of high school journalism in the early 1990s. His comments are more about the layout and design of the report than the actual content.

Konkle, B. E. (2003, January). *The origination and early years of the South Carolina Scholastic Press Association: 1936-1961*. Research paper presented at the AEJMC Scholastic Journalism Division mid-winter meeting, St. Petersburg, Fla.

The author covers the growth and development of the South Carolina Scholastic Press Association.

Konkle, B. E. (2003, January). *Dr. Laurence Randolph Campbell (1903-1987): His writing and research efforts on behalf of scholastic and professional journalists*. Research paper presented at the Association for Education and Mass Communication summer conference, Scholastic Journalism Division, St. Petersburg, Fla.

This paper explains how Laurence Campbell contributed significantly to scholastic journalism for almost a half-century. In addition to his research, he wrote more than 200 articles for advisers and journalists and devoted countless hours presenting at workshops and judging publications.

Konkle, B. E. (2008, August). *Periodical pursuits: A bibliographical listing of scholastic journalism articles published in noteworthy national education journals*. Research paper presented at the Association for Education and Mass Communication Convention, Chicago, IL.

In the 1900s, more than 700 articles appeared in 33 national education/curriculum periodicals. The articles, in such publications as School Activities and High School Journal, provided hands-on instruction and historical overviews.

Konkle, B. E. (2012, August). *High school and collegiate journalism: The ties that bind (through an AEJMC division, and beyond)*. Research paper presented at the Association for Education and Mass Communication summer convention, Denver, Colo.

This paper examines AEJMC's creation of a Secondary Education Division and almost 80 scholastic journalism articles in AEJMC periodicals.

Konkle, B. E. (2013, August). *A preliminary overview of the early history of high school journalism in the U.S.: 1775-1925*. Research paper presented at the Association for Education and Mass Communication mid-winter meeting, Scholastic Journalism Division, Washington, D.C.

The author offers a look at a century-and-a-half of journalism education and publications. Konkle provides a set of appendices, including the starting dates of hundreds of high school and college publications, articles by Laurence R. Campbell, scholastic journalism articles from 1900-1925, pre-1926 journalism books, theses and dissertations, starting dates of relevant associations and other resources.

Kopenhaver, L.L. & Click, J.W. (2001). High school newspapers still censored thirty years after Tinker. *Journalism and Mass Communication Quarterly*, 78(2), 321-339.

This study revisits Kopenhaver & Click's 1984 and 1988 studies on censorship of high school newspapers. It included schools from 47 states and questioned both newspaper advisers and school administrators. The study found censorship of high school newspapers is widespread, and that three-fourths of all principals questioned said their newspapers are censored.

The study expands on the issues found after Hazelwood and delves into the question of advisers censoring newspapers (only 27 percent of the respondents said their papers were not censored by the principal or the adviser). Both large and small school administrators said the adviser has a professional obligation to eliminate any item in a newspaper that might embarrass the school. The report clearly shows that high school journalism is not free.

Lauffer, K.A. (1997). *Examining the state of high school journalism in Michigan nine years after Hazelwood v. Kuhlmeier* **(Master's thesis). East Lansing, MI: Michigan State University**

This master's thesis examines the impact the 1988 Hazelwood v. Kuhlmeier case had on high school journalism classes nine years after the U.S. Supreme Court decision.

Lifetouch Yearbooks. (2014). Workshops. Retrieved from http://year-books.lifetouch.com/workshops

In 2014, Lifetouch offered three summer workshops in the following states: Tennessee, California and Connecticut.

Maine Department of Education. Commissioner of Education. (2002). *Chapter 127: Instructional Program, Assessment and Diploma Requirements.* **Retrieved from** http://www.maine.gov/sos/cec/rules/05/071/071c127.doc

This document outlines basic instructional requirements, including instruction in research skills, for public elementary and secondary schools in the state of Maine.

McConnell, R., Lira, L.L., Long, K., Gerges, M. & McCollum, B. (2011, September 16). How we think: Thinking critically and creatively and how military professionals can do it better. *Small Wars Journal,* **1-7.**

The authors summarize how cognitive theorists have described critical and creative thinking, in general, and how some military practitioners have applied this kind of thinking. They also propose principles of critical and creative thinking that may be applicable to the military profession, offering a common vocabulary to describe the type of thinking military professionals do.

McCoy, M.L. (1932). Why offer a course in high-school journalism? *School & Society, 36*(921), 244-246.

The author describes how school newspapers provide valuable services to the high school, the students and the community. However, a good newspaper adviser is key, the author says. She advocates for courses in journalism and for lessening the burden for those who advise the student newspaper.

McSweeney, M. T. (1947). High school journalism, *Education, 67*(5), pp. 291-294.

Michigan Interscholastic Press Association. (2004). *History of MIPA.* *In 2004-2005 membership handbook.* **Retrieved from** http://mipamsu.org/wp-content/uploads/pdfs/association/MIPAHandbook05.pdf

This membership handbook provides a brief history of the Michigan Interscholastic Press Association.

Missouri Group (Brooks, B. S., Kennedy, G., Moen, D.R. & Ranly, D). (2002). *News reporting and writing* (7th ed.). **New York: St. Martin's Press.**

The Missouri Group presents a comprehensive textbook on writing for journalism with discussions on what news is (and is not), the basics of writing for multiple journalistic formats, how to interview, how to properly cite resources, placing information in context, reporting with numbers, how to write to be read by the target audience, and basic story and beat writing, among other issues.

Missouri Group. (2014). *News reporting and writing.* **(11th ed.). Boston, MA: Bedford/St. Martin's Press.**

This textbook teaches students how to "work in the new world of digital journalism by using the enduring skills and current savvy that all reporters need." The book tracks stories across different platforms.

Moe, M. W. (1915). Amateur journalism and the English teacher. *The English Journal, 4*(2), pp. 113-115.

Monahan, B.D. & Scoland, G. (1983). Using the computer in high school journalism. *Computers, Reading and Language Arts, 1*(2), 27-29.

The authors describe the use of word processing and database management programs to encourage student involvement in school newspaper and yearbook production.

Moore, M. & Kohlmann, K. (1986). More than we ever wanted to know about high school journalism. *The English Journal, 75(*1), 56-59.

A high school journalism adviser and his senior student editor look back on a year of starting from scratch and how both learned about journalism.

The article shows the frustration of an English teacher who is thrust into the position of also dealing with a journalism class and the occasional crisis that ensues due to inexperience. The teacher decided to run the class in a democratic fashion with the students voting on issues. The opinions of administration and other teachers/staff are expressed in terms of "the newspaper should be a cheerleader for the school." The comments by the editor are enlightening from a student perspective, especially concerning the technical side of production.

Morse v. Frederick. (2007). 551 U.S. 393. Supreme Court of the United States. Retrieved from *LexisNexis Academic* http://www.lexisnexis.com/hot-topics/lnacademic/

The court determined Principal Deborah Morse did not violate Joseph Frederick's First Amendment rights by punishing him for displaying a "Bong Hits 4 Jesus" banner at a school event. The court concluded even though the school board did not demonstrate the banner caused a disruption of the school's educational mission, school boards have the right to prevent speech that encourages illegal drug use.

Nelson, J. (1974). *Captive voices: The report of the Commission of Inquiry into High School Journalism.* **New York: Schocken Books.**

This is a comprehensive look at the state of high school journalism in America circa 1974. The study focuses on censorship, minority participation, and journalism education. The study also makes recommendations to make corrective actions in the three areas. The Commission of Inquiry into High School Journalism concluded that most workshops are too short and "they seldom deal with problems of censorship or minority access. Also, because of tuition requirements, they attract few minorities."

Although some of the materials are now very outdated, some of the information/issues still ring true and have yet to be addressed, especially in terms of how professionals view and interact with high school journalism, the ability to entice racial minorities into the field and the issues of censorship by school administrations.

Newspaper Association of America Foundation. (2008). *High school journalism matters.* **Arlington, VA: NAA Foundation.**

This work in an update to the Dvorak, Lain and Dickson (1994) study that shows a correlation between academic performance and whether a student reported having been involved in high school journalism. This research was sponsored by the NAA Foundation, and the reports were widely distributed to high school teachers.

Olson, L.D., Ommeren, R.V., & Rossow, M. (1992). *The nation's scholastic press association directors describe the state of high school journalism.* **Presentation at the Association for Education in Journalism and Mass Communications annual conference, Aug. 5-9, 1992.**

This is a national survey of Scholastic Press Association directors and their attitudes of encouragement or skepticism about the future of high school journalism.

Olson, K. E. (1938). The province of high school journalism. *NASSP Bulletin, 22*(26), 26-32.

This is a call by the director of the Medill School of Journalism to increase high school journalism programs. He calls on educators to find the best and the brightest students as candidates for the profession. He also calls on high school journalism to remain non-professional in scope so that it helps to vitalize and reinforce English lessons, but he points out the new profession needs well trained professionals and that should be left to the newly-minted journalism schools in colleges and universities.

Olson makes an eloquent appeal for the qualities journalism can teach, especially critical thinking and a broad general knowledge. He also makes an excellent case for how journalism reinforces other lessons/courses including English, civics, economics, world affairs and history. He does, however, call for journalism to remain in the English curriculum.

Oregon Department of Education. (2005). *Career-related learning standards and extended application standard guide for schools to build relevant and rigorous collections of evidence.* **Retrieved from** http://www.ode.state.or.us/teachlearn/certificates/cam/pdfs/implemguide/implementationguide200304.pdf
The Oregon Department of Education published this guide to help teachers and administrators in implementing assessment for the Certificate of Advanced Mastery (CAM) Career-Related Learning Standards (CRLS) and Extended Application Standard (EA). The guide also provides information to help schools meet the state of Oregon's 2006-2007 diploma requirements.

Overbeck, W. (2006). *Major principles of media law: 2006 Edition.* **Belmont, CA: Thomson/Wadsworth.**
This textbook is an overall reference to all topics regarding media law. The chapter cited here discusses the reaction caused by the 9th U.S. Circuit Court's final opinion in Hosty v. Carter , the case in which the court ruled college newspapers were subject to the same amount of school control allowed under the Hazelwood decision.

Partnership for 21st Century Skills (2009). *P21 framework definitions.* **Retrieved from** http://www.p21.org/storage/documents/P21_Framework_Definitions.pdf
This page from the Partnership for 21st Century Skills explains its overarching framework, including the four Cs that are discussed in this book — creativity, critical thinking, collaboration, and communication. The framework also includes information, media, and technology skills and a discussion of how core subjects integrate into broader 21st century learning outcomes.

Patten, J. (1990, September/October). High school confidential: The alarming aftermath of the Hazelwood decision. *Columbia Journalism Review*, **29(3), 6-10.**
This article explores issues facing high school journalism teachers since the Hazelwood decision, how the decision has a dampening impact on school news coverage and how the ruling is causing many students to simply accept prior restraint as a fact, leading to an increase in underground school newspapers.

Paul, R. & Elder, L. (2009). *The miniature guide to critical thinking: Concepts and tools,* **(6th ed.). Tomales, CA: The Foundation for Critical Thinking.**
This pocket-sized booklet includes a definition of critical thinking and sections on thought, reasoning, intellectual standards, problem solving and how to analyze and assess assignments that are meant to display critical thinking. The first guide was published by The Foundation for Critical Thinking in 1999.

Perry, F. M. (1919). The supervision of school publications. *The English Journal, 8*(10), 617-622.

The author discusses (or rants about) the issue of censorship in student publications and how an adviser can deal with the low standards on the high school newspaper without censoring student work. Perry suggests a "press club" as an extra-curricular activity. A faculty leader will guide discussions about content in the club's newspaper.

Perry Education Association v. Perry Local Educators' Association. (1983) 460 U.S. 37. Supreme Court of the United States. Retrieved from *The Oyez Project at IIT Chicago-Kent College of Law* http://www.oyez.org/.

The Perry Education Association was approved by the Indiana school township's teachers as their official union. The collective bargaining agreement forbade the Perry Local Educators' Association, a competing union, from using the school district's internal mail system to distribute materials even though it had that privilege during the pre-election process. The court said the school district had the authority to regulate the use of its mail system and exercising that authority did not violate the First Amendment or the equal protection clause of the 14th Amendment.

Peterson, J. W. (1989). *High school principals and the high school journalism program.* Paper presented at the Association for Education in Journalism and Mass Communication Annual Midwinter Meeting.

A study asked selected high school principals to respond to statements about the value of high school journalism to the high school student and about the rights and responsibilities of the high school journalist. These responses were then checked against such information as whether or not the high school principal had worked on a high school publication and how the principal valued that experience.

Results indicated that years as a principal cannot be used to predict a principal's response to the rights of the student journalist; knowing whether the principal worked on a high school publication can help predict how the principal values high school journalism 20 percent of the time; knowing how principals rate their own high school publication experience can help predict how they value high school journalism today 16 percent of the time and how supportive they are of high school student rights 10 percent of the time. (Seventeen tables of data are included.)

Phillips, B. (2012, Jan. 25). *The 11 things that journalists consider newsworthy.* Mr. Media Training website, retrieved March 10, 2014 from http://www.mrmediatraining.com/2012/01/25/the-11-things-that-journalists-consider-newsworthy/

Provided by a PR firm, this is a succinct list of the 11 elements journalists consider as news worthy, without which there is no news story.

Pylayev, M. (2014, May 1). *10 skills to thrive in today's job market. AOL Jobs.* Retrieved May 6, 2014 from http://www.nextavenue.org/article/2014-04/10-skills-thrive-todays-job-market?utm_source

This describes 10 skills needed for the current job market, which includes many taught in journalism classes, such as accepting criticism, flexibility, problem solving, self-confidence, working well under pressure, teamwork, time management and good communication.

Reavis, W.C. (1922). Student publications in high schools. *The School Review, 30*(7), 514-520.

The author stresses the importance of being thoroughly organized before starting a school publication—from having the right teacher to having the administration's support. The nuts and bolts of operating the student publication are also discussed.

Redford, E.H. (1935). *Bibliography on high school journalism.* **Washington, D.C.: National Association of Student Editors.**

The book is a collection of articles, mimeographs and reports relating to high school journalism and printing high school newspapers. The work is inclusive through 1933 and exempts articles from the Scholastic Editor, the School Press Review and Quill and Scroll.

Redford, E. H. (1940). A philosophy for high school journalism. *School & Society, 51*(1308), 83-86.

The author reports "it is time for (high school) journalism and for us journalism teachers to grow up, get ourselves a philosophy and start to work in term of the ends we are seeking." He believes unorganized thinking about the teaching of high school journalism has occurred because of its quick growth. He offers a list of 23 suggestions for beginning a statement of philosophy for high school journalism, so the curriculum can be justified beyond mere enthusiasm for the topic.

Reinardy, S., Maksl, A., & Filak, V. (2009). A study of burnout and job satisfaction among high school journalism advisers. *Journalism & Mass Communication Educator, 64*(4), 345-356.

The researchers used the Maslach Burnout Inventory to measure burnout among journalism advisers. They found that in general high school journalism advisers are not experiencing burnout at any level. Instead, advisers feel a great deal of satisfaction in what they do.

Richard, P. (1997). *A brief history of the idea of critical thinking,* **Foundation for Critical Thinking, Retrieved from http://www.criticalthinking. org/pages/a-brief-history-of-the-idea-of-critical-thinking/408**

Starting with Socrates, the author examines the history and importance of critical thinking and the results of the collective contribution to human knowledge.

R.O. v. Ithaca City School District. (2009). Case No. 5:05-CV-695. U.S. District Court for the Northern District of New York. Retrieved from *Lexis-Nexis Academic* http://www.lexisnexis.com/hottopics/lnacademic/

The court determined the school district had a legitimate educational reason for denying publication in the student newspaper of a cartoon featuring stick figures in various sex acts because it constituted lewd speech as determined in Bethel School District v. Fraser. Further, the district was justified in refusing to allow distribution of an independent student newspaper featuring the cartoon because it could cause a disruption of the school environment.

R.O. v. Ithaca City School District. (2011). 645 F. 3d 533. 2nd U.S. Circuit Court of Appeals. Retrieved from *LexisNexis Academic* http://www.lexis-nexis.com/hottopics/lnacademic/

The appellate court upheld the Northern District's opinion and said the school district's actions were consistent with the authority granted it in Bethel v. Fraser and Hazelwood v. Kuhlmeier.

Russo, E. M. (1991). Prior restraint and the high school free press. *Journal of Law & Education, 18(*1), 1-25.

This article uses a comparison of the Tinker case to the Hazelwood decision, and states that Tinker did not strip school officials of all authority to regulate high school free speech and created a comparison of students' right to publish versus the traditional defense of school administrators to control content. The article also looks at the legal implications for schools following the Hazelwood decision, focusing on the wording: "material disruption of classwork or involves the disorder or invasion of rights of others."

Ryan, C.M. (1924). A project in high school journalism. *The English Journal. 13(*2), 129-130.

This details the problems of developing a high school newspaper from an English composition class.

Saltzman, J. (1997, January). High school journalism: Downsized into oblivion. *USA Today, 125* (2620).

A university professor writes an essay giving kudos to those trying to keep high school journalism alive.

Schaub, L. (1993). High school journalism programs need support of professional journalists. *Editor & Publisher, 126*(51), 56.

The author offers a list of suggestions on how the professional press can help high school journalism programs. One of the suggestions includes providing classroom volunteers to help with writing, editing, layout and design, and photography.

Schulman, A. (2011, Spring). Hazelwood goes to college. *Student Press Law Center, 33*(2), 36-40.

This legal analysis discussed the effect on federal U.S. appellate courts in determining student press rights after Hazelwood v. Kuhlmeier when the U.S. Supreme Court refused to hear the case. The Student Press Law Center, based in Washington, D.C., is a national advocacy organization for students' First Amendment rights.

Sherwood, H.N. (1924, January). The value of high school publications. *The Educational Review*, *67*, 20-21.

The author discusses the pronounced interest in high school publications in Indiana—so much so, that a state high school press association was created. That said, Sherwood explains why publications are worthwhile: They teach students the art of meeting responsibilities, they bring the community and the school together, they record a permanent record of school activities, and finally, they "create men of worthy ideals."

Simons, M., & Forgette, A. (2013). *Survey of NSPA pacemaker and CSPA crown finalists.* **Unpublished manuscript.**

This is an unpublished survey collected via a Google Form shared by Forgette with Jeff South for chapter 8 in this book.

Sloan, W. D. (1990). Willard Bleyer and propriety. In *Makers of the media mind: Journalism educators and their ideas.* **Hillsdale, NJ: Lawrence Erlbaum Associates.**

Willard Bleyer is one of 38 journalism educators profiled for their contributions to the field. The six areas of specialization are practitioners, historians, philosophers, legists, theorists and methodologists.

SNO Sites. (n.d.) *School newspapers online.* **Retrieved from** http://www. schoolnewspapersonline.com/clients/client-list/high-schools/

This site provides links to all online high school newspapers that are affiliated with School Newspapers Online, which is headquartered in Burnsville, Minn. The links are organized alphabetically by state.

Society of Professional Journalists (2014, May 21). SPJ calls on Pennsylvania school district to restructure high school publications policy. Press release. Retrieved July 1, 2014 from http://www.spj.org/news.asp?ref=1247

In this press release, SPJ leaders expressed dismay at censorship of a school newspaper and asked the board to reconsider their policy since it did not comply with the First Amendment or Pennsylvania's student press rights law.

Society of Professional Journalists. (2002). High school releases journalism teacher. *The Quill*, *90*(6), 47.

A high school journalism teacher in Maryland was slated to lose job after school paper temporarily shut down because of controversial stories in student newspaper.

State of Maine. (n.d.). Department of Education, Commissioner of Education, *Chapter 127: Instructional program, assessment and diploma requirements.* Retrieved from www.maine.gov/sos/cec/rules/05/071/071c127.doc

This document outlines the instructional program requirements, local assessment systems requirements, and secondary school diploma standards for the public schools of the state of Maine, and for private schools that do not receive school approval through accreditation by the New England Association of Schools and Colleges.

Student Press Law Center. (2005, December 7). *High school paper's oral sex article garners mixed reactions.* **[Online forums comment]. Retrieved from** http://www.splc.org/article/2005/12/high-school-papers-oral-sex-article-garners-mixed-reactions

The Columbus North High School newspaper received both praise and criticism after it printed a feature on oral sex. The medical and psychological risks of participating in oral sex were discussed, and the article included statistics about the number of U.S. teenagers engaging in the behavior.

The Poynter Institute for Media Studies. (2014). Website. Retrieved from http://www.poynter.org

Center for media training for journalists ranging in experience from junior high through secondary schools, higher education and professional development. Poynter is dedicated to teaching journalists and inspiring media leaders through webinars, seminars and the interactive NewsU online classroom. Poynter promotes excellence and integrity in the practice of journalism and stands for a journalism that informs citizens and enlightens public discourse.

Thompson, R. & Bowen, C. (2009). *The grammar of the shot.* **Burlington, MA: Focal Press**

A textbook, "Grammar of the Shot," teaches broadcast journalists the skills they need to build a successful visual story that flows smoothly and makes sense to the audience. The basic building blocks essential for successful shot composition, screen direction, depth cues, lighting, screen direction, camera movement, and many general practices that make for richer, multi-layered visuals are included.

Tinker v. Des Moines Independent Community School District. (1969). 393 U.S. 503. Supreme Court of the United States. Retrieved from *LexisNexis Academic* http://www.lexisnexis.com/hottopics/lnacademic/

This is a 1969 decision by the U.S. Supreme Court that decided a case of free speech in high schools. In it, the court ruled high school students do have the rights guaranteed under the First and Fourteenth Amendments, and that schools cannot implement rules against personal expression unless it can be proven the expression would substantially interfere with educational activities.

Turnbull, A. T. & Baird, R.N. (1956). Summer publications workshops idea succeeds. *School Activities, 27*(9), 299-300.

These authors, from Ohio University, describe that college's summer workshop, which by the mid-1900s was the largest in the country with 943 people representing 229 schools from 11 states.

United Amateur Press Association. (n.d.). *Membership guidelines and detailed description of the united Amateur Press Association of America.* **Retrieved from** http://uapaa.jarday.com/guidelines.html

This contains history and membership information for anyone who wishes to join the association, which comprises creative writers, poets, printers and desktop publishers.

University Interscholastic League. (n.d.). *History of the UIL.* **Retrieved from** http://www.uiltexas.org/history.
The University Interscholastic League was formed in 1913. As the article states, the UIL "has grown into the largest interschool organization of its kind in the world."

Walsh, M. (1994). Barriers faced by student newspapers detailed. *Education Week, 13*(24), 6.
The author discusses the main points of the Freedom Forum's report on the status of high school journalism in the early 1990s. He points out that the report stresses high school journalists face censorship challenges.

Walsworth Yearbooks. (2014). *Workshop central.* **Retrieved from** http://www.walsworthyearbooks.com/idea-file/conventions-workshops/workshop-central/.
Walsworth held 30 workshops from March to October 2014 in 20 states.

Warren, J. (1986, April 20). A festering Fallbrook awaits next hatchet job. *Los Angeles Times.* **Retrieved from** http://articles.latimes.com/1986-04-20/local/me-1100_1_hatchet-job
Warren's article covers the controversy surrounding Fallbrook High School's underground newspaper, the Hatchet Job. Administrators believed the material was obscene and suspended the publishers, who subsequently sued on the grounds that their First Amendment rights were being violated. The ruling in favor of the students ultimately opened up a larger discourse about free speech rights in the school.

Watts, L. (2003, April). The case they've waited for? *American Journalism Review, 25*(3), 16.
This is a look at the case of the Wooster Blade in Ohio, in which a high school newspaper staff was hoping to overturn the 1988 Hazelwood decision by suing the school district for violating the student's First Amendment rights.
The case involves prior review, which the students argued was the same as prior restraint; the school administration argued the school newspaper was a limited public forum.

Weigle, C.F. (1957). Influence of high school journalism on choice of career. *Journalism, & Mass Communication Quarterly, 34*(1), 39-45
The author conducts a survey of California High School advisers about career suggestions made to students. Weigle finds they underestimate journalism as a career, and there is a predominance of girls on publication staffs. When former high school newspaper editors are interviewed during their first year of college, only 10% say they are considering journalism as a career.

Weinberg, S. (1996). *The reporter's handbook: An investigator's guide to documents and techniques.* (3rd ed). New York: St. Martin's Press.

This is a handbook on how journalists can use documents to more accurately report. The work includes using paper trails, secondary sources, computer resources (such as databases, depository libraries and government data resources), international resources and how to investigate government, for-profit and not-for-profit organizations.

Wells, G.C. & McCalister, W.H. (1930*). Student publications.* New York: A.S. Barnes and Co.

This book describes methods of organization for media staff and the staff's duties. Four kinds of publications are discussed and have chapters: newspaper, yearbook, handbook and magazine. It was created as a "practical handbook" for the teacher-adviser.

Williams, T.M. (2013, January-February). Education for critical thinking. *Military Review. 93*(1), 49-54.

The importance of teaching critical thinking is especially applied to military education but applicable to all secondary education. The article specifically states methods of teaching and applying critical thinking exercises which are separated from knowledge and content, focusing more on the ability to question and argue.

Widmar v. Vincent. (1981). 454 U.S. 263. Supreme Court of the United States. Retrieved from Cornell University Law School Legal Information Institute http://www.law.cornell.edu/

The court determined a student religious organization could not be prohibited from using public university facilities for meetings because such a regulation is not content neutral and the university did not show a compelling state interest for the restriction by invoking the constitution's establishment clause.

Winitch, V. (1981). *Centering on: The study of newspaper journalism in the high schools.* New York: New York City Teacher Centers Consortium.

This booklet is divided into two sections, the first of which focuses on the purpose and importance of newspapers in a free-thinking democratic society. The first section also discusses responsibilities of journalists, a code of journalism standards, approaches to writing news, slanted reporting, objective reporting, elements of news stories, the 5 W's and H in news stories, news leads, news story structure, feature stories, techniques of interviewing, and provides a checklist for news stories and feature stories.

The second section presents guidelines for community-focused journalism projects.

Yang, N. (2014, March 11). Critical thinking. *Editor & Publisher.* Retrieved from http://www.editorandpublisher.com/PrintArticle/Critical-Thinking2014-03-10T12-26-34

Two journalists – a college senior and a near-retirement editor – discuss the importance of critical thinking in their work. Both contend journalists are at their best when they combine intelligence, critical thinking skills and curiosity, no matter what the delivery format of the news.

Yearbook Architecture. (1947). Hamilton, OH: The Champion Paper & Fibre Co.

This hard-cover publication was provided to yearbook staffs by an Ohio printer. Practical guidelines are provided on how to build an annual. The book also discusses trends in yearbook publishing.

Yoon-Hendricks, A. & Rodriguez, M. (2013). *A brief history of cherubs: The Medill cherubs program through the years.* Retrieved from http://cherubs. medill.northwestern.edu/2013/a-brief-history-of-cherubs/

"Cherubs" is the nickname for students who have attended the Medill-Northwestern Journalism Institute, which was started in 1934.

Zeeck, D.A. (2006, May-July). *Transforming high school journalism. The American Editor*, Columbia, MO: American Society for Newspaper Editors, p. 2.

This is a report on six years of ASNE high school journalism initiatives focusing on online and skills-based programs for teachers. The project targeted instructing and empowering high school advisers to produce better newspapers, inspiring future journalists and knowledgeable readers, and incubating school newspapers to help produce a diverse pool of professional talent.

The report is a bit sparse in real data. Much of the information came from two advisers in Tacoma, Wash., and New York, N.Y. The only comments from advisers were positive, and there were no negative or dissenting opinions; it did not include any teachers who gave information about their programs.

Profile 6

CHICHI PIERCE

Miami Beach Senior High (Public; 2,500 students, grades 9-12)
Miami Beach, Fla.
TV Production/Film teacher

Broadcast and film adviser Chichi Pierce expends a lot of energy keeping the lid on what she calls "chaotic creativity." From three contiguous rooms she monitors her 35 students' progress the best she can, bouncing like a pinball from one student to another.

"It's a madhouse," she said. "When you come into my classroom – when it looks like no one's busy – everyone's actually doing

their part of a larger thing. Some days it takes me the whole period, working with kids, to move across the classroom."

Pierce, 57, a former New York TV producer, just finished her eighth year teaching. It's her second year at Miami Beach Senior High, and she said she loves the energy of her students, yet there are roadblocks to doing the job the way she'd like.

"One of my biggest challenges," she said, "is how the class is labeled, not as academic, but as an elective. It's not considered a serious subject by some of the students, the administration, and even other teachers."

And because it's an elective, she said, the class sizes are large, and many students who have little interest in TV or film, but have few other choices, land in her class. This overcrowding, she said, can lead to behavioral problems.

"Part of the problem is the physicality of my room," Pierce said. "My room is off the library, and there are two separate smaller rooms and a studio we use. The space isn't meant for more than 18 kids."

To attend broadcast classes at her former high school, William H. Turner Technical Arts High School in Miami, students had to be accepted into the program, Pierce said. TV was a respected concentration of study, and the administration made sure everyone at the school watched the broadcasts, she said.

"At MBSH, technically, it doesn't even get to all rooms, and if it does, some teachers don't even turn it on," Pierce said.

And that can be disappointing for the five classes of TV students Pierce works with, she said, from beginning students to those who shoot, write and edit magazine-style segments for the weekly broadcast, "The View at Miami Beach," at WMBH-TV.

"My 11th-grade students are really into it," Pierce said. "They get excited about it and are good at it. We just need to get people to watch it."

The 11-minute program includes world, national and local news, sports, school announcements and "Hey, Miami!", a cultural piece that explores weekly events in the cosmopolitan city. MBSH, with more than 2,500 students, is a diverse community in itself, Pierce said.

"It's like 66 percent minority – maybe more. There's a large Latino population, some blacks and Chinese, and lots of Europeans

– Turkish, French, Italian. They all deal with each other, too; they seem to take interest in each other. And the Miami Beach culture is different than anywhere else," Pierce said.

This diversity allows for creativity at many different levels, she said.

"We try to do a show that's a little more hip," Pierce said, "a la Stephen Colbert. We have a couple students who are really smart, and really funny."

That sense of humor has sometimes landed the broadcast students and their adviser in a bit of hot water. Pierce said the administration has been critical about a few of the students' choices, and has made efforts to control content.

"A lot of times we went overboard, and I understand them being upset," Pierce said, citing a segment that featured a mafia shooting to preview an upcoming event in the city. "It, unfortunately, ran the same week of the Connecticut shootings," she said.

"And there were the recurring bits about the missing plane."

Still, Pierce said, there are many things of which to be proud.

One achievement she's particularly happy about is the growth of the broadcast program, and the increasing student interest in her classes, she said.

"But when I teach, it's a serious thing," she said. "I guess it's because I used to do this professionally. When I got here last year, I almost walked out. There were fewer kids, and many of them were looking for an easy A."

"I make the kids take a film history class, and in the introductory classes, we spend a lot of time learning the paper part of it, script writing and production management. Kids also learn basic camera and editing skills," Pierce said.

Students who stick with TV and film classes also can take part in an annual film festival at the school.

"We just finished the second one," she said, "and the films were really, really good. It was a packed house; I asked professionals I know to judge the films."

Pierce said her biggest wish is that students understand "what an amazing medium" TV is. "It's not just entertainment. There are so many ways to make a living, whether you're working on the Web, or streaming video or audio."

Before becoming a teacher, Pierce worked with NBC journalist

Linda Ellerbee, produced shows for Nickelodeon, and ran her own production company. She said she thinks it's important to involve her students in real, outside projects, so they can see opportunity.

She and her students have recently worked with the Cleveland Orchestra to produce an educational documentary, and were filmed by a local filmmaker as they shot an Art Deco walk in Miami. Students are currently working on the MBSH graduation video.

"Once you know how it works, you can use it for anything," Pierce said.

Addendum A

The status of high school news media in the 21ˢᵗ century

(20 years after Death by Cheeseburger and 40 years after Captive Voices)
Questionnaire for high school teachers and/or those advising student media[1]

Demographic Information
(including instructor/adviser background in journalism)

Please answer the following questions about yourself

1. Do you have journalism education certification through an outside organization, such as NSPA (National Scholastic Press Association)?
    Yes
    No

2. If yes, which specific organization; if no, skip to the next question.

    _____

3. Do you have professional media experience?
    Yes
    No

4. If yes, explain briefly; if no, skip to the next question.

_____

5. Did you take journalism courses in college? If so, approximately
    how many classes?
    1-3
    4-6
    7-9
    10 or more
    Not applicable

6. How many journalism workshops have you attended since be-
    coming a high school journalism instructor and/or student media
    adviser?
    None
    1-5
    6-10
    11-15
    16-20
    20+
    Not applicable

7. What are the requirements for teaching journalism in your state?
    None
    Below 15 hours of course work
    Between 15-19 hours of course work
    At least 20 hours of course work
    Other (please explain if your state includes another variation of
    requirements not included above) _____
    _____
    Don't know

8. In which state do you currently teach?

    _____

9. Do you believe your journalism course(s) or your school's student
    media are in danger of being eliminated?
    Yes
    No
    Don't know

10. If yes, why? Check all that apply. If no, skip to the next question.
Lack of funding
Lack of student interest
Emphasis is on required (common core) curriculum
Lack of resources (equipment, space, etc.)
Antagonistic administration
Resistance from school board
Resistance from high school student council/government
Resistance from Parent-Teacher Association
Belief of many that journalism is "dying" and no longer relevant
Other/Optional Comment _____

11. What do you believe is the *most* important purpose of having student media in high schools? **(Check only one.)**
Promote positive things about the school
Report both the good and the bad
Publicize school events, activities
Provide forum for student expression
Teach skills, such as the JEA's "communication, critical thinking, creativity and collaboration"
Prepare students for a mass communications career
Other (please state) _____

12. How worried are you that your journalism teaching and/or student media advising will be reprimanded because of student-created work that creates a controversy?
Constantly
Sometimes
Not at all

13. You became a media adviser or journalism instructor because (Check one.)
You were hired to do the job.
You were assigned to do the job.
You applied when you were hired.
You applied while already teaching.
Other (please state) _____

14. What best describes your situation? (Check one.)
I am a full-time journalism teacher; all my classes are journalism-related.
I teach journalism and other subject areas.
I teach no journalism classes; student media work is done outside the school day.
Other (please state) _____

15. How are you paid for your student media duties? (Check one.)
    In addition to my basic teacher pay, I receive a stipend for the student media I advise.
    I receive basic teacher pay with no additional stipend for the student media I advise.
    I am not a teacher, but I am paid a stipend for the student media I advise.
    I volunteer my time working with student media.
    Other (please state) _____

16. Sex: Male _____ Female_____

17. Age:_____

18. How many years as a high school teacher? _____

19. How many years as a high school journalism course and/or student media adviser? _____

Please answer the following questions about your school

20. Which of the following approximately describes your school's setting? (Check one.)
    City with a population of 150,000 or more
    Smaller city or suburb with a population less than 150,000
    Rural or consolidated school district
    Other (please state) _____

21. How many students are enrolled at your high school?
    Fewer than 100
    101-500
    501-1000
    1001-1500
    1501-2000
    2001-3000
    3001-4000
    4001-5000
    5001+

22. My school is a
    Public school
    Public charter school
    Private school

23. What is the approximate breakdown of minority/non-minority students at your school?
Predominantly minority
Predominantly nonminority
Roughly an even balance
Don't know

Please answer the following questions about student media and/or journalism courses at your school

24. Do you and others who teach and/or advise journalism students follow the four C's of the Journalism Education Association: Critical thinking skills, collaboration, creativity and communication? (Check one.)
Yes
No
No, but we follow this: _____
Don't know

25. Media literacy is taught in your course(s)
Taught in a separate course
Taught as a section in other courses
Other (please state) _____
Don't Know

26. Does your school publish a literary magazine?
Yes
No
Don't know

27. Does your school offer film studies?
Yes
No
Don't know

28. Does your school have a radio station that plays *only* music?
Yes
No
Don't know

29. Does your school belong to any scholastic student media or journalism associations, national or state?
Yes
No
Don't know

30. If yes, which one(s)? (Check all that apply.) If no, skip to the next question.
Journalism Education Association
National Scholastic Press Association
Columbia Scholastic Press Association
A regional scholastic press association
A state scholastic press association
A local scholastic press association
Other (please state) _____

31. Have your student-created media been entered in any contests in the past five years?
Yes
No
Don't know

32. If yes, how successful have your students been? Check all that apply. If no, go to the next question.

Local award(s)
Regional award(s)
State award(s)
National award(s)

33. What contributions to your high school student media are made by university journalism programs? Check all that apply.
Guest speakers
Teaching materials
Scholarships
Workshop sessions
Other help (please state) _____
No contributions

34. What contributions to your student media are made by working professionals?
Guest speakers
Funds for materials
Workshop sessions
Internships
Scholarships
Other help (please state) _____
No contributions

35. ***Approximately*** how many journalism courses ***per school year*** are offered at your high school?
None
1-2
3-4
5-6
7-8
9-10
11 or more
Don't know

36. ***Approximately*** how many students are enrolled in journalism courses during each semester?
1-25 students
26-50 students
51-75 students
76-100 students
More than 100 students
Don't know
Not applicable

37. Which of the following subjects are discussed as part of your journalism course(s) or student media advising? (Check all that apply.)
Freedom of the press and the First Amendment in general
Censorship in general
Freedom of the press as it relates to student journalists
The role of the news media in a democratic society
Ethics
None of the above
Not applicable

38. How would you assess the ***ability range*** of your journalism students or staff? (Check one.)
A diverse mixture
Mostly high achieving
Mostly low achieving
Don't know

39. How would you assess the motivation of your journalism students or staff toward creating news media in any form? (Check one.)
    A diverse mixture
    Mostly high motivation
    Mostly low motivation
    Don't know

40. In the journalism courses you teach and/or with the student media you advise, what skills are being taught? (Check all that apply.)
    Use of social media
    Use of video editing equipment
    How to shoot video
    How to shoot photos
    Use of design software
    Use of photo-editing software
    How to create Audio
    Other (please state) _____

Now please answer questions about specific media that you advise at your school. If a section does not pertain to you, you will be asked to skip to the next one. Please complete the sections that pertain to the area in which you teach or advise. Finally, after answering the appropriate section(s), you will be asked to answer four questions. The sections go in this order:
- Newspaper (print and/or online)
- Magazine (print and/or online)
- Television News (broadcast in-house, on cable and/or online [with social media such as YouTube])
- Radio News (broadcast and/or online [with social media such as YouTube])
- Yearbook (print and/or online)

NEWSPAPER. If you advise or teach students who publish a student newspaper (hard copy), an online newspaper or both, answer the following questions. *If not, skip this section, and go to Question No. 55.*
41. What are the requirements, if any, for students to participate on newspaper staff?
    Must be enrolled in the relevant journalism course
    Must have taken a journalism course
    Anyone welcome
    Other (please state) _____

42. Who in the school has the ***very final OK*** of student-created work to be published?
    The student editor
    The student media adviser/instructor
    The school administration
    Other (please state) _____

43. What is the frequency of the print publication?
    More than once a week
    Once a week
    Every two weeks
    Monthly
    Less than monthly
    Not applicable

44. What is the frequency of online publication?
    Daily
    More than once a week
    Once a week
    Every two weeks
    Monthly
    Less than monthly
    Not applicable

45. Do you as instructor or adviser place any limitations on what can be published?
    Yes
    No

46. If yes, what limitations? (Check all that apply.) If no, skip to the next question.
    Potentially libelous/libelous
    Invasion of privacy
    Obscenity/sexual content
    Language or visuals that cause a material and substantial (physical) disruption to the learning process
    You (or others) have a legitimate pedagogical concern about the language or visuals
    Too controversial, inappropriate for our school community
    Too controversial, inappropriate for our broader community
    Content critical of the school (its employees, student clubs, athletics, etc.)
    Other (please state) _____

47. Does the administration do a pre-publication review?
   Always
   Sometimes
   Never

48. What kinds of stories are typically covered? (Check all that apply.)
   Sports
   Extracurricular
   Local educational problems or issues
   School social news
   Local community news
   National issues
   International issues
   Profiles
   Other (please state) _____

49. Do you believe your student newspaper represents student opinions?
   Yes
   No
   Don't know

50. Do you believe your student newspaper adequately covers topics of interest for your student body?
   Yes
   No
   Don't know

51. Do you have any written guidelines that help you and your staff decide which topics are appropriate for a high school audience?
   Yes
   No
   Don't know

52. If yes, who created these guidelines? If no, skip to the next question.
   Within the school by faculty
   Within the school by administration
   By county or local Board of Education
   By state Board of Education
   Other (please state) _____

53. Because previous research shows concern about the lack of minority participation in high school student media, could you *estimate* the amount of minority participation within the medium you advise?
Predominantly minority
Predominantly nonminority
Roughly an even balance
Don't know

54. How is this student medium funded?
School administration
Advertising
Fund-raising efforts among students and/or community
Mixture of the above
Other (please state) _____

MAGAZINE. If you advise or teach students who publish a student *magazine* **(hard copy), an online** *magazine* **or both, answer the following questions.** *If not, skip this section and go to Question No. 68.*

55. What are the requirements, if any, for students to participate on magazine staff?
Must be enrolled in the relevant journalism course
Must have taken a journalism course
Anyone welcome
Other (please state) _____

56. Who in the school has the *very final OK* of student-created work to be published?
The student editor
The student media adviser/instructor
The school administration
Other (please state) _____

57. What is the frequency of the print publication?

Once a week
Every two weeks
Monthly
Less than Monthly
Other (please state) _____
Not applicable

58. What is the frequency of the online publication?
Once a week
Every two weeks
Monthly
Less than Monthly
Other (please state) _____
Not applicable

59. Do you as instructor or adviser place any limitations on what can be published in the magazine?
Yes
No

60. If yes, what limitations? Check all that apply. If no, skip to the next question.
Potentially libelous/libelous
Invasion of privacy
Obscenity/sexual content
Speech that causes a material and substantial (physical) disruption to the learning process
You (or others) have a legitimate pedagogical concern about the speech
Too controversial, inappropriate for our school community
Too controversial, inappropriate for our broader community
Content critical of the school (its employees, student clubs, athletics, etc.)
Other (please state) _____

61. Does the administration place any limitations on what can be published?
Always
Sometimes
Never

62. What kinds of articles are typically covered?
Sports
Extracurricular
Local educational problems or issues
School social news
Local community news
National issues
International issues
Profiles
Other (please state) _____

63. Do you believe your student magazine represents student opinions?
Yes
No
Don't know

64. Do you believe your student magazine adequately covers topics of interest for your student body?
Yes
No
Don't know

65. Do you have any written guidelines that help you and your magazine staff decide which topics are appropriate?
Yes
No
Don't know

66. If yes, who created these guidelines? If no, skip to the next question.
Within the school by faculty
Within the school by administration
By county or local Board of Education
By state Board of Education
Other (please state) _____

67. Because previous research shows concern about the lack of minority participation in high school student media, could you please *estimate* the minority participation with the medium you advise?
Predominantly minority
Predominantly nonminority
Roughly an even balance
Don't know

68. How is this student medium funded?
School administration
Advertising
Fund-raising efforts among students and/or community
Mixture of the above
Other (please state) _____

TELEVISION NEWS. If you advise or teach students who broadcast a television news show in-house, on cable or online, answer the following questions. *If not, skip this section and go to Question No. 86.*

69. What are the requirements, if any, for students to participate on television news staff?
    Must be enrolled in the relevant journalism course
    Must have taken a journalism course
    Anyone welcome
    Other (please state) _____

70. Who in the school has the *very final OK* of student-created work to be aired?
    The student editor/producer
    The student media adviser/instructor
    The school administration
    Other (please state) _____

71. Frequency of on-air (via any method: local cable, in-house, online)?
    Daily
    More than once a week
    Once a week
    Every two weeks
    Monthly
    Less than Monthly

72. Do you as instructor or adviser place any limitations on what can be aired?
    Yes
    No

73. If yes, what limitations? Check all that apply. If no, skip to the next question.
    Potentially libelous/libelous
    Invasion of privacy
    Obscenity/sexual content
    Language or visuals that cause a material and substantial (physical) disruption to the learning process
    You (or others) have a legitimate pedagogical concern about the language or visuals
    Too controversial, inappropriate for our school community
    Too controversial, inappropriate for our broader community

Content critical of the school (its employees, student clubs, athlet-
ics, etc.)
Violation of FCC rules/regulations
Other (please state) _____

74. Does the administration place any limitations on what can be
aired?
Yes
No

75. What kinds of stories are typically covered?
Sports
Extracurricular
Local educational problems or issues
School social news
Local community news
National issues
International issues
Profiles
Other (please state) _____

76. Do you believe your student television programs represent student
opinions?
Yes
No
Don't know

77. Do you believe your student television programs adequately cover
topics of interest for the student body?
Yes
No
Don't know

78. Do you have any written guidelines that help you and your staff
decide which topics are appropriate to cover?
Yes
No
Don't know

79. If yes, who created these guidelines? If no, skip to the next question.
Within the school by faculty
Within the school by administration
By county or local Board of Education
By state Board of Education
Other (please state) _____

80. Because previous research shows concern about the lack of minority participation in high school student media, could you please *estimate* the minority participation with the medium you advise?
Predominantly minority
Predominantly nonminority
Roughly an even balance
Don't know

81. How is this student medium funded?
School administration
Advertising
Fund-raising efforts among students and/or community
Mixture of the above
Other (please state) _____

RADIO NEWS. If you advise or teach students who broadcast a radio news program in-house or online, answer the following questions. *If not or if your radio station plays only music, skip this section and go to Question No. 95*.

82. What are the requirements, if any, for students to participate on radio news staff?
Must be enrolled in the relevant journalism course
Must have taken a journalism course
Anyone welcome
Other (please state) _____

83. Who in the school has the *very final OK* of student-created work to be aired?
The student editor
The student media adviser/instructor
The school administration
Other (please state) _____

84. Frequency of programming?
Daily
More than once a week
Once a week
Every two weeks
Monthly
Less than monthly

85. Do you as instructor or adviser place any limitations on what can be aired?
    Yes
    No

86. If yes, what limitations? Check all that apply. If no, skip to the next question.
    Potentially libelous/libelous
    Invasion of privacy
    Obscenity/sexual content
    Language that causes a material and substantial (physical) disruption to the learning process
    You (or others) have a legitimate pedagogical concern about the language
    Too controversial, inappropriate for our school community
    Too controversial, inappropriate for our broader community
    Content critical of the school (its employees, student clubs, athletics, etc.)
    Violation of FCC rules/regulations
    Other (please state) _____

87. Does the administration place any limitations on what can be aired?
    Yes
    No

88. What kinds of stories are typically covered?
    Sports
    Extracurricular
    Local educational problems or issues
    School social news
    Local community news
    National issues
    International issues
    Profiles
    Other (please state) _____

89. Do you believe your student radio programming represents student opinions?
    Yes
    No
    Don't know

90. Do you believe your student radio programming adequately covers topics of interest for your student body?
    Yes
    No
    Don't know

91. Do you have any written guidelines that help you and your staff decide what topics are appropriate?
    Yes
    No
    Don't know

92. If yes, who created these guidelines? If no, skip to the next question.
    Within the school, by faculty
    Within the school, by administration
    By county or local Board of Education
    By State Board of Education
    Other (please state) _____

93. Because previous research shows concern about the lack of minority participation in high school student media, could you please *estimate* the minority participation with the medium you advise?
    Predominantly minority
    Predominantly nonminority
    Roughly an even balance
    Don't know

94. How is this student medium funded?
    School administration
    Advertising
    Fund-raising efforts among students and/or community
    Mixture of the above
    Other (please state) _____

YEARBOOK. If you advise or teach students who publish a student yearbook (hard copy), an online yearbook or both, answer the following questions. *If not, skip this section and go to Question No. 106.*

95. What are the requirements, if any, for students to participate on yearbook staff?
    Must be enrolled in the relevant journalism course
    Must have taken a journalism course
    Anyone welcome
    Other (please state) _____

96. Who in the school has the *very final OK* of student-created work to be published?
    The student editor
    The student media adviser/instructor
    The school administration
    Other (please state)

97. Do you as instructor or adviser place any limitations on what can be published in the yearbook?
    Yes
    No

98. If yes, what limitations? (Check all that apply.) If no, please skip to the next question.
    Potentially libelous/libelous
    Invasion of privacy
    Obscenity/sexual content
    Language or photo that causes a material and substantial (physical) disruption to the learning process
    You (or others) have a legitimate pedagogical concern about the language or photo
    Too controversial, inappropriate for our school community
    Too controversial, inappropriate for our broader community
    Other (please state) _____

99. Does the administration do a pre-publication review?
    Yes
    No

100. Do you believe your student yearbook represents students'
wishes?
Yes
No
Don't know

101. Do you believe your student yearbook adequately covers topics
of interest for your student body?
Yes
No
Don't know

102. Do you have any written guidelines that help you and your yearbook staff decide what topics are appropriate for a high school
audience?
Yes
No

103. If yes, who created these guidelines? If no, skip to the next question.
Within the school, by faculty
Within the school, by administration
By county or local Board of Education
By state Board of Education
Other (please state) _____

104. Because previous research shows concern about the lack of
minority participation in high school student media, could you please
estimate the minority participation with the medium you advise?
Predominantly minority
Predominantly nonminority
Roughly an even balance
Don't know

105. How is this student medium funded?
School administration
Advertising
Fund-raising efforts among students and/or community
Mixture of the above
Other (please state) _____

Almost Done! Final 4 Questions

106. If you believe something hinders your job as a journalism instructor and/or student media adviser, what do you think is the problem? Check all that apply.
No support from other faculty
No support from administration
No support from school district
No support from state Board of Education
No support of parents
Interference from parents
No interest from students
No money for updating necessary equipment
Not applicable

107. If you are willing to be interviewed for our report on the status of high school journalism, complete the following information. If not, skip to the next optional question, No. 107.
Name:
School:
City:
Phone:
Email address:

OPEN-ENDED QUESTION (Optional)

108. Do you have suggestions on how scholastic journalism can be improved?

109. If you would like to be entered in the drawing to win one of five $100 Visa gift cards, please enter the following information:
Name:
Email address:
Phone:

Endnotes

1. Some questions for this survey were modified from questions used in the 1974 report *Captive Voices: High School Journalism in America* convened by the Robert F. Kennedy Memorial, prepared by Jack Nelson and distributed by

Schocken Books, New York, and from questions used in the 1994 report *Death by Cheeseburger: High School Journalism in the 1990s and beyond* convened and published by the Freedom Forum.

Addendum B

The status of high school news media in the 21st century

Questionnaire for high school teachers and/or those advising student media

Feb. 8, 2014

Dear high school journalism teacher and/or media adviser:

      You have been chosen from the membership of the Journalism Education Association to participate in an important survey about the current status of high school journalism. No matter what type of media you advise or what kind of journalism courses you teach, the survey, which was created by a member of the Society of Professional Journalists' Education Committee, should take less than 10 minutes to complete, and your anonymity is guaranteed.

      The survey does offer you an opportunity to comment at the end of the survey via an open-ended question; this is optional, however. Also, for those participants who wish to be included, the researchers will hold a drawing for five $100 Visa gift cards.

- If you are a Newspaper advisor, please follow this link:
- If you are a Magazine advisor, please follow this link:
- If you are a TV advisor, please follow this link:
- If you are a Radio advisor, please follow this link:
- If you are a Yearbook advisor, please follow this link:

- If you advise more than one medium, please answer the multi-advise link:

Why this study now? Forty years ago, the Robert F. Kennedy Memorial created a commission to investigate the status of high school journalism; the members published their report *Captive Voices: The Report of the Commission of Inquiry into High School Journalism* and expressed concerns about administrative censorship, low minority participation and ill-prepared instructors, making suggestions for improvements in general. Twenty years later in 1994, the Freedom Forum created the publication *Death by Cheeseburger: High School Journalism in the 1990s and Beyond,* investigating the status of scholastic journalism 20 years after the Kennedy study; those who created the study expressed similar concerns and also made suggestions for improvements.

Now, 20 years after *Cheeseburger*, the education committee of the Society of Professional Journalists wants to look again at the status of high school journalism. Has anything changed? Ultimately, the survey seeks to find answers to how SPJ can help high school teachers accomplish their goals for their journalism teachers. To take the survey:

If you have questions about the survey, call one of the researchers listed below. Thank you in advance for your participation!

Sincerely,

Rebecca Tallent, Ed.D.
Associate Professor
School of Journalism and Media
University of Idaho
(208) 596-9507(cell)
rtallent@frontier.com
(On sabbatical this semester)

Lee Anne Peck, Ph.D.,
Associate Professor
Journalism and Mass Communications
School of Communication
University of Northern Colorado
(970) 351-2635 (office)
leeanne.peck@unco.edu

The Authors

Tracy Anderson teaches journalism at Central Michigan University. She has more than a decade of reporting experience and continues a significant freelance career. She discovered her passion for journalism as a high school junior when she attended events organized by the Michigan Interscholastic Press Association. Anderson holds bachelor's and master's degree from Central Michigan University.

David Burns, Ph.D., is an associate professor in the Communication Arts Department at Salisbury University. He is a past president of the SPJ Maryland Pro Chapter, member of the SPJ Education Committee and occasional contributor to *Quill* magazine. A former television producer, Burns has taught journalism and communication courses and conducted new media workshops to mid-career corporate and media professionals and college students in the United States, Poland, Russia, Jordan, the United Arab Emirates, Qatar and Afghanistan. Burns also has led summer television reporting workshops for middle and high school students for the Maryland Scholastic Press Association. He got his start as his high school's yearbook photographer.

Butler Cain, Ph.D., is an assistant professor of Mass Communication at West Texas A&M University in Canyon, Texas. He received his B.A. and M.A. degrees in Journalism, and a Ph.D. in Media History, from the University of Alabama. Butler spent several years as a broadcast journalist, including a decade as news director of Alabama Public Radio in Tuscaloosa, Alabama. Before arriving at West Texas A&M, he taught English language writing skills in South Korea. He has been a member of the Society of Professional Journalists since 1997. He began his career in journalism as the humor columnist for his high school newspaper.

Kym Fox is a senior lecturer and coordinator of the journalism sequence in the School of Journalism and Mass Communication at Texas State University. She worked at the San Antonio Express-News as the deputy metro editor before joining the Texas State University faculty in 2002. Fox served two terms on the national board of directors of the Society of Professional Journalists as campus adviser at-large and is a member of the SPJ education committee. Fox holds a bachelor's degree in journalism from Arizona State University and a master's degree from the University of the Incarnate Word in San Antonio. She was editor of her high school paper, the Centurion at Layton High School in Utah.

Suzanne Lysak is an assistant professor of broadcast and digital journalism at Syracuse University's S.I. Newhouse School of Public Communications. She has previously taught at Virginia Commonwealth University and the University of Southern California. A former reporter, producer, executive producer and news director, Suzanne received two regional Emmy awards in her 24 year local television news career.

June O. Nicholson is a professor of journalism and director of graduate studies in the School of Media and Culture at Virginia Commonwealth University in Richmond, Va. Nicholson's scholarship has focused on diversity issues. Before joining the VCU faculty, she was an award-winning reporter and editor for more than a dozen years in North Carolina and Virginia. She holds a master's degree in public affairs journalism from The American University in Washington, D.C., and a B.A. degree in journalism from the University of North Carolina at Chapel Hill. In 2008, she was recipient of the Robert Knight Multicultural Award for promoting diversity in America's newsrooms, given by AEJMC's Scholastic Journalism Division. That award was given in part for her work for more than 20 years in directing the summer Urban Journalism Workshop for minority high school students at VCU that was co-sponsored by the Dow Jones News Fund and the Richmond Times-Dispatch. Nicholson was recipient of the Distinguished Service Award of VCU's College of Humanities in 2007 for contributions to VCU and the journalism profession.

Adam Maksl, Ph.D., is an assistant professor of journalism at Indiana University Southeast, where he teaches journalism courses and advises student media. Maksl's research and service focus primarily on youth media and media literacy. He has worked as a high school journalism adviser and continues to be involved in outreach programs for high school teachers and students.

Jimmy McCollum, Ph.D., is associate professor of communication and journalism at Lipscomb University. He also is faculty adviser to Lipscomb's student news service and the campus chapter of the Society of Professional Journalists. Formerly coordinator of the Alabama Scholastic Press Association, he has served since 2009 as director of the Tennessee High School Press Association, based at Lipscomb University.

Mac McKerral has served as an associate professor and Journalism Unit coordinator in the School of Journalism & Broadcasting at Western Kentucky University since 2005. He is a past national president of the Society of Professional Journalists and a recipient of SPJ's Wells Key, the society's highest honor, and a recipient of SPJ's National First Amendment Award. He twice received the Florida Press Association's highest honor, the Joseph Roosenraad Award for writing in defense of the First Amendment. He holds a bachelor's degree in Secondary Education/History from Arizona State University and a master's degree in journalism from the University of Illinois. He has been a journalist and journalism educator since 1980 and has worked as a reporter, city editor, managing editor and editor in Illinois, Florida, Indiana and New York. From 1988-1998, he served as director of the annual Hall School of Journalism High School Workshop at Troy State University, which drew 400-500 students from Alabama, Georgia and Florida. From 2006-2008, he served as the director of the Dow Jones Newspaper Fund/Xposure High School Journalism workshop hosted by the SJ&B at WKU.

Lee Anne Peck, Ph.D. is a professor of journalism in the School of Communication at the University of Northern Colorado. Before becoming a full-time instructor, she worked as a reporter and editor for more than 20 years at publications in Colorado, Illinois, Florida, Ohio and Delaware. She worked on school yearbooks every year from eighth to 12th grades, and she also published three issues of an "underground" newspaper with friends during her senior year in high school—a newspaper that outraged members of the administration.

Jeff South is an associate professor and director of undergraduate studies in the Richard T. Robertson School of Media and Culture at Virginia Commonwealth University. In recent years, he has served as a Fulbright Scholar in China and a Knight International Journalism Fellow in Ukraine. Before moving into academia in 1997, he was a reporter and editor for 20 years on newspapers in Texas, Arizona and Virginia. South got his start in journalism working on the Conroe (Texas) High School newspaper.

Leticia Lee Steffen is an associate professor in the Department of Mass Communications at Colorado State University-Pueblo. Steffen teaches the Introduction to Journalism, Digital Publishing, Women and Media, Feature Writing, Gender and Film, and Advanced Media Lab courses. Steffen's research interests include critical thinking within, and critical analysis of, mass media. She got her start in the field of journalism as co-editor of her high school newspaper, The Chieftain, which was a single page published each week in the community newspaper of New Hampton, Iowa.

Rebecca J. Tallent, Ed.D., is an associate professor at the University of Idaho's School of Journalism and Mass Media. She is a former reporter and editor of financial and petroleum industry news, plus she held various public relations positions with science-oriented groups. She was chair of the Society of Professional Journalists national Journalism Education

Committee from 2010-14 and was the coordinator of this work. She is also a member of the SPJ board of directors as a Campus Adviser at Large. Tallent was editor of the Sandtonian newspaper at Charles Page High School in Sand Springs, Okla., taught high school journalism for a year at Bishop McGuinness High School in Oklahoma City, Okla., and since 2010 has been director of the annual UI High School Journalism Workshop in Moscow, Idaho.

Nerissa Young is a lecturer in the E.W. Scripps School of Journalism at Ohio University. She has taught or practiced journalism in Mississippi, Oklahoma and West Virginia. Young has worked in radio, newspapers and magazines. She is the author of "Mass Communication Law in West Virginia, 2nd Edition." Young grew up on the family farm in southern West Virginia. Her interest in student media comes from being a former adviser to a campus newspaper.

Index

Mencher, Mel, 159
Miami Beach Senior High School, 251-252
Michigan Department of Consumer and Industry
    Services, 143
Michigan Interscholastic Press Association,
    162-163
Michigan State University, 47, 143
micro videos, 130-133, 135
microblog, 124-125, 130-131, 133-135
military service, 152
Miniature Guide to Critical Thinking, The, 150
Minneapolis Star Tribune, 76
Minnesota High School Press, 162
Missouri Interscholastic Press Association, 162
Missouri School of Journalism, 109
Moe, Maurice W., 62
Montana Interscholastic Press Association, 162
Monument Mountain Regional High School, 75
Moore, Michael, 71-72
Mordue, Norman, 89, 91
Morse v. Frederick, 93
Motamedi, Beatrice, 182
Mountain Vista High School, 104-106, 117,
    181, 204
Murphy, Joseph M., 164
Murrow, Edward R., 165
MySpace, 134

N

NAA, 25
National Association of Black Journalists J-
    SHOP, 200
National Education Association, 154
National Geographic, 13
National High School Institute, 166
National High School Journalism Convention,
    36, 171
National Public Radio, 56
National Scholastic Press Association (NSPA),
    49-50, 77, 104, 106, 112, 163, 171
NBC, 254
Neiman Reports, 158
Nelson, Jack, 24, 43, 197-198, 200
Neshaminy (Pennsylvania) High School, 7
New England High School Journalism Col-
    laborative, 200
New Expression, 25, 77
New York Times, 146, 164, 173, 208
New York World, 164
Newport Miner, 99
News and Observer, The, 180
news writing, 124
Newsday, 173
Newspaper by the Bay, 182-183
Newsweek, 103

newsworthy, 122-123
Newton, Mark, xi, 104-106, 117, 137-147, 171,
    175, 181, 185, 187, 189, 194, 204-205
niche workshops, 180-182
Nicholas, Sarah, 114-115
Nichols, Casey, 170
Nickelodeon, 254
No Child Left Behind, 57
North Carolina Scholastic Media Association,
    180
Northern High School. 107, 213
Northern Interscholastic Press Association, 162
Northwest Missouri State University, xiv
Northwestern University, 166, 168
Northwestern University, Medill, 68
nut graph, 125

O

Ohio University, 168-169, 195
OIPA, 185
Oklahoma Educational Television Authority,
    128-129
Oklahoma Interscholastic Press Association, 162
Oklahoma University, 162
Olman, Gloria, 88-89
online
    high school newspapers, 157
    publications, 124
Orange & Black, The, 117, 144
Orange Glen High School, 202-203
Oregon Department of Education, 155
Oregon Scholastic Press, 162
Orlando Sentinel, 77
Overby, Charles, 27

P

Palo Alto (Calif.) High School, 174, 183
pan, 132
Partnership for 21st Century Skills (P21), 138-
    141
Path, 130
Patterson, Franklin, 24
Paul, Richard, 150
Pella Community High School, xiii-xv
Pella Publications, xiii
Pelladium, The, xv
Pennsylvania's student press rights law, 7
PerfSpot, 134
Perkins grants, 37
Perry Education Association v. Perry Local
    Educators' Association, 83
Perry, Frances M., 61
personal management, 155
Philadelphia Inquirer, The, 76, 173

X

Xing, 134

Y

Yang, Nu, 159
Yearbook Architecture, 65
Young Latino Journalism Scholars Program, 202
YouTube, 130

Z

'zines, 124
zooms, 132

Made in the USA
Coppell, TX
11 January 2024

27589240R00171